The Beef Industry

The BEEF

INDUSTRY

What They Don't Tell You

John Peirce, DVM

SUNSTONE PRESS

SANTA FE

Sunstone books may be purchased for educational, business, or sales promotional use.
For information please write: Special Markets Department, Sunstone Press,
P.O. Box 2321, Santa Fe, New Mexico 87504-2321.

Book and cover design › Vicki Ahl
Body typeface › Minion Pro
Printed on acid-free paper
∞
eBook 978-1-61139-408-5

Library of Congress Cataloging-in-Publication Data

Peirce, John, 1945- author.
    The beef industry : what they don't tell you / by John Peirce, DVM.
    pages cm
    ISBN 978-1-63293-084-2 (softcover : alk. paper)
    1. Beef industry. I. Title.
    HD9433.A2P45 2015
    338.1'76213--dc23
                        2015029692

Sunstone Press is committed to minimizing our environmental impact on the planet. The paper used in this book is from responsibly
managed forests. Our printer has received Chain of Custody (CoC) certification from: The Forest Stewardship Council™ (FSC®),
Programme for the Endorsement of Forest Certification™ (PEFC™), and The Sustainable Forestry Initiative® (SFI®).

The FSC® Council is a non-profit organization, promoting the environmentally appropriate, socially beneficial and economically viable
management of the world's forests. FSC® certification is recognized internationally as a rigorous environmental and social standard for
responsible forest management.

WWW.SUNSTONEPRESS.COM
SUNSTONE PRESS / POST OFFICE BOX 2321 / SANTA FE, NM 87504-2321 /USA
(505) 988-4418 / ORDERS ONLY (800) 243-5644 / FAX (505) 988-1025

Dedication

Great men have always stepped forward when the time came, and the need was there. Whether it was blazing cattle-trails to the Kansas railhead; or simply willing to lend an ear, and extend a hand of support regarding new ideas and philosophies. The philosophy of "Genuine Care & Concern for the Individual" could not have happened without the support and leadership of Larry Bilberry, past manager of Garden City Feedyard, Garden City, Kansas. He is a man among men; a beacon of integrity. To my valued friend and great feedyard manager, I say: "This one's for you."

Contents

Foreword

Most people are presented opportunities from time to time to enhance their knowledge base concerning a topic that impacts them on a weekly basis; yet, most of these opportunities are not realized. We as a people infrequently take the time to read, to educate ourselves, and update our beliefs with actual facts and figures. We make major decisions based simply on emotion; it feels, or it seems, like the right thing to do. It is no wonder that we find our nation and many nations around the world, in such an economic plight.

Most of you will be positively impacted by what you read in this book. It is an open, educational, and in-depth view of the beef cattle industry. No issues are intentionally avoided. This effort is not the creation of a scholar, academician, or a well-known industry figure. It is the creation of a professionally trained veterinary feedyard consultant with a lifetime of experience within the cattle industry. A feedyard consultant is a workingman's title. We share the same environment as the cattle, good and bad. Our efforts, including the comprehensive efforts of the feedyard, are ongoing—seven days a week, 365 days a year. In spite of weddings, funerals, little league games, doctor appointments, Thanksgiving, or white-out blizzards, the cattle must be fed, have access to water, monitored, and managed appropriately.

When we domesticate animals—all animals—we assume great responsibility. Let me share with you the industry that most of us have for dinner. You are the only one capable of looking out for yourself. Do it through education, and efforts designed to reveal the facts. As long as you are lazy enough to be spoon fed garbage—you will be. Make the effort to glean the facts. Recognize the scope and invasiveness of marketing. Recognize hidden agendas to direct your decision making. Make the individual effort to become informed, one subject at a time. Today's subject is beef. It is a broad, diverse, and challenging industry to understand. It is no wonder that beef and its consumption has such diversity of understanding and appreciation among our peoples nationally and internationally.

This fact based excursion through the beef industry entails personal history, industry history, and efforts designed to focus on the individual wellbeing of the source cattle that ultimately deliver their product to your plate. Learn what very few (outside the industry) know about the how and why of the beef industry. You will ultimately know a whole lot more than a lot of people even within the industry. Within just a few hours of reading your decision making regarding beef will be well founded; your family better protected; and your money better spent. Beef, the red meat you need to know more about.

Introduction

Our world, our very lives, are in transition every day. Take a moment and look back, two years, five years, or even ten years. Within the time frame of these relatively brief periods, you will realize just how much has changed—similar to the ever changing hands of a clock.

For someone my age, I look back twenty-five or even fifty years. Fifty years ago, post WWII, our lives were much simpler, and our roots more rural. In those days most of you still had family and friends on the farm. If memory serves me over 40% of the population was involved with agriculture. Did you know that today that number is very close to 2%? It is no wonder that you find yourself at least three generations removed from the farm. You no longer have family and friends to ask questions of.

What you know of our beef industry likely has come from the voices of our critics, or the media whose fragmented stories are typically directed at hot-button, emotional issues that garner viewer/reader response, rather than share the full story including the facts. I want to change that. I want you to know the facts regarding the production of beef. It is certainly in both our interests for us to get re-acquainted; and, enable you to be able to access avenues of communication back into specific areas of beef production that you might have interest in.

There are over 760,000 locations across the United States alone that raise beef. The same scenario exists in other countries. The U.S. is the largest beef producer with Brazil being second largest. But, the U.S. does not have the most cows. India has 281 million head; Brazil has 174 million head; China has 106 million head; U.S.A. has 95 million head; European Union has 88 million cows; Argentina has 56 million head; Australia has 28 million head; Mexico has 27 million head; Canada has 13 million head; and Uruguay has 12 million head of cattle. All of these countries participate nationally and internationally in the movement and consumption of beef. The vast, vast, vast majority of these cattle production sites are owned and managed as family operations.

No individual aspect of attaining the facts concerning our industry is more important than you realizing that farm and ranch operations are very largely, family operations. Most are single family operations; a few are larger, extended family operations that might include brothers, sisters, sons, daughters, or even grandkids. These families make up the production segment of our industry.

When beef transitions into the fabrication segment of the beef industry it is typically owned by large companies or giant corporations who are very profit motivated. If greed exists in the beef industry it is certainly not in the production segment where economic survival is in the forefront of our minds.

In the U.S. the three largest meat (beef) packers own or control about 70% of the cattle in finishing operations (feedyards). When an entity owns and controls 70% of the marketplace, they pretty well dictate the markets. In a real sense they set the fat-cattle (finished carcasses) price. Then because they are buying 70% of feeder calves (going into the feedyards), they are now, largely, setting the price there as well. When one controls both of these markets, they certainly have the mechanics in place to squeeze the smaller, independent (family owned), feeding operations out of business. The number of independent feedyards has been shrinking for many years. This recent upsurge in beef prices has at least momentarily reduced the economic pressure on the independent feedyards.

In our world today consolidation and buying out the competition is the name of the game. Many people in many countries have lamented the loss of national sovereignty as we become a part of something larger. For some time now, world-wide consolidation of power has been a primary goal of most, larger companies. It is disguised in many ways, but giant corporations are quickly gaining control of the world. That may sound a little crazy; I wish it were.

When you, our urban consumer, look at the cattle industry in particular and pointedly chastise beef producers as being giant corporations who are stuffing, fluffing, and injecting hormones like crazy, without regard for animal welfare—you are out of touch with reality. Giant companies who own production level enterprises in other segments of food production may be guilty. But, that is not the case in beef production. That thought process is not even on the same planet, regarding the facts as they relate to beef cattle production.

The world-wide marketplace for beef has changed enormously over the last few years. It seemed to begin with the fact that Americans can no longer afford beef like they used to be able to. Historically, we consumed the "middle meats" (where most of the better cuts of beef come from) of the beef we raised here in the states. That is no longer the case. Many markets across the globe can now better afford these middle meats, than we. So, a growing percentage (monthly) is now going abroad. We are actually now importing "middle meats," but they are certainly not of the same quality as that being exported.

You may not like the aspect of finishing cattle in feedyards. Your perception of that activity may not be positive. It should be, if you knew the facts. That, to a significant degree, is why I chose to spend two years writing this book so that you might understand the attention and the care levels of the cattle in question. It is the one place that we can meet every need that they might have as determined by a variety of true experts in nutrition and animal health. The decision makers can manage most any group of calves to maximize their potential as feeder calves. Not all calves can be fed to prime, or even choice. Some few don't even have the immune system to stay in this environment. A part of my own work was to identify these individuals as quickly as possible, and remove them the next day to a low-exposure environment where they could be successful and happy. Yes, it's a word we use.

Until two years ago, beef consumption, per capita, was going down. Largely, because we Americans in particular cannot afford it as we used to. But, also because critics of beef are touting it as unhealthy. This question too will be thoroughly addressed within the context of this effort. While beef in general has taken some verbal assaults here in the U.S., the rest of the world who are now enjoying our beef, are singing its praises. In my personal opinion no one else in the world comes close to feeding cattle as well, as efficiently, or as professionally as American feedyards. And, very importantly, we do it with great regard for individual animal care. This book is all about the why, how, and where the activities occur that produce the world's greatest beef.

Very importantly, YOU should never forget that in today's world, everything is marketing, and marketing is everything. Meaning that every product manufacturer has an entire staff devoted to finding ways to sell their product even if it is not a very good product. Marketing in today's world has inundated our daily life. We don't realize just how invasive marketing has become. Who would have ever believed that pharmaceutical companies would be marketing to prospective patients, so they would then go tell their doctor what pill they want? Few things are as real, as unadulterated, as healthy, as green, as natural, or as wonderful as they are presented as being. Marketing departments are wonderfully successful at what they do.

Fresh beef you can trust. Family beef production operations including independent feedyards, you can trust. By the time you finish reading this book you are going to know the people who produce your beef. It will be a heartwarming story that will open your eyes. It will allow for the creation of a knowledge base from which you can make good buying decisions regarding beef. You'll know the facts of the industry; and how to interact with the professionals within this great industry. If this effort is successful, the next effort will be for you to personally get to know the men and women who are actually producing your beef.

Most aspects of this book focus on current issues and actualities as they exist today. The first four chapters are about the product: beef. The next four chapters are the industry as seen through my eyes. The last four chapters are the specific issues I think you are perhaps most interested in learning about.

In order for many of you to appreciate the industry through my eyes, you must get to know me better: where I come from, what I've done, and how I arrived at many of the goals, objectives and dreams I have for the industry I love; and the animals within that I want the very best for. Thus, there will be some family history, a few stories, distinct challenges, critical developments, and a dream for the future—all will become evident as you proceed forward.

Opening

My great granddad owned cattle. My grand-dad (1863–1923) was a cowboy. My dad (1910–1973) was a cowboy. I was ranch raised among the last of the great American cowboys. My dad used to say that "pickups and trailers ruined a lot of good horses." Meaning that when horses began to get hauled around from place to place, they were not getting the miles put on them that made good horses.

As I grew up (born in 1945) hauling horses was common. My early memories include an old Dodge Power-Wagon, and a trailer often referred to as the "log-wagon" because it was made of rough, heavy timbers, designed to travel over very rough country. The ranch we lived on at the time was 42,000 acres—sixty-six square miles. It was seventeen miles from our house, out near the highway, down to the only set of cattle working pens on the east side of the river. We hauled horses down to this set of pens, and rode from there out into the various pastures to gather or check on the cattle as needed. Our usual mode of transportation was a plain Jane, single cab pickup and a gooseneck styled, twenty-foot trailer.

The ranch was split almost in half by the South Pease River. You probably would not even describe it as a river. It was up to a quarter of a mile wide, much narrower in most places, and ran a little water all of the time. During decent rains over the area, it ran a lot of water—bank to bank and would easily wash out all the fence-lines. Thus the term "water-gaping" came into play as we had to put the wire and staves (very small diameter cedar posts) back up and into place to hold the cattle in their respective pastures. Out of the river bed on both sides were good, strong corner posts that anchored the barb-wire (suspension) fence that we called a water-gap. This sandy river bottom had a lot of areas that were locally known as quicksand. When we crossed the river we always followed "cow-trails" to avoid the quicksand. Once in it, inadvertently, the horses raised around this river would flop down on their side and roll out of it. The saddle was an encumbrance, but they managed. The rider had to look out for himself.

My brother Joe (two years younger) and I were with dad every day that we were not in school. On days we actually gathered cattle, there would commonly be from twelve to seventeen cowboys present. This ranch was brushy, mesquite country, and the cattle would be considered wild by just about anyone's standard. Though this historic old ranch had been sold a few years before, we still had significant numbers of maverick bulls, and a few assorted cows that had never been gathered after the ranch sold. If these cattle were branded at all, they carried the "one-winged V," reflecting the ownership of the now defunct Matador Ranch.

James Koonsman standing behind the gate (in front of the cook-house) that displays the one-winged V (used on cattle), and the 50 (used on horses) brands that were used on the historic Matador Ranch. These brands continue to be used by today's Matador Ranch, owned by the Koch family.

I do not remember what the grown men (day-workers) got paid, but Joe and I got six dollars and eight dollars per day, respectively. It seemed like a lot of money at the time. It is odd sometimes at the things we remember when we look back many years later. One that often comes to mind is having to get up an hour earlier if we were working on the other side of the ranch—across the river. When working that side of the ranch men would ride (horseback) in from at least a couple of different directions to reach the designated meeting place for the day's gathering (of the cattle). First one there commonly built a small fire as it was still dark at that time of the morning.

An old gentlemen named Red Payne (the last wagon-boss of the Matador's) most commonly led this group of cowboys, dropping off a man periodically as we went around the back side of the pasture to be gathered. About the time there was just four or five of us left (behind Red), daybreak would just begin lighting up the eastern sky. Red would most commonly drop Joe off next to Dad, and send me around the outside, staying in contact with the outside fence. Meaning, that Dad would be there to help Joe, and Red would keep me where I needed to be. We were the only kids ever present at these workings. Gathering cattle in rough, brushy country, and trying to stay in line with all the other cowboys was not always an easy thing to accomplish for a kid. If you got too far ahead or too far behind, cattle would "leak-out" (slip out between cowboys and not be gathered). Some of these cows were real crafty in avoiding the gather. I have seen many a cow and her calf in heavy brush, standing still as a statue, trying not to be seen, just a few feet away. Once they knew they had been seen, all you would hear was the "popping" noise she made as her horns hit the brush, making a mad dash, trying to escape. The old seasoned horses that my dad put Joe and me on knew what to do. We just had to hang on, trying to avoid any limbs that would drag us off the horse. Often a little help would show up from one side or the other to get the cattle turned in the proper direction. It was a bad no-no to find yourself out of position (on the wrong side of the cowboy next to you). We would each top-out (ride to the top of small hill nearby) as we could to see where the cowboys on each side of us were. Otherwise we would simply "sing-out" (making a little verbal noise) occasionally to let others know where we were. Sometimes we might just be thirty or forty yards apart, and at other times considerably more than a hundred yards apart. There always seemed to be an event or two (more if it was a difficult gather) that necessitated a mad rush through the brush to head off some cattle determined not to be penned. I do not know that we ever got them all. Pasture head counts were just an approximation. It was not unusual to pen calves in the fall at shipping time (movement towards the feedyards) that had not been penned at the spring branding.

It varied as to the size and shape of the pasture, and how much trouble we had; but normally we would have the cattle penned by 10:30 or 11:00 AM. If it was a spring branding, the calves would be cut off from the mothers (separated into a different pen), leaving just a few cows with the calves. They were more comfortable if a few cows were still present. Spring working consisted of applying a hot iron to prove ownership, dehorning, castrating the bull calves, and administering vaccinations to prevent sickness.

Only the older (perhaps 50 years old and above) cowboys got to "drag calves" to the fire. This involved roping the calves (larger ones by the hind feet, and smaller calves around the neck), and bringing them out of the mass of calves, and up to where the cowboys (the flankers) could access them. "Flankers" worked in sets of two men each, using techniques taught to them by their fathers as fairly young kids—on small calves of course. These men would gain control of the calf, quickly removing the rope, allowing the dragger to quietly return to get another one.

Calves separated and ready to be worked.

Calves quietly awaiting procedures.

First calf brought to
the flankers.

Routine procedures
accomplished
efficiently.

Process quickly
continues.

Most commonly we would have two if not three men dragging calves; each utilizing at least one set of flankers. With the calf properly restrained a "brander" (also a senior individual) would apply the hot iron. De horning and castration of bull calves was accomplished by "experienced" (middle aged) individuals. The vaccine gun might be managed by someone a little younger. Kids and young men were always on the flanking crew. Early on Joe and I handled the smallest calves. By about the sixth grade we were split up and teamed with a very experienced young man, handling whatever calves came our way. It might vary as to whether it was a bull or a heifer, and how big they were, but commonly it took from thirty seconds to a minute to complete all the necessary tasks for each calf.

In the early days (late 1950s and early 1960s) we had a lot of "screw-worms." Many parts of the southwestern U.S. became very familiar with these flesh eating parasites (fly larva) that were attracted to any open wound. They would kill a calf, or a cow for that matter, if left untreated. My brother and I had learned to rope (Saturdays and every summer day that we were not "working" cattle) "prowling" the pastures with dad, looking for cases of screw-worms. Screwworms were slowly eradicated by a government program that consisted of dropping small boxes of sterile (irradiated) flies out of airplanes. These boxes opened up when hitting the ground, releasing the flies. These sterile flies stopped reproduction. There were labs along the Mexican border that produced these flies, and made them ready to be dropped anywhere a screwworm report occurred. It all sounds strange but it worked. We missed all the roping, but everyone felt a lot better that the cattle did not have to suffer the consequences of screw-worm infestations.

The ranch was a great place for a kid to grow up. There were many positives associated with the environment. When I look back one of the things that always comes to mind had to do with the morning chore that Joe and I shared. Every other morning Joe and I changed jobs. One morning one of us went after the horses, and the other milked. You would think that we would both strongly prefer using the "night horse" to go gather the horse-herd we kept near the house. It was kind of cool because it would be completely dark, and though we could see nothing, our horse could. We would just give him his head, and pretty soon he would find the other horses. Before long he would "nicker" (a common sound that horses make when acknowledging other horses) and others would respond. Without ever seeing anything, you would hear the drum-beats of all the horses loping for the barn. Another aspect you learned very young was not to lope in (back to the barn) behind the horse herd; but rather trot in behind the others. That would fall under the cardinal rule category.

For some reason I rather enjoyed the mornings I milked, while Joe went after the horses. We just had two cows—a spring calver and a fall calver. Having one calving (giving birth) in the spring, and one in the fall, gave us fresh milk and cream year around. At least half of the year we only had to milk one; and then, only had to milk two quarters, leaving the other two quarters for her calf. After feeding everything, we would take the milk to the house, strain it, and then Mom would put it into the refrigerator. By the time we cleaned up and ate breakfast, the school bus would be fast approaching.

But always at the top of my list for favorite memories of my youth, was that regarding the quality of the cowboys (men) that we had the opportunity to grow up around. These were all quiet, mild-mannered men who had great respect for each other. They were in my eyes, the best of the best—the last of a few. There were handfuls of these men in other locations as well. The Waggoner Ranch, near Vernon, Texas always had them present. Newt O'Keefe, who spent several years there, was my dad's old compatriot. Other than knowing dad from being around him every day, I learned all the good stuff about him from Newt. These men might kid each other about an old episode or story, but they rarely told the story themselves. Even in my limited perspective of the world, I knew there were more of these men scattered across northwest and west Texas, as well as New Mexico and Arizona. Where else I did not know. These men were our heroes. It is no wonder that a lot of very bright kids did not want to go off to college. They knew what they wanted to be.

Perhaps the greatest negative associated with staying on the ranch as an adult had to do with economics. Ranch jobs did not pay very well. It was hard to raise a family on what these jobs paid. The most I ever remember dad making was $250 a month. Ranch jobs did commonly provide housing, utilities, beef and a milk cow. Still, with kids requiring clothes, school supplies, food for the family and having to make some kind of old car payment—it was not easy. It was great for the kids; perhaps we did not know any better. Most of the ranch kids were about the same. But, I know it had to be a little hard on the parents. On one particular Saturday night while Joe and I were in high-school, we decided we wanted to go to town. We asked Dad if he had any money. He gave us the last fifty cents he had. Joe and I drove up to the highway, turned around and came back to the house. We were not going to spend the last fifty cents.

My dad was particularly interested in us four boys going to college. He, having quit school in the seventh grade, wanted us to have more options. Though each of us had to eventually earn our way through school; we all managed; TCU, Texas Tech, South Plains College, and Texas A&M for me. I figured that if I had to go to college, I wanted to be a veterinarian. The thought process was that if at any time they (the university) told me I couldn't—I would go back to the ranch.

Years later having completed my initial college registration, I went to pay out and found that I was fifty dollars short. Someone suggested that I go over to the former students association and talk to them. There I visited with an elderly gentleman by the name of Mr. Locke. Thirty minutes later I left with a check for fifty dollars and assurances that if I had any trouble finding a job, to let him know. Six years later I left with two degrees, including a Doctor of Veterinary Medicine.

After entering veterinary practice, It took a few years for me to get back to cattle, but I did. I spent seventeen glorious years in what I referred to as a "remote ranch practice," located in the panhandle, south-plains and west Texas, as well as the southeastern quadrant of New Mexico. A ten year drought finally broke me, and sent me scurrying for a job. The Lord blessed me mightily when I went to work for AzTx Cattle Company, Hereford, Texas—the fifth largest cattle feeding company. AzTx had five feedyards located in three different states, with one-time feeding capacity approaching 250,000 head.

I found home in the feedyards. I wished that I had found them twenty years before I did. Feedyards are all business. It is a data-rich environment; everything, anything can and usually is measured. We will get into a lot of the specifics later, but suffice to say I had the opportunity to prove much of what I had long believed—that if you would treat the cattle kindly (elevating and sustaining their sense of wellbeing), they would pay you back with enhanced performance parameters. This was the beginning of many years of personal trials and data collection. My boss gave me the leeway to try about anything I wanted, but often cautioned: "it had better work." He did finally draw the line (years later) when I approached him about putting some "playground" equipment in some Holstein feeder cattle pens. There, I believed, this equipment would have relieved some of the boredom commonly seen in cattle while in a confined feeding operation. I am sure this project would have given us at least two-tenths of a pound a day of additional gain (per animal). He looked at me, smiled, and said: "I refuse to become the butt of jokes across the industry, concerning playground equipment in some of my feeding pens." He knew I was not talking about slides and teeter-totters; just something they could not tear up, nor get injured by; yet, be entertained.

Over the years we accomplished a great deal. Ultimately, a new philosophy emerged: "Genuine Care & Concern for the Individual" (trademarked). Much of this book encompasses the details of this new philosophy. The total program creates a win/win scenario for all involved. The cattle win because their sense of wellbeing is significantly elevated during the feeding period. The owner wins because the performance parameters of the cattle have been elevated; thus presenting the opportunity to either make more money, or loose less money, as the case may be. The consumer wins because "you" desire that your beef source cattle have been kindly treated. The industry wins because we have come a long way in minimizing at least one of the issues regarding beef "sustainability." This international issue revolves around five or six issues, but the two you are likely most interested in are *humane treatment and low-environmental impact.* Both of these items and others will be covered in this book.

My great-grandfather's cattle era was far different from that of his sons. His son's era was far different from that of my dad's era; and, my dad's era far different from that of my own. Much has changed. We have moved from a producer-driven industry to a consumer/retail-driven industry. You, the consumer, are in a position to lead the band. You tell your retailers what you want and you should get it. The "should" rather than the "will" is at the discretion of the major packers who slaughter and fabricate 82% of the beef in America. Small packers will go out of their way to bring you what you want. The large packers do whatever makes themselves the most money. They own or control over 70% of the cattle in the finishing phase of production (the feedyards). It is monopolistic in every sense of the word. Apparently, our politicians have been bought off.

The large packers are just one of our three great challenges that our industry faces. Regulatory oversight, often written for other industries (that we fall under), in conjunction with agents (government representatives) that know nothing of our industry who attempt to interpret the federal policy as it applies to us; and, our lost lines of communication with you, our consumer.

Through no fault of your own, you (urban consumers) have lost contact with agriculture in general, and the beef cattle industry in particular. You are at least two generations removed from having family back on the livestock farm or ranch. These lost lines of communication and its associated knowledge base, have made you vulnerable to misinformation. Most of you have two sources of information: our critics, and the media. The production aspect of the beef industry cannot go through the packers to reach you to share information. The primary reason behind this book is to provide you the opportunity to restore that lost knowledge base concerning beef. Here you will find an in-depth and honest view of the inner workings of our industry and its people. We are not perfect; we never will be. But, we are proactively and aggressively trying to earn your trust. Some of you think in terms of factory farms. Nothing could be farther from the truth regarding the beef industry. The production segment of our industry is almost completely owned by individuals and families—just like AzTx Cattle Company. The exception of course is the segment of cattle feeding operations owned by the major packers.

As you read this book you will actually feel the efforts made by family operations in providing you safe and wholesome beef. You will understand who, where, and specifically how your beef arrives at the grocery store or restaurant where you shop and eat. I will walk you through our industry from the birth of a calf to harvest. These are food animals—not pets. But, you will see and feel the actual efforts made in caring for these individuals that may surprise you.

Ours is a way of life; a lifestyle that most of us were born into. It is what we want to do. It is not about the money. If it were, most of us would be doing something else. You will get to know us, our efforts, and our significant challenges as you progress through these chapters. This is not a novel designed to entertain. Some chapters you will enjoy more than others because it must necessarily be educational. But, when thoughtfully consumed you will reach real understanding regarding our industry, and have a knowledge base from which you can make good buying decisions. You decisions will then be based on fact, not emotion. It is then that you will fully appreciate your own invested time and money, relative to this book. The first few chapters are specifically about the beef industry and its product. The middle chapters are more per-sonal in nature involving areas of activity as seen through my eyes and my experiences. The final chapters are about you and your concerns relative to our industry.

A Personal Word from the Author

I know cattle. I have spent over sixty years of my life involved with cattle from conception to consumption. Of recent years I have been involved with developing concepts that would allow beef producers to bring to the marketplace (in a verifiable and auditable manner) that specific product that you might desire—beef produced from calves that spend their entire life under an operational philosophy of "Genuine Care & Concern for the Individual" (trademarked). It is a rather long story and you will find much of it in this book. Our beef industry has long needed to reestablish communication links directly with you (our consumers). The more you know of us the better off we both become. The more we know about you, the more we can fine-tune the specific beef of your desires and bring it into the marketplace.

Today, our continuing sphere of activities and our hope for the future resides around you. The realization is stunning that we have allowed you to become so isolated from our industry. You are inarguably widely diverse regarding your knowledge of the beef cattle industry; widely differing as you your point of view; and significantly divergent in your personal level of concern regarding our impact on the environment, as well as the care level of the cattle under our charge.

Your questions might actually be few in number, yet widely divergent in how they are phrased, and the depth to which you seek answers. I cannot answer every question that you might have. But, I can share detailed information regarding my own experiences in the cattle industry. There are many, many people who know more than I about specific subject matter within the beef cattle industry; yet very few with my level of knowledge from "conception" to "consumption."

I will share this information in an open and frank manner. You may not appreciate everything that we do, from your current perspective. But, almost without fail, you would appreciate what we do if you were in our position for a few years. Work under our constraints and challenges (long enough to know them), and your appreciation of our efforts would vastly escalate.

Yes, we have critics; actually, a variety of critics. Some of our critics actually support the demise of animal production agriculture. Most of these critics hide behind the banner of humane treatment. Some of our critics are more philosophical in nature. These may believe that the cost of food production, including importing feed for animals, and disruption to the energy efficiency of the ecosystem, can be more harmful to ecosystems than simply importing food. Wow. We live under the effects of imported oil (gasoline) every day. Would you really want your food operating under this same system, originating off-shore?

Some of our critics are very bright people in their own field of study; but they often make false assumptions regarding the beef cattle industry, and then build a "case" on a false foundation. Others simply "think" they know something that others are not aware of, and they want to share it. Yet other critics believe that we all should simply avoid meat consumption, period.

It is easy to champion negativity to the uninformed. Earlier models of beef production more easily facilitated (between producers and consumers) issues regarding trust, accountability, and transparency. In that day lines of communication were intact. Then, you either had family still on the farm, or a local butcher (at the meat shop) with whom you could converse. You had someone to answer your questions. Today, you are isolated and without interactive lines of communication. It behooves our industry to rectify this situation as quickly as possible. Your lack of knowledge makes you vulnerable to misinformation.

We have nothing to hide and are not apprehensive about being judged on our merits. But, we do want you to judge us from a base of knowledge. Decisions based simply on emotion are often regrettable decisions. Sort out the facts for yourself. If you have interest, find out what is happening and why. This book and the website list in the back will give you that opportunity.

You will find as you traverse the chapters of this book that my efforts and my energies were directed on behalf of the cattle under my care. I wanted to tie together all the issues that negatively affected the cattle's immune system; identify all issues that diminished their sense of wellbeing; and identify social-ization issues involving cattle. Pure science does not always reveal answers. But, for my answers to be real; they had to be measurable.

My quest began (at the feedyard) simply as augmenting procedures (vaccination protocols) that would minimize sickness in the feedyard. We cre-ated and proved a protocol (Doing the Basics Perfectly); and then encouraged our source producers (cow/calf operations sending us their yearly calf-crops) to utilize the same program. It proved to be a great starting place.

Next, I looked at the issues of "stress" affecting the cattle prior to, and during their time at the feedyard. Stress is the #1 enemy to good health. Sources of stress were rather easily identified, but harder to quantify; yet we persevered. At this 90,000 head feedyard where this program was developed, 80% of the cattle were already going through the feeding phase of production without having received any antibiotics. The other 20% were primarily issues of immuno-suppression (weakened immune systems for a variety of reasons). Some of these calves could still be successful feeders, while others of them, could not. A new program, Selective Culling, was created to identify (and quickly remove from the feedyard) individuals with weakened immune systems. Placing these identified individuals, immediately into low-exposure, pasture environments, gave them an opportunity to be successful—regaining their health. This incremental achievement allowed us to ultimately focus on 5%-7% of the cattle population, regarding health issues that had to be more intensively managed.

Socialization issues were among the last to be focused upon and identified. Yes, these issues are real, and measurable. All of this will be discussed in later chapters.

All of these individual programs and others ultimately created an operational philosophy that I called "Genuine Care & Concern for the Individual." It is a program that works. It requires us to thoughtfully consider how to manage stress factors, and the way we handle cattle. "Quiet and Gentle, Low-Stress Handling" was introduced to us by Dr. Tom Noffsinger, a feedyard consultant from Benkelman, Nebraska. It became a core-activity. The industry is always searching for safe ways to enhance performance parameters. Thus, our efforts, elevating and sustaining their sense of wellbeing, ultimately met an industry desire.

The term humane treatment was at no point a targeted area. I actually backed into the subject material through efforts involving the elevation of their sense of wellbeing for economic reasons. Sense of wellbeing is a much more quantifiable term; and one that we can all debate without raising voices. Producers are "touchy" about the subject of humane treatment. This is principally because cattle care already rates above that producer's family desires. Johnny's dental issues and Mary's college fund are already secondary to cattle care requirements. Beyond shelter and food for the producer family, the cattle have always come next on the priority scale. It is the cattle that ultimately pay for everything. To short them is to short yourself. Understandably, they (producers) are sensitive to the issues of humane treatment as handled by our "critics."

In this new era of consumer driven interests our industry is occasionally finding itself in untenable positions. Let me share a case in point. Many years ago we looked at the issues involved in stopping and resting cattle which are involved in cross country transits to the feedyard. On the surface it seems to be the thing to do. That was proven not to be the case. Morbidity (sickness) was appreciable higher (as was death loss) in cattle that were stopped for a few hours of rest, feed and water. We as an industry are always concerned with the numbers. Everything is measured. Today, we know that we need to focus more on getting those animals full (freshly fed), and properly hydrated prior to being loaded for such a long trip. Other than that, we focus intently on having that transit occur as quickly and efficiently as possible. This means that the drivers should be well rested before the cattle are loaded. Stops in route should be strictly limited to fuel and checking on the cattle.

Now, our critics want us to stop and rest the cattle every so many hours. We are caving in on some of these issues so we do not appear to be hard-hearted. Sickness is going to be more prevalent; death loss will be higher. The cattle will suffer more and longer; but the critics will be happier. Personally, you (our consumer) are the only voice I am interested in. If you know the issues and still want it—you get it. Hopefully, you can appreciate that we long ago tried that alternative and proved that it did more harm than good. We need to stay focused on what is best for the cattle—not our critics. My voice and my vote are always on the best interests of the cattle involved. It is another reason why I wanted to make the effort to write this book.

There is an old saying: "walk in their footsteps before judging." No beef cattle producer would do anything to limit an animal's performance ability, knowingly. No producer wants to do anything to create sickness, lameness, pain, or suffering. It all robs that animal's ability to be successful.

I want to be your missing link (of communication) to the beef cattle industry. I want to share with you efforts that are being made to enhance our cattle's sense of wellbeing. Happy Cattle is a term coined in California. It does not roll off the tongues of beef producers very well; but it should. Happy cattle make us more money. That should be reason enough. Getting to feel good about our actions and efforts—involving "doing the right thing"—is simply icing on the cake.

There will be a test at the end of the book (just kidding). But I will answer some tough questions posed by one of your fellow consumers (a developmental editor), who presents herself to be representative of my targeted audience: urban, educated, and a little skeptical; but she desires to know what the facts really are concerning the beef cattle industry—particularly as to how we impact the environment. It is my fondest hope that by the time you get to the back of the book, you will actually understand the answers. Invariably, I will fail to cover every subject that you might have a question regarding. But, if you will but review the outline of chapters, you will see that I have certainly tried. In all likelihood, if you will be patient, your subject of interest will be openly explored.

You will get to know our people, our challenges, and our operations. I believe that you will get to know yourself a little better as well. The information contained herein will be enlightening and I hope at least a little entertaining. Join us, won't you, as we walk through the pages of "THE BEEF INDUSTRY, what they don't tell you."

1

Development of an Industry—from 1655 to the Present

Cattle have a long and ancient history. Four-thousand year old wall drawings have been found in Egyptian tombs depicting cattle. Through history cattle have been used for a wide array of purposes: as beasts of burden, elevated religious symbols, slaughtered for food, and slaughtered simply for their hides (leather), and tallow (fat used in making soap and candles), as well as their bones (fertilizer).

Early American colonists often survived on what could be caught from rivers and streams, wildlife, and domesticated farm animals. William Pynchon of Springfield, Massachusetts, became the first American devoted to the packing business. In 1655 he started by driving cattle into Boston, offering fresh meat to the residents. He was also packing large numbers of hogs by 1662. In those days, beyond the limited supply of fresh beef for local consumption, beef was salted or smoked, and packed into wooden barrels or boxes for storage and shipping—most commonly by sea. Hence, the term "meat packing" became a part of our language.

It was common in these colonized settlements for domesticated farm animals to be utilized as sources of trade or cash. While waiting on crops to mature, it was farm animals that gave quality of life to these meager households. In many parts of what was to become America as we know it today, small farm animal operations flourished. Each met the needs of the families involved and often sold or bartered their animals/production to others. Some drove animals or otherwise moved fresh meat, as well as milk and eggs, into nearby towns. But significant movement of beef in particular was limited to ships along the coast, until the later 1830s.

Spanish cattle roamed Texas well before the eighteenth century. Longhorn cattle arrived in Texas in the 1820s and the 1830s (from the mid-west). Slowly, some commercial use was made of these cattle, though predominately, they were used individually, as needed, for food. The earliest markets involved sailing ships into ports of call like Galveston, New Orleans, eastward around the gulf, and north along the Atlantic coastline.

Trail drives to distant markets were the next step in finding markets for these Longhorn, and Longhorn-Spanish crossed cattle. In 1836, the Beef Trail became the route to New Orleans. In the 1840s the Shawnee Trail was utilized to move cattle to Sedalia, Missouri. In 1854 there was even a California Trail established. As markets emerged, though often distant, ranches emerged, depending solely on the cattle for their livelihood. Many of these ranching operations became stable, while others failed, due to weather issues including drought, and erratic markets.

As the fight for Texas Independence (from Mexico) came to a close in 1836, men who had served were issued script for land in the new republic. Land was an abundant commodity. Though money was scarce, the land given to these soldiers became the center of their economic future. Location was immensely important. Areas prone to drought, and well away from marketing avenues, made these ranching operations a roll of the dice.

George Ware Fulton traveled from Indiana to Texas to aid Texas independence. Though he arrived just after the Battle of San Jacinto (ending the fight), he enlisted in the republic's new army as a second lieutenant. He was promoted to captain during his enlistment. When he completed his enlistment, he received warrants and land script for 1,280 acres of land. After his service he went to work for the provisional governor of Texas, Henry Smith. George worked in the land office. The two of them became friends, and soon were considering mutually advantageous business ventures. Their focus centered in the coastal-bend area (mid Texas coast) where George had his acreage. In 1840 he moved to the area, and married Smith's oldest daughter, Harriet.

After six years and three kids, they moved back east. Proper education of the children was a primary reason for the move. He soon became a railroad superintendent, and later a practicing civil engineer of significant note. He was lauded "a universal genius, capable of building a locomotive, running one, or comprehending anything in the range of science, mechanics, or anything that required hard work and management."

As the Civil War between the states ended, Harriet longed for Texas. Henry Smith had died in 1851, and had left Harriet 28,000 acres of land. In 1867 the Fulton family moved back to the coastal town of Rockport, Texas. In 1868 George constructed a wharf to load beef onto sailing ships, and a small meat packer business. A dozen other meat packeries began in Rockport, and Fulton, as it was coming to be called. It was hoped by all the local ranchers that these packeries would become the principal market for their cattle.

1865 proved to be the year that changed everything, concerning Texas cattle moving into the market place. That year Armour & Company had opened a large, modern plant in Chicago that heralded the expansion of the packing industry. Swift was soon to follow.

In 1871 George entered into a partnership to form Coleman-Mathis-Fulton Pasture Company, encompassing 115,000 acres of land. George worked to strengthen the cattle company by becoming diversified. The pasture company served as agent for the large, ocean transport company, Morgan Steamship Company. This company shipped preserved beef as far as Liverpool, England. Salt beef, the traditional way of curing beef, served a purpose, but was never fully appreciated. The next feasible alternative for George was refrigeration. He experimented with mechanical refrigeration until he found success, and received a patent in 1869. In 1871 he opened the first refrigerated meat packery in the country.

After the Civil War, three to six million head of cattle roamed loose over Texas. With local markets pricing cattle at $2 per head or less, cattlemen had little choice but to pursue new, additional markets. Armour & Company had become the most desired market for their cattle. The westward expansion of the railroad became the new target area to get their cattle to Chicago.

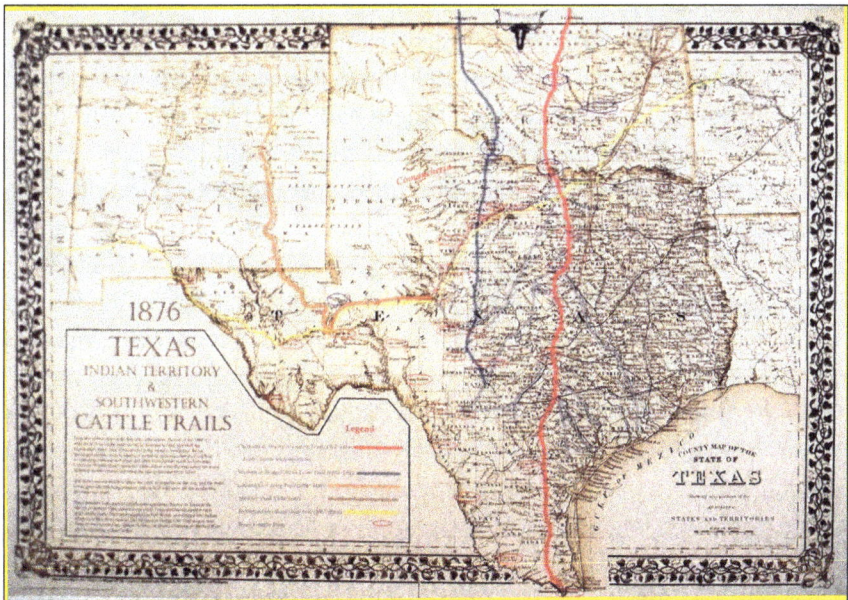

Historic map of trail drive routes.

The Chisholm Trail was the early first choice. One point five million head of Texas cattle were trailed to Ellsworth and Abilene, Kansas, between the years of 1873 and 1886. In 1876 much of the traffic shifted over to the Western Trail that ended in Ogallala, Nebraska. The other primary trail, the Goodnight-Loving Trail, usually ended in Cheyenne, Wyoming. These particular drives often over-wintered in a boxed canyon just north of Colorado Springs, Colorado. Getting cattle to these aforementioned markets enabled prices of up to forty dollars per head. Between the years of 1866 and 1886, twenty million head of Texas cattle were moved to distant markets.

In 1875, G.H. Hammond designed the first practical, refrigerated railcar for use in transporting fresh beef. The demise of the cattle trails was also caused by two additional factors. Texas Cattle Fever, a tick-borne disease, caused great resistance regarding the movement of Texas cattle through Missouri in particular. However, the ultimate factor was "barbed wire."

Glidden & Ellwood's Barbed Fence Company received a patent in 1874. In 1878 John Gales, a company representative, held a demonstration in San Antonio, Texas. He held a group of wild Longhorn cattle in a barbed-wire fenced corral. He touted the fence as "light as air, stronger than whiskey, and cheaper than dirt." Sales grew quickly, and barbed wire permanently changed land uses and land values in Texas. Fenced property lines changed the landscape, vastly limiting cross-country movement of cattle.

In the latter 1800s and early 1900s many large, historically significant Texas ranches were created. Some of these had ownership groups from England and Scotland. Some few of these ranches are still in existence today. These survivors generally became diversified operations. Gas and oil exploration enormously helped a few. The King Ranch, one of the very earliest, still exists and is well diversified. The Waggoner Ranch, Vernon, Texas, is the largest contiguous ranch in Texas, and is still intact, but family feuding has limited its performance significantly. However, oil and gas checks have kept it on solid financial ground. Two other historically significant ranches, the XIT (1885–1912) and the Matador Land and Cattle Company (1879–1951), were broken apart and sold for much the same reason: investors losing interest. The XIT totaled three million acres and ran up to 150,000 cows. The Matador Ranch's locations totaled just over 1.5 million acres; 900,000 of which was worked out of the headquarters at Matador, Texas. More about this ranch will follow as a footnote at the end of this chapter. Another, very notable early ranching operation was the Bar C Ranch that had control over a large portion of the north-eastern corner of today's Texas panhandle. In 1885 a late, freak snow-storm hit in early April. Cow numbers were devastated during this three day blizzard. Seven hundred cows remained out of fourteen thousand head. The ranch did not survive. This acreage of over 500,000 acres was broken up into several smaller ranches, most of which still operate today. At that time the only source of available water was the Canadian River. Virtually all of these newer operations were situated such that each had at least some access to the Canadian River, or its tributaries that commonly held pools of water.

I might mention that large ranches existed elsewhere besides Texas. Even though these other ranches were large individually, the sheer numbers of available cattle to be marketed beyond the region were small. The big numbers to serve significant portions of the nation came from Texas, and truthfully, from Mexico as well. Even today, Texas still has the largest resident population of cattle. Most of these early ranches are now in their third and fourth generation, and are still in the family and well managed. The families who own these operations today take great pride in their heritage, and hold traditional ranching values dear to their hearts. No one loves their land more than these people. It may not look as pretty to visitors, regarding lands they are more familiar with; but it is beautiful to the descendants of those who created this ranching operation.

Occasionally, one of these good ranches is bought by another individual or an oil company that transforms it into a bird (quail) or deer hunting operation. Though most of them do bring back a few cows to keep forages (grass) under control. Few things remain just as it was. We are all in some form of transition, one way or another. But, the heart of a cowman is still alive and well wherever cattle are located.

By the 1950s the Chicago meat industry had reached its peak. Its fall from prominence was caused by the fact that most of their facilities were now old; and it was now more economical to ship beef carcasses, than live animals. There had always been small, local meat packers serving county residents. But, as the big packers began to leave Chicago and spread out, many medium sized, independent packers came into existence, serving regional areas. Some of these grew into very sizable companies. During more modern times the original packers began to buy out their competition, and the age of consolidation began.

As beef production intensified a new center of activity was created. The first commercial "feedyard" was built in Hereford, Texas in 1960. It was designed to receive country, pasture cattle in "range condition," and fatten them on corn based diets to make the beef a more pleasurable eating experience. This initial confined feeding operation was the creation of Paul Engler, founder, owner and operator (at the time) of Hereford Feedyard. Mr. Engler went on to become an icon within the industry, creating a huge cattle feeding operation known as Cactus Feeders. Hereford, Texas was to become the "Wall Street" of the cattle feeding industry. Over three million head of cattle on feed can be found within thirty-five miles of Hereford; and over ten million head within 135 miles of Hereford. Other feedyards sprang up in many other mid-western and western states—anywhere corn was grown. If you look at exactly where the major packers have packing-houses today, just look at locations where there are significant numbers of cattle on feed: the panhandle of Texas, Kansas, Iowa, Nebraska, Colorado, and California.

Today's meat processing has become "highly sophisticated." Modern, computer-age business practices and the application of scientific knowledge, as well as technology, has allowed efficiency to prevail across the workplace. No one works harder at staying out of the news, than packing houses. The last thing they want is to become involved in a bacterial contamination issue. There are not many things I like about their industry, but I love their rigid focus on cleanliness. Their attention to the smallest detail, regarding the movement of contaminated surfaces, from one part of the facility to another, is impressive. Your rubber boots are going to stay wet from walking through sprays, foams, and pools of disinfectant solutions. Even the surface of the finalized hanging carcass is decontaminated, before moving into the cooler. The plant that I was in used "steam," but there are other ways as well.

Doing their job of harvesting cattle is not the problem. They do the work of harvesting beef and fabricating beef cuts as well as anyone in the world. Having a virtual monopoly is the problem. They control well over 70% (approaching 80%) of all cattle on feed (in the feedyards). Now they are heavily influencing the feeder-calf market because they are buying most of the calves. That puts them in a position to control profitability among the independent feedyards (23% of fed-cattle volume). The current state of mind regarding the independent feedyards is depressing. They are not optimistic about the future. You, the consumer, only become a packer priority when a negative news story breaks, involving recalled beef. Competition has always been good for the American marketplace. In today's world, international competition between mega corporations seems to be where the focus is. Consolidation of an industry gives great leverage to the few companies left. I am not at all sure that is good for consumers in particular.

Regarding The Matador Land and Cattle Company

I thought perhaps some specifics as to the people, and how such a ranch developed might be of interest. It will additionally serve as a foundation material for Chapter 5: Your Beef Producers.

Lessening Indian conflicts allowed ranching activities to begin at different times across the west. Though other ranches were already located in north-western Texas, H.H. Campbell selected Ballard Springs as his new headquarters for the developing Matador Cattle Company. Initially, two "dugouts" served to shelter the men while cattle were being purchased.

As plans and activities proceeded with the ranch, Mr. Campbell wanted to initiate local government. In order to patent a site for a county seat, the General Land Office required a settlement with at least twenty business establishments. Ranch-hands opened up the required number of businesses using supplies "borrowed' from the ranch commissary. Their town, to be called Matador, was granted the patent, and became the designated county seat.

Officially organized in 1879, the Matador Cattle Company began with five men, including Campbell, each subscribing $10,000. A.M. Britton of Fort Worth served as president of this newly formed corporation; S.W. Lomax, also of Ft. Worth, served as secretary and treasurer; and H.H. Campbell serving as general manager of ranching operations. Mr. Campbell, who on several occasions had traveled much of the western lands, claimed that this land from the waters of the Brazos to the Red River and for 40 miles under the Cap Rock (to the south), was the best cattle breeding country in the United States.

Mrs. Campbell accompanied the freight wagons (loaded with timber to build a new home) from Ft. Worth to the ranch headquarters in March 1880.

On arrival, she would not live underground, as she termed the dugout. So, she camped in a tent until the house was finished. Over the ensuing years she would become the local nurse tending to whatever elements might occur, gained fame as a ranch hostess, and become the post-mistress when the local post office opened up. She was a real lady that served her community well, and loyally secured the family bonds through good times and bad.

The first cattle had arrived in late December of 1879. They carried a

"V" brand, and had originated in south Texas. This brand was to become the famous "one winged V" of the Matador Ranch. In those days the men driving the newly acquired herd were most commonly considered an inheritance—acquired with the cattle. In May of 1880 the famous Jingle Bob cowherd of John Chisum was purchased. Also customary at the time was assuming the lands that had been home to the cows at the time of purchase. Their next acquisition was the lands and cattle of Coggins and Wilie, ranging on the head-waters of the South Pease River; then the Houston and Lemond herd was acquired in 1881; as well as the T-41 herd and lands ranging on the lower waters of the South Pease River—on Tee Pee Creek. Purchased next were the Tobe Odom cattle in 1882 (lower down on the South Pease River in Cottle County). Next were the black cattle ranging in the Croton Breaks in Dickens County, which were tributary waters of the Brazos River. Thus within two years a range of just about a million acres was acquired.

To facilitate the purchase of these lands Mr. Britton had gone to Scotland where money was cheaper (interest rates). There a syndicate was formed in 1882 which absorbed the Matador Cattle Company at a price of $1,250,000. The ranch then became known as the Matador Land and Cattle Company.

Scottish Syndicate visiting the ranch, circa 1881.

Mr. Campbell continued on in the new company as manager, and was authorized to acquire additional lands at a rate of ten cents per acre. He shouldered the wrath of the Scotch syndicate when he acquired properties near

Clarendon that were to become his northern boundary. He gave eighty cents per acre knowing that if someone else bought it, a variety of ensuing conflicts were likely.

In the mid 1880s Mr. Campbell began fencing the range. The creation of "camps" (locations for cowboys or a man and his wife, to live while caring for the fences and cattle in his designated area) occurred over the lands in appropriate areas allowing for efficiency of travel through the pastures. The Matadors, as it was commonly called, had at least twenty-five of these camps. Most all of these camps began as dugouts. In time they were renovated and enlarged, but most did not become wooden structures for many years.

Before renovations of "turtle hole" dugout.

After renovations to the "turtle hole" dugout.

The ranch employed as many as 150 men during peak work periods. Working men had to be fed. In order for breakfast to be ready at 4:00 am, the wagon cook had to be up tending his fires as early as 3:00 am, practically every morning of the year. Twenty-five to thirty men were commonly fed.

Matador ranch hands branding cattle—circa 1881.

Matador ranch hands—circa 1881.

Most of these ranch-wagon cooks were much appreciated, and were considered to be excellent cooks. On one particular day they had 140 men to cook the noon meal for. Two chuck-wagons pulled up side by side; one handled the bread line, and the other the meat. Other pertinent chores were divided between the two wagons. It seemed a big chore for just two men, and it was. But, the meal was served on time.

Every chuck-wagon had an accompanying "hoodlum wagon." Its driver furnished the wood for cooking, and water for the chuck wagon, cowboys and branding crew. He also hauled the branding irons, as well as other over-flow items that could not fit in the chuck-wagon. The chuck-wagon was commonly referred to as simply "the wagon."

Chuck & Sheri Bowden photograph, Lamar, CO, circa 1903; "Just Camped."

Chuck & Sheri Bowden photograph, Lamar, CO, circa 1903; titled "Roll Out Boys."

Standard Ranch cowboys, circa 1907.

Ranch branding, circa 1940s.

JA Ranch cowboys, circa 1907.

Another important person was the horse wrangler. His duty was to keep the remuda (saddle horses), which often numbered 150 head of horses. He would day-herd them over good grass and take them to water in the evening. At night he had to bunch them close by so the cowboys could access them for an early morning start.

Where there were cowboys, there was a need for boot makers. In 1884 a young man by the name of McLaughlin came to the Matador Ranch. Someone in Ft. Worth had suggested he go to the Matador Ranch; surely they needed a boot maker. His arrival occurred during spring branding season when there was an abundance of cowboys present. They all wanted boots. The young man took foot measurements for several days. Having no way to purchase all the necessary materials, he approached Mr. Campbell concerning his dilemma.

Mr. Campbell asked him to make up a list of all needed materials, and the costs involved. The figure turned out to be $600. Mr. Campbell remarked after seeing the bill: "When I send for that order I will have to send a wagon especially for this stuff. It is an expensive trip. Colorado City is the nearest railhead. Better double those items." Mc Laughlin gasped. "I had just come from the north, where people were chilly as could be. I know I could not get credit for $600 in 600 years. But I did not know *Old Paint*," as the cowboys called Campbell. McLaughlin ultimately made boots for cowboys all over the panhandle of Texas. Over the years other boot makers followed him in the business of making boots. Hand-made boots continued to be made in Matador until the 1990s.

By 1891 things began to change between H. H. Campbell and the Scottish Syndicate. Mr. Campbell felt that change was in the air. With a little incentive many new settlers could be brought into the area. His plan was to systematically divide a small portion of the ranch into many small ranches of four sections (square miles) each, and make them available to men of good character. He felt that this concentration of many small ranches, some of which would be turned into farmland, would have allowed Motley and surrounding counties to economically dominate the entire area—allowing prosperity to become wide-spread. He wanted every ranch employee to own acreage of their own. They could continue to work for the Matadors (as it was commonly called) while they paid for the land. He wanted them to look to the future and own more than just their saddle.

Remuda, catching mounts for the day.

The Scottish syndicate opposed his idea; they did not want more settlers. They wanted their "cash cow" to continue. Mr. Campbell finally accepted that it was not to be. At his last annual Christmas Ball for all employees and their ladies, he addressed the issues that he considered important, and shared that the following day would be his last day in a managerial capacity for the Matador Ranch.

In a tearful presentation that his wife had to ultimately finish reading for him; he spoke from the heart with such eloquence that most thought it would be remembered forever. For the listening audience it immortalized the man; it confirmed what they already knew of the man. To them there would never be another H. H. Campbell; he epitomized honor, integrity, and appreciation of his fellow man. His talk should have lived in infamy; it did not. You judge for yourself for it (drawn from a book written by his son, Harry Campbell, about the history of Motley County) shall follow in its fullness. I think you will be more than a little surprised at his eloquence, and his grasp of the future. H. H. Campbell was a great ranch manager, a great friend, and a great family man. Here are his words that fateful night in December 1891.

I am heartily glad to greet you, one and all, this evening. These festivities are always seasons of freedom from care, good fellowship and happy reunion. But this particular occasion is fraught with special, almost painful, interest to me. The flood gates of thought are opened up, and the lights and shadows of years filled with joys and sorrows, battles and victories, successes and failures, chase each other in rapid succession across the field of consciousness. You my friends, have all traveled far enough along the journey of life to have observed that nothing is permanent, and that change is everywhere prevalent. The winds of heaven that blow across our limitless plains change continually. The sleepless rivers that roll on to the ocean are continually carving out new channels and gnawing at the banks that confine them. Old ocean himself is restless and unceasing in his lashings of the coast that confines his angry billows. Our lives are full of changes: First we are cooing infants in the arms of doting and devoted mothers, then prattling and mischievous children, whose lives are filled with careless joys and short-lived sorrows; next we are grown-up boys and young men with stronger sinews and budding ambitions for higher achievements, and then comes mature manhood with its grave responsibilities, high aspirations and ardent labors. But not only do changes take place in our physical beings, in our places of abode and in our surroundings; there are also changes in our occupations and in the business and social relations that we sustain to each other. This brings me directly to the thoughts that are uppermost in my mind, and possibly in yours too, at this time.

You are doubtless aware that important changes in the management of this splendid property are impending; changes that will probably change the currents of several of our lives into different channels, and in a greater or less measure, for better or for worse, affect the community that has for so long been the scene of our labors. Before the revolving wheel of time shall have made another circuit and ushered in another holiday season, our present business and social relations will have been forever severed. I feel that this is a fitting occasion to review the past, contemplate the present, and cast the horoscope into the shadowy and uncertain future for a prognosis of coming events. I cannot deny myself a free and soulful talk with you at this time—you whose skill, energy, endurance and courage have contributed so largely to the building up of this, the most successful and possibly the most famous ranch in all the imperial domain of Texas. I also want to take advantage of this, our last annual reunion, to express to you my appreciation of your unswerving fidelity to myself, your courtesy and kindness to my wife and child, and your faithfulness and devotion to the interest of your employers.

The age in which we live, gentlemen, is preeminently an age of specialties. The day of glittering generalities is a thing of the past; there is no room for the Jack-of-all-trades in our modern business economy. He who would succeed in any undertaking, profession or enterprise, must do so by careful preparation and unceasing devotion to that calling in its minutest detail. All modern mechanical wonders existed in the minds of their inventors as purely mental conceptions before they assumed tangible shape. The railway engine, the electric light, the ocean steamer and the cotton gin were at first but intangible ideas in the minds of their respective inventors, till they were clothed with material form to bless and benefit mankind. This is no less true of the splendid property, known nearly all over the civilized world as the Matador Land and Cattle Company. It was at first but a figment of the fancy, to be brought into existence, developed and perfected into its present mammoth proportions through years of patient toil on your part and mine, backed up by the liberal endowment given it by foreign capital. Twenty-two years ago, just as the country was beginning to recover from the effects of the civil war, we started out, with the Matador a mental picture, photographed upon our mind, to find a place and the means to clothe it with the garb of materialization. The Pacific Slope, the Sierra Nevada Mountains, and the Great Northwest were all carefully searched for these essentials. At last a proposition was made to a capitalist by the name of A. P. Haws for the building up of such a property. This proposition was favorably received and the prospects looked encouraging for a while, but resulted in disappointment. Negotiations were then entered into with Chicago capitalists that for a time promised good results, but these, too, resulted in disappointment. We then turned to acquaintances of our boyhood days who had grown wealthy, and had large means at their disposal, but inordinate demand for a guarantee of sixty percent per annum on their money invested in the enterprise courted disappointment and invited disaster from the start, and rendered worse than hazardous any enterprise established upon such costly capital. Then it was that, with pride wounded by a lack of confidence on the part of those of whom we had a right to expect the most, we turned our eyes to foreign lands in search of the necessary capital, at a low rate of interest, to establish this enterprise upon a firm basis, and through the financiering ability of Col. A. M. Britton, secured the necessary means, located the maturing grounds for our product, and successfully inaugurated the enterprise that has grown into the splendid and world-famed property, known as the Matador Land and Cattle Company.

In this connection we wish to call your attention to the various efforts that have been made in our State and Nation to prejudice the minds of our people against foreigners and foreign capital. We would also impress upon your minds the fact that, but for this cheap foreign money, Northwest Texas would still be a desert, the refuge of bandits and outlaws. It is this cheap foreign money that has enabled you, gentlemen, to subdue the country, make the desert blossom as the rose, drive out the thief and the bandit, and prepare the way for the splendid civilization that is now taking possession of this fertile and beautiful country over which you, gentlemen, have already established the supremacy of the law and the dominance of right and justice. And while we would admonish you to devotion to your country above all things else, and to let your lives be in strict conformation with the highest and purest patriotism, we would also counsel justice to those foreign capitalist who have so liberally placed their money at our disposal to accomplish these results. We would earnestly entreat you to be faithful to them in the future as in the past, both in work and in deed, defend them when their good name is traduced and their intentions misrepresented by malignant ignorance, and protect their property from abuse and destruction by the vicious and the dishonest. In this vast and fertile country we have the natural resources for wealth and widespread prosperity, but we have not the capital to develop and render available these riches. We must combine our knowledge, skill and resources with the cheapest money that we can find, and whether that be home or foreign capital, it is but right and justice that each should have his equitable share of the proceeds of this combination of resources; therefore we would admonish you to broad and liberal views in regard to the investment of outside money in ranching, or in railway or other public enterprises in this country, that will tend to the development of the natural resources of the country. Be true to yourselves, but also be broad and liberal in your views, and just to those who furnish you the means to enable you to achieve results otherwise unattainable.

At the outset I remarked that we must concentrate, if we would succeed; that we must familiarize ourselves with the details of our business; that we must grow up into it, as it were, and if you will pardon for a moment the introduction of personalities into these remarks, we will state that our first experience in the stock business was the riding a goat in our father's lane. We never repeated the experiment, we never want to. It didn't hurt the goat, but somehow the ground just flew up and hit our pistol pocket so hard that we have ever since been firm in the conviction that there was an earthquake on that particular day. We are against the goat. With the assistance of two sympathetic brothers, our next venture in the stock business was the breaking in of a calf. It was more successful; there was no earthquake that day. This particular calf became the object of our constant care and solicitude. It was a companion; we studied its wants and its habits and became intimate with its every instinct as it grew into mature ox-hood. This was but the beginning. From this time on, our life was constantly associated with cattle, both in driving and tending herds and in the handling of oxen. Whatever measure of success has attended our management of the Matador Ranch, must to a very great extent be attributed to our intimate knowledge of cattle, their wants and their habits, acquired by careful observation and study in early life. The lessons we wish to inculcate by this recital is that, whether you continue in the cattle business, or engage in some other occupation, you must familiarize yourselves with the details of your business if you would succeed. We trust that we may not be considered egotistic if we assume that what it has taken us 40 years to learn cannot be grasped by others as an inspiration, and you, gentlemen, must not hope to embark in the cattle business or other avocation and grasp by inspiration the knowledge of that business that will guarantee success. It must be acquired by patient toil, investigation and experiment. But just here we would observe that these are the very instrumentalities that make the good citizen, the useful man and the wise counselor.

Perfection of management and execution must not be expected of imperfect beings. We of the Matador Ranch have made mistakes, probably many and serious mistakes, but when we look around us at the hopes that have been wrecked and the fortunes that have been squandered by others in fruitless efforts to succeed at the same line of business, we can but congratulate ourselves that we are associates with an enterprise that has weathered the storms, paid regular and legitimate dividends, and landed safely in the harbor of financial security, while thousands have shipwrecked on the same sea.

The prudent man is rarely content with the present, but desires, as far as possible, to peer ahead and see what the future promises. We have already remarked that everything is characterized by change. How often have we seen this truth verified by personal observation in this country? First the Indian and the buffalo; then the cowboy and the herd, and finally the settler and civilization. The cowboy—how shall I pay a proper tribute to his courage, his fortitude and his kindness? He has defied the torrid heats of summer and the frigid blasts of winter without shelter and at times almost without food and clothing. He has braved the fury of savage beasts and still more savage men. He has turned his back upon the comforts of home and the love of kindred to sweep across the trackless desert in the face of dangers seen and unseen, to pave the way for advancing civilization. He has endured every hardship, scorned every danger and surmounted every obstacle that rude and untamed nature could throw in his pathway. Civilization owes him a debt of gratitude greater than is conceivable and one that will never be either fully realized or repaid.

In this connection I will speak but briefly of the little government that you, gentlemen, have built up in the four counties included in the Matador. You came into this country when it was infested with bandits and outlaws. You had every temptation to lead lives of recklessness and debauchery; but to your credit be it said that you chose the better part, proved better than your surroundings, dislodged and drove out the robber and the renegade, ostracized violence and rapine, seated justice upon her throne, and established a community, the virtue, peace and happiness of which was predicated upon the honor of the individual and the gentleman, and the few instances in which it has been violated is a lasting tribute to cowboy government.

But, gentlemen, in doing all this, you have brought about a condition of affairs that is revolutionizing the country. The homeless sons of the East have heard of your fertile lands and sunny skies; they have heard of the expulsion of the Indian, the thief and the robber, and they are coming by hundreds and by thousands to convert your vast pastures and ranges into homes and farms, and the question is, "What are you going to do about it?" Our advice in the premises is to reap the benefits of a condition of affairs that your own courage and fortitude has brought about, secure a body of this rich land that is attracting the attention of the world and that is so rapidly enhancing in value, and next invade the home of one of these good settlers for whom you have prepared the way, capture his daughter for a companion and trot in double harness down the rest of the pathway of life—in other words, settle down and be happy. The best of the domain is being rapidly absorbed, and unless you act promptly in the matter, the opportunity will be gone. You are on the ground, and are familiar with the country, and can make a living if anyone can. If benefits are to accrue from the settling of the country, you are certainly entitled to reap them, and now is your opportunity and it won't last long. Understand me, I am not advising you to leave the employ of the company; but your remaining so employed will not prevent your taking a section of land. I hope you will remain in the employ of the company and be faithful and true to them in the future as in the past, and use your earnings to improve your land that is to be your future home. And when there is no longer employment for you on the ranch, settle down amid the scenes of your early hardships and show to the world what a useful, thrifty and honorable citizen a cowboy can be.

I have before remarked that this is our last annual reunion as co-workers for the Matador. We have had many difficulties to overcome and many rough roads to travel. Heat and cold, hunger and privation have each and often assailed the citadel of our manhood. Under these trying ordeals it is but natural that little asperities should be aroused and hot and hasty words be spoken, but I am proud to know that through it all the milk of human kindness has run, and the wounds inflicted in moments of passion have been more than healed in days and hours of magnanimity and manly reparation, and mutual forgiveness and forgetfulness.

It is with mingled feelings of pride and sadness that I sever my business relations with this company—pride, pardonable pride I trust, that it has flourished and prospered during my connections with its business management and that in a measure my ideal of a cattle ranch has been realized; sadness that I must sever my connection with an institution in which I have so greatly prided and in the interest of which a number of the best years of my life have been spent, and upon which all the thought of my years of greatest mental activity has been expended.

The currents of our lives, yours and mine, have run side by side through many years, many hardships and privations, many victories and defeats. "Tis with sadness I see these long established associations severed, associations rendered sacred by many severe tests of both manhood and friendship. And my good wife, who has been my comfort and support in all these years of toil, exposure and privation—she who has been your friend and comfort in many a gloomy hour, when far from the tender sympathies and administrations of your own loved ones, has a warm place in her heart for each and every one of you, and heartily joins me in admonishing you to continue steadfastly in the paths of truth, honor and duty, ever aspiring to higher and nobler manhood, and it is needless for me to add that she also joins me in wishing you all the prosperity and happiness that this world can bestow upon a set of deserving boys."

The Matador Ranch continued well after the resignation of H. H. Campbell. Murdo Mackenzie managed the operation very successfully until 1912; then he went to work for Brazil Land, Cattle, and Packing Company. His nephew, John McBain, managed for many years. The very last manager, John V. Stevens, was the man my dad worked for at the Adams Ranch. It was one of many smaller operations that evolved after the sale of the Matador Ranch. The historic headquarters and sizeable acreage of over 100,000 acres was acquired by the Koch family out of Wichita, Kansas. Originally Rock

Island Ranch, it is now known as Matador Land and Cattle, and continues to use the one-winged V brand.

Consumers, I want you to know that we have always had men who inherently wanted to do the right thing; just as we have always had individuals solely focused on return on investment. H. H. Campbell was a man of strong conviction trying to do the right thing for everyone involved—not just the ownership, and not at the expense of ownership either. He was an honorable and noble man with a vision for the future.

I believe that our industry and agriculture in general has had over its many years a preponderance of men like H. H. Campbell; all seeking to lend a helping hand without regard for their own best interest. I sincerely hope that through the course of these chapters you will glean an appreciation for the men and women who make up our industry—past and present; perhaps even admire their strong sense of character. I know I do. Having spent time in the area where his (H. H. Campbell) footsteps linger, I can tell you that his strength of character is still alive and well in his descendents, as well as the descendents of those who worked for him.

The beef cattle industry is a wonderful industry to be a part of. The appeal of its people and the quality of life issues that surround us are much more valuable than simple return on investment. I hope this particular story of the ranch and the man who made it possible, will give you specific insight in supporting the generalities of Chapter 5: "Your Beef Producers."

2

Beef Specifics

Where does your beef come from?

Beef (cow/calf) production in the United States is wide-spread, occurring in every state. Though the number has declined 20% over the last twenty years; there are still nearly 765,000 farms and ranches that have a beef cattle inventory. Though most of these operations are small (almost 80% have less than fifty cows), they provide, collectively, a huge number of beef source cattle.

The ranches that I have personally worked with in Texas, Oklahoma, New Mexico, Louisiana, and Florida are among much larger operations. Regarding these operations, less than 500 cows would be small; less than 1000 cows would be medium sized; and over a thousand cows would be large. The largest is 44,000 cows. There are a goodly number of ranches in the six to sixteen thousand (mother cows) head category; and many in the two to six thousand head category. With the exception of the very largest, all are owned individually or by family operations. The largest is owned by the Mormon Church.

Many different breeds are utilized by these ranches. Primarily they select a breed (or a cross-breed) that fits the specifics of their country: temperature fluctuations, humidity, environmental pest issues, water issues (scarcity), as well as type and available forage issues. In some parts of the country a cow may have to walk two miles, or more, to water. The fertile grounds of the mid-west are vastly dissimilar to the drought-prone southwestern states. The gulf coast country is vastly dissimilar to that of the northern mid-west. Well managed operations will have a base cowherd that fits their particular country. Also in well managed herds, each individual cow unit is, largely, treated as an independent business. Those individuals that prove themselves to be less efficient regarding production standards are culled from the cowherd at a convenient time. Today's high production costs force us to make good business decisions regarding keeping our cowherds efficient.

Thompson Ranch near Munday, Texas.

Spade Ranch keeper-heifers, Levelland, Texas.

Bradshaw Ranch, Shattuck, Oklahoma.

Cougar Mountain Ranch, Corona, New Mexico.

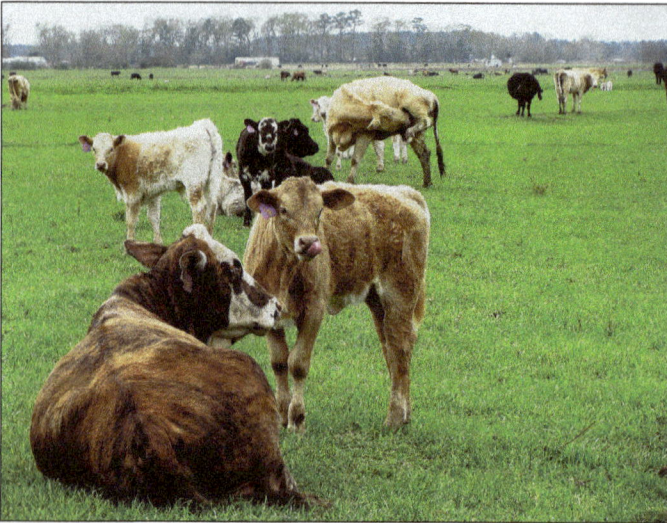

Fournerat Cattle Operation, Basile, Louisiana.

South Florida Cattle Operation.

Thompson Ranch near Munday, Texas.

Spade Ranch keeper-heifers, Levelland, Texas.

Bradshaw Ranch, Shattuck, Oklahoma.

Cougar Mountain Ranch, Corona, New Mexico.

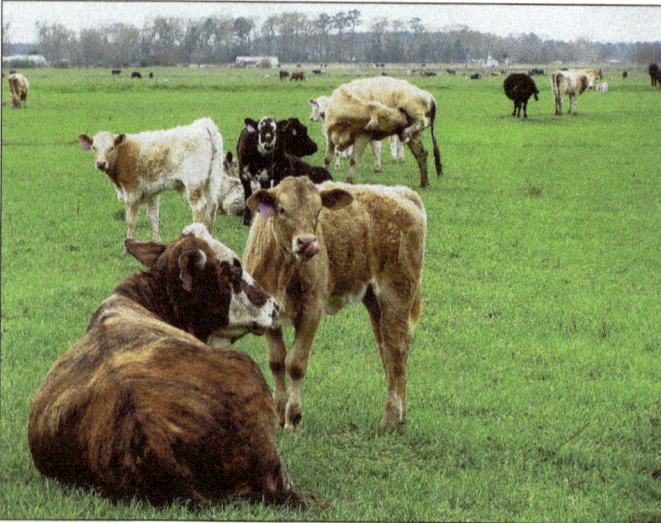

Fournerat Cattle Operation, Basile, Louisiana.

South Florida Cattle Operation.

Thompson Ranch near Munday, Texas.

Spade Ranch keeper-heifers, Levelland, Texas.

Bradshaw Ranch, Shattuck, Oklahoma.

Cougar Mountain Ranch, Corona, New Mexico.

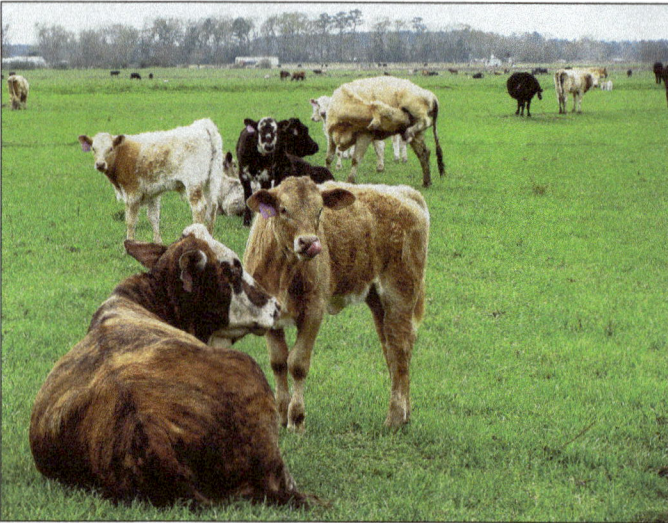

Fournerat Cattle Operation, Basile, Louisiana.

South Florida Cattle Operation.

Generally speaking, if you are in the cattle business, you are doing one of two things. You are actually raising "replacement cattle" (high quality individuals that will be going back into someone's cowherd to become breeding animals); or you are raising beef source cattle destined for the feedyard. Even though the calves you raise may go to a local sale-barn (for auction), or bought by a local cattle buyer; the vast preponderance of all calves will wind up in a feedyard of some description, somewhere. Just at the feedyards that I have been associated with, we have received cattle from all the western states, most of the mid-western and central states, virtually all of the south-east, and at least a couple of the north-eastern states (from Pennsylvania and New York we received Holstein calves). There are good calves that will produce very good carcasses from every part of the country. That said each part of the country has a certain reputation regarding the kind of cattle we are expecting upon arrival at the feedyard. This would not apply as much to feeder Holsteins as they are much more consistent. From the south and south-east, we commonly expect a cross-bred calf with some Brahman influence. We refer to these cattle as being thin hided and little hair. Meaning they need to go to a feedyard in Texas, Arizona or California. They can be fed in more northern climates but should arrive during the summer, allowing more time for winter acclimation. Cattle from Kentucky can certainly be of good quality, but are going to be very inconsistent as to color and breed. Do not get me wrong, they feed just fine; it is just that no two of them look just alike. Cattle from the north-west and north central states will be very uniform, common breed and color, with a heavy hair-coat, and are most commonly of very high quality. Cattle from out west (California, Nevada, Utah and perhaps southern Idaho, will generally be of good quality, but often appear just a little plain. They likely feed best in moderate climates.

The reason that a part of the country creates cattle that become representative of their own locale, has to do with the necessity of having a base cowherd that can do well—given the specific climatic conditions—in that part of the country. Also, many areas just have small cattle operations. If that is the case, when they are put together in truckload lots going to a feedyard or grow operation, they are obviously going to look different from one another.

Some of these calves arrive at the feedyard as single source calves (all having been raised together as part of the same calf crop, at the same location). Some (probably the majority) will arrive as "put together cattle," most commonly of sale-barn origin. If these latter calves are freshly assembled and quickly shipped to the feedyard, they do just fine. When that is not the case, they can and often are, much more of a challenge to get "straightened out" and performing well in the near term. Some few calves never reach a commercial feedyard, but are fed-out at home (on the farm) for local consumption. There is also some "niche" marketing of grass-fed cattle that we will cover later in the book.

Regarding the production of the cowherd, most of us (not raising replacement cattle) are attempting to raise a calf-crop that is desired by the cattle feeder (feedyards). The feedyards want a calf (calf-crop) that will stay healthy. This requires a good preventative health program back at the ranch. Feedyards want an efficient feeder (calf)—converting feedstuffs to pounds of gain. Feedyards want a calf that has some "stretch." The "middle meats" (premium cuts of meat) principally come out of the back and loin areas of the carcass. So, the most desired calf will be a fairly long bodied calf. Many feedyards have a breed or color preference. Often this preference is noticeable across the yard. More commonly, that preference is made known by what they offer for any given set of calves.

With over 700,000 possible beef source farm and ranch locations, you can see that the beef industry is far different from that of pork or chicken, where corporations have control over how they are raised. Yes, beef has inconsistencies—between breeds, between herds, even between individuals within the same herd. There are good carcasses produced by all breeds. Some breeds just have a higher percentage of very good carcasses, than others.

What is a good carcass? A good carcass is one that has a good dressing percentage (difference between the weight of the live animal, and the weight of the finished carcass) yielding an optimal percentage of marketable beef. A good carcass is going to grade well and be tender. A good carcass is going to result in a pleasurable beef eating experience. Meaning, we want that entrée to have the potential to excite sensory perceptions; and then deliver that which was anticipated.

Yes, beef has inconsistencies that pork or chicken does not have. But every individual cow must be able to be successful in her own, particular, environment. There is a vast array of environments in America. Thus, we have a vast array of cowherds—all special in their own right; and all appreciated for the challenges that they must endure.

Beef Consumption

Beef is a seventy-three billion dollar industry. US beef consumption in 2010 was 26.4 billion pounds. US production was almost identical: 26.41 billion pounds. US commercial slaughter was 34.2 million head; of which 27.1 million head were steers and heifers; and 6.5 million head were cull beef and dairy cows.

USDA estimates US per capita beef consumption at 57.4 pounds each, down 13% from ten years ago. It is down 25% from 1980 levels; and down almost 40% from 1960 levels. USDA prediction for 2012 is 54.1 pounds each. With domestic consumption of beef going down, exports generally must increase.

Let us look at why beef consumption has been trending downward rather dramatically. Cash strapped Americans are economizing. We cannot afford the beef entrees at restaurants, as frequently as we used to. The more expensive cuts (middle meats) that used to be almost totally consumed in America are now expanding their presence in the "world" of fine dining. Additionally, our portion sizes have shrunk for a variety of reasons. We are not eating as much at a time as we used to. Also, we are not cooking at home like we have in the past. The meals our young people, in particular, consume are often in the junk-food category, lacking quality protein of any kind. Processed meals (ready to eat) often rely more on food chemistry and bi-products, rather than identifiable food products we recognize. Lastly, there is the category of people that find beef unsuitable to eat. Some do not want to eat any beef that has a name, like T-bone or sirloin. Some think of these animals as pets. Many consumers are simply judging the beef industry based on emotion, rather than from a base of knowledge. Any prospective beef consumer not consuming beef based on ethical reasons is a reflection of a complete lack of knowledge concerning the beef industry.

The good thing concerning the last two categories of consumers that do not like beef for their own personal reason, is that they are not a substantial part of the reason for beef consumption to be going down, per capita. America's eating habits have changed enormously over the last fifty years. The degree to which we "cook" has changed enormously over the last fifty years. Even though we are individually eating less beef than fifty years ago, there are a lot more of us. Today, bottom-line, Americans are cutting back due to economic pressures. I love beef, and I have to cut back. I simply cannot afford beef at the frequency I could in the past. With rising retail costs here, and efforts to tackle chronic but preventable ailments such as obesity and diabetes, meat companies are increasingly developing and catering meat products to fit the taste of foreign consumers. Later in this book you will know that fresh beef is not a part of the obesity problem. The key point being, the people we are selling our beef to are not in serious economic trouble. They can afford our beef. Asia, in particular, is still on a very strong economic path. Top markets for US beef include Japan (351 Million pounds), Mexico (500 Million pounds), South Korea (277 Million pounds), Canada (390 Million pounds), and Russia is expanding their cowherd base with American cattle.

Supply and demand are the principal driving forces regarding price. World-wide beef consumption is dramatically up; and is expected to remain in good demand through 2050. Only two countries in the world can expand base cowherd numbers more than 10%—Brazil and Argentina. Our U.S. cowherd numbers continue to drop for a lot of different reasons: state and federal lands restricting cattle grazing opportunities, encroaching urbanization (huge factor in the state of Florida), next generation does not want the hassle of managing a few cows, and escalating land prices. It is very difficult for young people who desire a cattle operation, to be able to afford to do so. Current tax laws are making it very difficult to pass the land to the next generation without having to sell some off to pay the taxes.

(Note: Although total U.S. boxed beef availability has decreased by 72,000 metric tons, the other big-three have increased their supply: Brazil (242,000 metric ton increase), India (633,000 metric ton increase), and Australia (162.000 metric ton increase). These numbers were courtesy of Dr. Grant Dewell, Beef Cattle Extension Veterinarian, Iowa State University. Our usual supply partners (Canada and Mexico) simply have no significant, available numbers to send to the U.S. Another interesting change involves ground beef. Historically, the category of steak has been priced at two and a half times that of ground beef. Today, it is only one and one-half times the price of ground beef; yet, we continue to buy the ground beef because it is what we can afford. At many sale barns today, producers cannot afford to buy replacement cows because the price that the packers are willing to pay is above what they can afford to give for these cows. The demand for ground beef is that significant.

Our ranch lands and small stock operations are shrinking in size and numbers. Consequently, our cow herd numbers are shrinking as well. To compound the issues involved, a wide-spread drought across Middle America has contributed, rather dramatically, to this shrinking cowherd. The National Agricultural Statistics Service reported on 7/4/2012 that the numbers of cattle and calves in the US totaled 97.8 million head. That is 2% less than the year previous. Beef cattle numbers were down 3% at 30.5 million head counted, while dairy cow numbers remained unchanged at 9.2 million head. Overall, it is the smallest cattle inventory since the agency began a July count in 1973.

The nation's calf crop was also 2% smaller than the year previous. The other key indicator, replacement heifers, will be low as well, when the drought related numbers are re-tabulated. These two factors indicate that cow numbers will not recover soon.

Those of you who enjoy beef should expect long-term pricing, regarding your favorite beef entrees to move upwards, exacerbating the issue of beef affordability. I am sure our "critics" will want to take credit for reducing cattle numbers. Do not believe it. Our critics (HSUS and PETA in particular) are irritating, and even occasionally infuriating; but their importance pales dramatically, compared to the real issues regarding our shrinking cowherds. If we prioritize all the issues affecting our cattle industry, you are at the top of the list—the most important of all. We need to get you up to speed regarding our industry. We need you to be informed, enabling choices based on fact. We need you to keep from being used by our critics. We need you to understand our challenges, and hopefully, to appreciate our efforts. You, quite simply, are the most important person in our lives. No one is going to work harder to earn your trust, than we are. Proof seems to come from the fact that US per capita beef consumption has actually started back up over the last two years.

The Science Of Beef

The sciences involving beef can quickly become overly complicated unless we narrow the scope of our focus. For this discussion we will limit the subject material to meat science. The broader definitions we will cover in later chapters.

Research and development of new "value added" beef products are constant and on-going. New products developed to fit the desires of an evolving consumer base, are constantly being evaluated. As these products are nearing the test-market stage, they must pass all governmental, food safety guidelines. Heat N Serve beef entrees, convenience packaging, portion controlled meals, seasoned and/or marinated beef products ready for the oven or grill, and single dish meals with a beef entrée, are regularly entering the marketplace. Modern food and food products are designed to be complex and multi-sensorial. We eat them for sensation. The food industry is trying to find the formulation that is going to make the greatest number of people want their product.

Here, we must separate the two subjects: fresh beef and beef product. Most of our discussion topics will focus on fresh beef. I trust fresh beef. I know what is in fresh beef. It is wholesome and nutritious. I do not know what is in beef product. I know that it has met governmental approval for safety; but, I question all the "chemistry" involved. Obesity is a serious problem in America. I suspect that all the chemicals, preservatives, flavor enhancers, and high fructose corn syrup that our food industry adds to most processed food products, has far more negative effects to our bodies, than we currently realize.

Regarding fresh beef, Michigan State University did a study on beef quality. From this public survey they found that "tenderness" was rated the most important component of a beef entrée. Second most important was flavor; and number three in importance was juiciness. Their work indicated that "the extent of post-mortem (after death) muscle fiber shortening and break-down, and the amounts of moisture, marbling and intact connective tissue left over after cooking, determined "tenderness." They also found that "flavor" was a result of fat and compounds that arise from muscle changes during the aging process. Lastly, that juiciness was principally associated with the degree of doneness.

The Iowa Beef Industry Council has also done some great work that I will share. Beef develops its desirable flavor and aroma during cooking. True meaty, umami flavor begins with the application of heat as it transforms proteins, carbohydrates and fats into their smaller amino-acids, sugars, and fatty acids. As heat denatures myofibrillar proteins causing them to gradually shorten or toughen, and release liquid, connective tissues solubilize, and begin to break down. When beef with low amounts of connective tissue, such as loin and rib-cuts, are cooked beyond 149 degrees Fahrenheit, the additional heat continues to toughen them. So, fast cooking at higher temperatures is preferred (dry heat).

Beef with higher levels of connective tissue (white strands), such as chuck and round cuts, need longer, slower cooking (moist heat) to allow time for the connective tissue to convert to gelatin and become tender.

Basically, all beef cooking methods fall into two main categories: dry heat (for tender cuts of beef), and moist heat (for less tender cuts of beef). Tender cuts come primarily from the middle of the animal—the rib and the loin. These muscles receive less exercise, and thus less connective tissue. Less

tender cuts of beef come primarily from the front and hind sections—the chuck and the round. They are less tender because these are heavily exercised muscles that develop more connective tissue.

Dry heat cooking methods would include broiling, grilling, oven roasting, and stir-frying. Moist heat cooking methods would include braising and pot roasting, as well as stewing and poaching. During long, slow cooking in moist heat, beef flavor components leach into the cooking liquid, creating delicately flavored meat. The lack of strong browned beef aromas, also reduce flavor intensity. So, ingredients such as broth and wine are often used in place of water to produce a flavorful, aromatic sauce or gravy. The difference between stewing (more liquid), and braising is the amount of liquids involved.

Let me leave moist heat cooking with this very important note. Browning of the meat (searing if you will), prior to placing in the liquid, should never be skipped. Why? Because browning creates beef flavors that can only be produced through dry heat; unique flavors and aromas that are not intrinsic to the beef itself. Browning the beef causes proteins (amino-acids) and carbohydrates (sugars) to caramelize into intense flavors and aromas. So, before using the moist heat cooking methods, brown your beef.

The French are noted for keeping their menus interesting. "Seasonality—eating the best at its peak—and seasoning—the art of choosing and combining flavors to complement food—are vital for fighting off the food lover's worst enemy: boredom, not calories. Eat the same thing in the same way, time and time again, and you will need more just to achieve the same pleasure. Think of it as "taste tolerance." Have just one taste experience as your complete dinner, and you are bound to eat too much, as you seek satisfaction from volume, instead of the interplay of flavors and textures that come from a well thought-out meal. The French master a few basic preparations, and leave the rest to improvisation, the art of tweaking an old stand-by into something seemingly different. They do it by slightly altering the preparation or seasoning, or by transforming lunch left-over's into something rather different for a later meal.

It is all about manipulating how the five senses are interacting with what is put before them. It can be as simple as choosing the more unusual yellow tomato over the standard red variety. Visual variety, color and presentation, are underestimated factors in food pleasure. They are the reason why freshness, quality and other sensations dictate how we feel about our food.

Most of us use the terms taste and flavor interchangeably; but they are actually different. Taste refers to the five basic receptors: sweet, salty, sour, bitter and umami (pronounced oo-MOM-ee). Flavor is a combination of taste, PLUS the other sensations that influence our perception of food, such as aroma, texture, juiciness, mouth-feel, and color.

The ability to detect these five tastes has been significant to our survival throughout the ages, directing us towards vital foods and away from potential poisons. SWEET means energy-giving carbohydrates. SALT indicates essential minerals for life-sustaining cell functions and wound healing. SOUR says to "proceed with caution," since many foods sour as they deteriorate. BITTER warns "spit it out," because many natural toxins taste bitter.

Umami, the fifth taste is described as meaty and savory or delicious. It is the taste of glutamates—the salts of an amino-acid, and other small molecules called nucleotides. The small protein compounds that trigger our umami receptors come from many sources. Meaty, savory umami flavors instantly bring to mind a great steak, but fruits and vegetables also contain these same proteins. Tomatoes, mushrooms, aged cheeses, green tea, and seaweed all stimulate our umami receptors. When these individual umami compounds are combined, they have a magnifying effect on each other. These fruits and vegetables that are at the peak of their ripening have increased umami flavor. That is why a truly ripe tomato, aged Parmigiano-Reggiano, and fermented foods such as wine and soy sauce, possess enticing, complex flavors, and also pair well with beef dishes. Some classic beef dishes loaded with umami-rich ingredients would include Steak Diane, Swiss steak, Steak De Burgos, Beef Bourguignon, and Beef Stroganoff. Now, you know why these classic pairings have withstood the test of time.

Beef Quality

Let me begin with the thoughts of Dr. Elizabeth Boyle, Department of Animal Science and Industry, Kansas State University. "When consumers eat a steak or slice of roast, they expect the meat to be tender, juicy and have a good flavor. But how do you determine if the beef displayed in the retail case at the supermarket, will have eating characteristics that you desire? It is important to recognize that there are many factors influencing the acceptability of the meat you eat."

Let us look at some of those influencing factors. First, we will look at the various breeds of cattle, and the gene-pool contained therein. No breed is perfect. One may be among the best at one point of the production chain, yet weak in another. Genetically, some breeds are going to consistently hang-up better carcasses than others. Some have inherent advantages regarding marbling (we will get into that later); yet, there are many outside influences that affect the ultimate quality of a finished carcass.

Can we say which breeds are better? Sure, if we are willing to narrow the subject question. Which breed is most efficient regarding feed conversions (the number of pounds of feed required to produce a pound of beef)? Which breed has higher tendencies toward marbling (fat deposition in the muscle)? Which breeds are noted for their tenderness? Which breeds tend to make the owner (of the cattle during their time in the feedyard) the most money? Yes, there is pre-disposition; but, it is also heavily influenced by variables that affect the individual and the calf-crop in general. That is why the "history" of the cattle is so important to the feedyard manager, or whoever is buying the cattle. Once we have fed a particular calf-crop (one year's production from the source cowherd), we "know" what they are worth. We then know the involved health issues, conversion data, as well as grade and yield issues regarding the finished carcasses. Now, we know their particular value, and how they should be marketed. This information will be reflected in next year's offering (price) for the calf-crop.

As a general rule, retail cuts of beef from breeds such as Limousin, Charolais, Gelbvieh, and Simmental are generally lean, and have acceptable tenderness. Beef from Angus and Hereford (English breeds), and their crosses, have very desirable eating characteristics. Crossbred cattle (having at least a hint of Brahman influence), that fit much of the country in the south and south-west, have much more variable carcass quality. Some of their carcasses are as good as any of the above; and some of them are poorer than any of the above. Dr. Boyle accounted for as many as seventy breeds (including crosses) of cattle used by producers, which obviously contributes to some of the variability regarding beef quality.

Economics, as they primarily relate to the packer (where harvest and the break-down of the carcass is achieved), always influences what is fed; how they are fed, and length of the feeding period. "Finished" beef animals can be sold (from the feedyard) into a grid, where the cattle are expected to fit the specific parameters of that grid (a particular market segment, most commonly). If they do in fact fit the grid, the cattle (economically) do well. Cattle can also be sold into the cash market, where the owner gets paid based on live animal weight.

Or, the cattle can be sold "in the beef," where the owner gets paid based on the quality of the individual carcass (high risk, high reward).

Very commonly, it is the "choice/select" spread (the dollar value difference between a "choice" graded carcass versus the dollar value of a "select" graded carcass) that determines how long cattle are fed. If the spread is narrow (between the value of a choice carcass versus the value of a select carcass), and the subject cattle are a little plain; it may make more sense (dollars) to market them as soon as the feedyard manager believes that they will qualify for the "select" grade.

With a little higher-end calf (higher quality) that is still feeding efficiently, that same manager may feed them a little longer, hoping to get more "choice" carcasses. Really high-end (high quality) calves will usually be fed toward a grading goal of "choice."

If cattle are not feeding efficiently (poor rate of conversion from grain ration to pounds of beef), they will go onto the "show-list" early. These cattle need to move on toward harvest, if at all possible. The show-list involves the pens of cattle that are available to packer buyers.

Some of the breeds with their particular body types, are simply going to finish (reach maximum acceptable fat levels) earlier than others. If the entire pen fits that description, it's great. They will all finish at the same time. Otherwise, you are going to have some individuals in the pen, finishing well ahead of the others. This is a poor state of affairs. These "finished" individuals become an economic night-mare, if they continue to be fed, while waiting on the other individuals to finish. Some feedyards create opportunities to pull out these early finishing individuals, and market them with others (usually a different owner), going to the packer. Yes, it does create extra work and extra bookkeeping.

Add the genetic variability to the marketing alternatives presented by the packer—not to mention packer discounts for things they do not like—and you can appreciate that feedyard managers are constantly evaluating and re-evaluating marketing options which best fit any particular set of calves currently being fed.

What other factors influence beef quality? Wild cattle never feed well. Well managed feedyards often do not accept, or will aggressively cull wild cattle. Wild cattle have higher injury rates; higher rates of lower leg lameness, poorer feed conversions, and endure higher stress levels, all of which negatively affects the quality of the meat. These attributes commonly reduce opportunity for profit by $60 per head.

Gender, also plays a role in carcass quality. A yearling heifer (rather than a younger, calf-fed heifer) is one of the hardest classes of cattle to feed. Most people would agree that "tenderness" is a common problem with this class of cattle. Many cattlemen prefer not to feed heifers in general, for this reason and others, including issues involving pregnancy.

Our industry used to feed a lot of yearling cattle. In those days it was common to leave the weaned calf-crop on the ranch, away from the cowherd, enabling additional time (usually 6 to 12 additional months) to grow before being sent to the feedyard for finishing. Today, we feed mostly calves—calf-feds, if you will. These calves are usually weaned (at about six months of age) from their mothers (at the ranch), and either sent to the feedyard, or to a stocker cattle operation for a few more months before going on to be finished. Carcass quality significantly improved when we started feeding six month old cattle, rather than eleven or twelve month old cattle. Length of stay at the feedyard only increased modestly. The average calf's life span (conventionally fed) is 442 days. Grass-fed cattle (not finished on grain rations) would have a significantly longer life-span. It takes them much longer to reach anything approaching harvest weight, simply grazing grass. This will be discussed in some detail within the confines of the environmental chapter of this book.

Nutrition is the last category we will consider regarding carcass quality. Specifics will be noted under "grass-feds" and "finished cattle," just a little later in the book. Suffice to say that availability and quality of feedstuffs does make a difference in carcass quality. I also believe that there are significant differences between consulting nutritionists. Some view cattle from ground level; while others view it from 1,000 feet or even 10,000 feet; meaning, that their perspective and focus may be on different things. Some are very good at helping the consulting veterinarian in minimizing the impact of bloat and GI (gastro-intestinal) disturbances; while others remain focused on maximizing performance parameters. Personality and chemistry are huge factors. We need to be able to collectively delve into a subject and find a direction, if not a solution. Bill Dickey, M.S. is a cattle nutritionist out of Lincoln, Nebraska that I worked with more than any other. He is brilliant and a joy to work with. Challenges are many at a large, commercial feedyard. Dedication, persistence and doing the right thing for every individual animal, no matter how many are present, are the tools for success in today's cattle feeding environment.

USDA Grade

If a beef animal is harvested and the meat is going to be made available to the public, that live animal, and the harvested carcass will have been inspected by USDA personnel, properly trained in all aspects of food safety. It is the law, and it is well understood by all individuals within the industry. For any reason inspection personnel can off-rail and hold a carcass for complete evaluation and testing if necessary. That carcass does not go back on the moving chain until all doubts are erased, and that inspector is comfortable that no adulteration has occurred. Some few do not go back on the rail.

On a work assignment in a packing house I saw two gorgeous carcasses cut-down (off the hook and into large chunks), and dropped a few feet onto a moving conveyor, exiting the immediate area. These carcasses had been condemned because of single buckshot, found just barely under the surface of the musculature. Some pheasant hunter (most likely) had shot in the wrong direction while hunting birds. This very likely had occurred several, if not many, months before. What a waste, not to mention economic loss. But, it is their job to maintain the integrity of our nation's food supply. I think they do a great job.

After inspection and final cleaning, the carcasses go into a cooler (large chill room) for a day or two before being graded. As these carcasses exit the cooler, they are knife-opened between the 12th and 13th rib, exposing the ribeye muscle. This is one of the focal areas utilized by USDA graders.

A quality grade is a composite evaluation of factors that affect palatability of the meat. Included would be carcass maturity, firmness, texture and color of the lean, and the amount and distribution of marbling within the lean (the exposed ribeye). Most people would consider degree of marbling and degree of maturity to be the more important criteria.

MARBLING (intra-muscular fat) is the intermingling or deposition of fat within the lean. Graders evaluate the amount and distribution of marbling in the ribeye muscle at the cut surface. Degree of marbling is the primary determination of quality grade. Desirable ribeyes will exhibit an adequate amount of finely dispersed marbling in a firm, fine textured, bright cherry-red colored lean. As an animal matures the characteristics of muscle change; muscle color becomes darker, and muscle texture becomes coarser.

MATURITY refers to the physiological age of the animal, rather than the chronological age. The indicators are bone characteristics, ossification of cartilage, as well as color and texture of ribeye muscle. At approximately thirty (30) months of age ossification centers in the "buttons" of the sacrum region of the vertebra, begin to appear. Carcasses are categorized as A (9 to 30 months), B (30 to 42 months), C (42 to 72) and D (72 to 96 months). Carcass maturity scores of B and above, require an increasing amount of marbling as maturity scores increase to remain in the same grade.

After the degree of maturity and marbling score has been determined, these two factors are combined to arrive at the FINAL USDA GRADE.

USDA PRIME: three different categories of "abundant" marbling (AB=abundant; MAB=moderately abundant; SLB=slightly abundant).

USDA CHOICE: Three categories of "modest" marbling. The upper category is sold at a premium due to the chronic shortage of Prime carcasses.

USDA SELECT: Two categories of "slight" marbling.

Yearly numbers regarding how many of each grade is produced will vary; but, commonly, the numbers might be represented by: 2% Prime, 57% Choice, 36% Select, and 5% NR (no roll) which is wholesome meat, just little to no exposed (visually notable) fat in the musculature.

A yield grade is also assigned to each carcass. Yield grades estimate the amount of boneless, closely trimmed retail cuts from the high-value parts of the carcass—the round, loin, rib, and chuck. A yield grade one (YG 1) has the highest percentage, and a YD 5 has the lowest percentage.

Ribeye areas are expressed as a measurement in square inches. These measurements typically may be as small as ten (10) and as large as seventeen (17). Negative economic adjustments are made (as to the value of the carcass) by the packer if they deem that number to be too small or too large. Histori- cally, the "trade" has desired a medium sized ribeye.

Yes, marbling is a huge factor in determining the value of a carcass. It is clearly a large part of the sensory beef eating experience. For those of you who are put off by the term fat or marbling, may I offer a comment about KOBE BEEF. This Japanese beef product is a highly prized and highly priced cut of beef. Many of you have heard how wonderful it is; and some of you have ac- tually enjoyed consuming it. It is marvelous. That said, even those of you who have tried it and loved it, would likely not buy it from a meat case if it were presented there. Visually, these steaks appear to be as much fat (marbling) as lean. To my eye they appear to be more white (fat) than red (lean). They are not pretty to look at. Few customers would buy them, even at a moderate price, if they did not already know the product. It is not something you want to eat regularly, but on occasion, wonderful.

Identifying American breeds that marble well would produce a variety of opinions. Much also depends upon their nutritional background. My own opinion would include Shorthorn, Jersey, and Angus, with a slight preference toward Red Angus.

There are some recently imported breeds that tout tenderness and marbling. I have no argument with their statements regarding the full-bloods (a purebred of the breed); but, arguments do exist regarding the half-bloods, if they are presented as being of the same eating quality. Variability does exist in half-bloods depending upon which breed with which they are crossed.

Now, let us move a little deeper into the subject. Some calves simply do not have the genetic potential to advance, efficiently into the "choice" category of beef. Feeding an average calf to "select" might make a profit of twenty dollars, for example. Feeding that same calf to "choice" might create a loss of twenty dollars, or more. Finding a window of economic opportunity and taking advantage of that opportunity, allows us to stay in business over the long-haul. The problem is that the variables continue to move. What was a great plan in conception turns out to be a disaster, 250 days later when close-out information is tabulated. Even long-term experience only helps avoid some of the pitfalls. There are many management philosophies out there in practice; but few that work in the long term, and most of them are based on break-evens. Corporate America would scoff at our returns. We are not wild about them ourselves; but, we want to feed cattle. We like feeding cattle. We do not expect to get rich, few do—and none in recent times.

The bottom-line is that we are often more focused on economic survivability (regarding the feeder cattle owner) than the quality grade of the beef involved. The last thing you should want to happen is for Corporate America and packing houses in particular, to do to cow/calf operators, what they have already done to the feedyard industry. The price of your steak would go through the roof.

Flavor, Collagen, Juiciness, and Color

Most of meat's flavor develops when it is cooked. The amount of fat in meat certainly influences its flavor; but a process called the "Maillard reaction" is likely responsible for the most distinguished flavors. Flavor can also be added through brining and marinating. The "Maillard reaction" occurs when the denatured proteins on the surface of the meat recombine with the sugars present. The combination creates the "meaty" flavor and changes the color. For this reason, it is also called the "browning reaction." This reaction occurs most readily between 300 and 500 degrees Fahrenheit.

In the early twentieth century, Louis-Camil Maillard was trying to figure out how amino-acids linked to form proteins. He discovered that when he heated sugars and amino-acids together, the mixture slowly turned brown. But it was not until the 1940s that scientists discovered the role the Maillard reaction plays in creating flavors and aromas. As many as six hundred components have been identified in the aroma of beef.

MARINADES:

Marinades are usually made up of three components: acid, oil, and herbs. The acid helps to partially denature the meat's proteins, opening up "tunnels" in the structure of the meat where flavor can seep in. Marinades do not penetrate very far. They work best on the less dense (than beef) muscle structure of chicken or fish. For denser meat (beef), marinades work best when the meat is cut into smaller pieces. However, if left too long, the action "cooks" the surface of the meat. Marinades work quickly on less dense meats, and take much longer for more dense meats.

BRINING:

Brining meat (placing it in a salt water solution) adds moisture through osmosis. Osmosis happens when water flows from a low-concentration environment, to a higher concentration environment, through a semi-permeable membrane. When meat is placed in a brining solution, the meat's cell fluids are less concentrated than the salt water in the brining solution. Water flows out of the cells in the meat, and salt flows in. The salt then dissolves some of the fiber proteins, and the meat cell fluids become more concentrated, thus drawing water back in. Brining adds salt and water to the meat cells. When the meat is cooked (where most water is normally evaporated out), there is still water left in the cells because water was added before cooking.

FAT:

Fat, an energy source stored in animal muscle, also contributes to the flavor of the meat. Water is the most prevalent component of meat, and most of the flavor-carrying, aroma molecules are "hydrophobic" (repelled by water). These molecules do however, dissolve in fat.

Meat's fat content varies from animal to animal and within each animal from part to part. Muscles that are often used, consume the stored-up fat; so the meat from these areas do not have much fat. Areas that are not used much, do not use up as much energy; so there is more fat in these cuts of meat. Age also plays a role. The older the animal, the more time it (the body) has to build up fat-pocket energy reserves in its muscles.

COLLAGEN:

Collagen (the white strands in beef) is a long, stiff protein that is the most prevalent protein in mammals. It is made up of three separate molecules composed of amino-acid chains, twisted around each other. Something like the way fibers are twisted around each other in forming a "rope." This structure is what makes the collagen so strong. This strength is also what makes it more difficult to break down. The more collagen there is in a piece of meat, the tougher it is to cut and to chew. Skin is mostly collagen, as are the tendons that connect muscles to bone. For cuts high in collagen content, cooking methods (moist) must be long and slow. Collagen is soluble in water, and when cooked slowly and with moist heat, it becomes gelatin. It can be made less of a problem by cutting the meat, cross-grain, into small pieces (easier to break apart).

JUICINESS:

With the exception of meats exposed to brining solutions, juiciness is almost completely a result of how well done you like your beef. Since juiciness is such a huge factor regarding the beef eating experience, many restaurant chefs will not cook it past medium—a few not past medium-rare. When one goes to the trouble of selecting and making available great steaks, these chef's want them to be the best they can be. Cooking past medium does not yield a product any chef can be proud of.

COLOR:

Grocery stores typically offer beef in one of two ways, at least regarding those cuts displayed in the meat case. "Trimmed and ready" steaks are most commonly presented in a Styrofoam tray, covered with an oxygen permeable film. This enables the color of the beef to be as cherry-red as possible. If your grocery store has a discounted meat area, it will be for those steaks beginning to lose that cherry-red color. That is where I shop. There is nothing wrong with the meat; and the color loss does not affect the taste. Fresh meat, including ground meat, that smells fresh and appears lightly brown in color, is safe to cook and eat; but, should be quickly frozen if you do not intend to consume it within a day. Use your nose; smell the beef you buy. You have to know what the fresh smell of beef is, in order to detect an "odor" that is associated with beef that has been poorly managed. Yet, I cannot ever remember buying beef from an American supermarket that was anything but fresh.

Larger cuts (perhaps whole ribeye rolls or tenderloins) are normally packaged in vacuum bags. This beef will have a purplish-red color while still in the package. Once the meat is removed from the packing and exposed to air, the surface of the meat will turn to bright cherry-red. The interior of the muscle will remain purple because oxygen cannot penetrate to the center of the meat. Both the purple and the red colors are natural for fresh meat in their respective containers.

Myoglobin is a pigment found in muscle that influences meat color. Beef has higher concentrations than pork or poultry. That difference causes beef to appear redder than pork, and pork to be redder than chicken. Muscles that were used for greater physical activity generally have more myoglobin; the dark meat of a chicken leg for example.

The meat from mature animals is most commonly redder than meat from younger animals. If you have had veal, you will remember it as being very pale in color. Spring lamb is pale in comparison to a mature sheep.

The sarcoplasmic proteins—hemoglobin and myoglobin—are also denatured during cooking. The color change in these pigments is the primary indicator for degree of doneness in beef. As the temperature of the beef increases, the muscle becomes progressively opaque, changing from red to pink to brown. The color of the beef juice also changes from pink to pale amber.

Labeling—Hamburger Versus Ground Beef

Shoppers are confronted with a variety of labels in the meat section that I call the hamburger meat area. Even though various governmental mandates have gone into place with the intent of clarifying the issue, they have largely proved unsuccessful. Most shoppers are still confused over all the differences, and the options presented. Beef purveyors have also made matters worse in their efforts to support the effort of "lean meat." Perhaps, I can help.

1. First, decide what grade of beef you desire. In the meat case you most commonly will find "Select." The select grade will be less expensive; thus it will be what most people buy. Personally, I consider the choice grade when buying a good steak: T-bone, ribeye and strip steaks in particular. Remember that tenderness may have little to do with USDA grade. USDA grade has more to do with the youth of the animal involved and the amount of fat in the musculature. If I am going to pay extra for choice, it must visually represent a difference to my eye. It literally must sell itself to me by its appearance, or I buy the select steaks. Some grocery store chains will have an excellent supply of "Choice" meats on display. If you desire other than what is displayed, ask the market personnel. They can very likely meet your request in whatever grade you desire.

2. Next, let us immediately discern the difference between "Ground Beef" and "Hamburger Meat."

"Ground Beef" is chopped fresh and/or frozen beef from primal cuts and trimmings. The maximum fat content allowed is 30% (70% lean). No water, no phosphates, no binders, or other red meat sources may be added, and still be labeled as "Ground Beef." The label may have an added qualifier: ground sirloin, or ground chuck, or ground round. If that is the case, the lean can only come from that particular source, and the fat included, must also come from that particular source. If I buy "Ground Sirloin" (which I usually do, because the sirloin is, in my opinion, the most flavorful part of the carcass) everything in that package will have come from the sirloin portion of the carcass. Not necessarily from that one carcass, but from many. It is a "pooled product."

"Hamburger Meat," on the other hand, can contain lean from several different parts of the carcass, and it can contain fat trimmings from other than the primal sources; meaning that the fat can also come from a variety of different sources (pertinent to the beef carcass)

3. Usually the label will express the fat content as a percentage: 30%, 20%, 15%, etc. Some grocery stores will turn that around, and express it as a percentage of lean: 70%, 80%, or even 90%. So, if it is labeled as 70/30, you know it is 70% lean, and 30% fat. The fat content can never be above 30%.

How much fat content do you like? For me, it is not a question of which is healthier, because I am not going to be eating it every day, anyway. I like the additional flavor of the higher fat product. I buy 70/30 ground sirloin. Yes, if you buy the leaner product, you can eat it more often. But, if you have to add oil in order to fry a hamburger patty, you are dismantling the thought process you used in buying that particular meat in the first place.

If I am cutting down on fats, carbohydrates and sugars (which I am), it does not mean I do not still eat them—I do. But, I do not eat them as often, and in lesser amounts. I will not forgo the "sensory beef eating experience," in particular, just because I am watching my weight. But, I will have fatty beef (ribeye steaks in particular) less often. The leaner ground product just does not have the natural flavor, and is a little harder to cook (without adding oil). I am a fan of all things natural. If mother-nature created it, I want it. I stay away from processed anything. That is not to say I never eat boxed ingredients, or frozen entrees, I do. But it is rare, and I am usually at someone else's house. I will eat whatever they serve, in limited portions.

4. Lastly, the subject of economics. If you are like many people who are closely watching their budget, do not run from hamburger meat. It is usually less expensive and perfectly nutritious. Most of us could not discern the difference when it is cooked. It may have a little less flavor, but I am sure you can season that issue out of contention. Do not beat yourself up over which meat to buy. Buy what you need to buy to stay in your budget. Times will get better. If they do not, we may all have to go "off-shore" to get a good steak.

3

Beef Handing Techniques

A base activity of bringing an animal protein to the marketplace has always been how do we make it better? Today, we add a new question—how do we make it safer? Though separate issues, each is a huge part of bringing beef into the marketplace "perfectly" ready to meet your desires. Let us examine some of those options in place today.

Aging

Post-mortem aging is usually limited to beef, due to the relative youth of pork, lamb, and veal. Aging is a natural process that usually improves tenderness. During this conversion of muscle to meat, natural enzymes (proteases) found in muscles, breaks down specific proteins in muscle fibers; a process known as proteolysis. Tenderization occurs at a relatively rapid rate for the first 7-10 days. Aging beyond 28 days results in little additional benefit concerning enhanced palatability.

Dry Aging

Dry aging occurs in refrigerated conditions: 32-34 degrees Fahrenheit. Relative humidity and air movement are especially critical. The beef itself can be whole carcasses or cuts of meat. Dry aged T-bones are very popular. Though some variation between facilities does exist, 85% humidity is most common. Air movement (velocity) is usually between .5 and 2.5 meters/second. Air velocity is essential in removing moisture from the room. Insufficient air flow will result in off flavors and possibly spoilage; while too much air flow results in weight and trim losses associated with overly drying of the meat surface.

Wet Aging

Wet aging is a process that occurs in vacuum bags under conditions of 32-34 degrees Fahrenheit. Because most beef is vacuum bagged at the site of carcass fabrication, wet aging is the predominant method of aging beef today. Most commonly we are talking about the middle meats (rib and loin cuts) that are wet aged. These cuts have less connective tissue, which is not broken down during the aging process. Obviously, air flow and relative humidity are not necessary requirements.

The average time that beef is wet-aged is seventeen (17) days. Beyond 28 days there is little beneficial effect. Because the fact that the wet aging process begins when placed in the vacuum bag, some marketing avenues plan on a 7-10 day arrival window at the retail store, allowing the wet aging process to be at least partially accomplished in transit.

Wet and dry aging both result in a similar degree of palatability, yet each produces distinctly different flavors. Wet aged beef can have a bit of a bloody and almost metallic flavor. Yet when properly prepared and delivered to the plate, these subtle flavors are much appreciated by most consumers. Dry aged beef has a brown-roasted flavor that is highly valued by many consumers. Dry aged beef usually costs more because there is some shrinkage to the product during the aging process.

While aging does optimize tenderness, it does not insure tenderness. The National Beef Tenderness Survey revealed that 15-20% of beef was undesirable relative to tenderness. To that end, very recently, tenderness can now be ascertained at the packing house with 94% accuracy. In theory, we are about to do something about the inconsistency of beef regarding tenderness.

While aging can have a profound effect on palatability; breeding, feeding, processing and preparation all play a very important role in consumer satisfaction. Improper preparation (cooking) can certainly negate a lot of worthwhile efforts expended to create a good steak. Steaks cooked to rare or medium-rare will be tenderer than steaks cooked to medium or medium-well.

Incidentally, the tenderloin has long been a popular choice because it is the tenderest part of the carcass.

Storing Beef

Historically, fresh meat, including beef, that was not going to be eaten in a day or two, would be preserved by curing, smoking and drying, or salted, and boxed (more commonly in barrels). Ice boxes and early refrigerated plants extended the period of time that fresh beef and meat in general, could be utilized as fresh beef. In the 1930s and 1940s, cold storage locker plants became widely available, extending the life of fresh beef—now frozen.

The ideal temperature to store fresh beef is 28-32 degrees Fahrenheit. As the temperature approaches 40 degrees, perishability increases. Today with modern refrigerators, freshly purchased beef should be utilized within a few days at most, or freeze it until it is needed. As a rule of thumb consider these guide-lines.

Beef cuts—store in refrigerator no more than 3-4 days.
Pork cuts—store in refrigerator no more than 2-3 days.
Raw Poultry—store in refrigerator no more than 1-2 days.
A package of lunch-meat, after opening—no more than 3-5 days.

Caution: freezing will not save meat that has already begun to deteriorate. Either utilize it in a timely fashion, or freeze it for later use; nothing in between. It if is going to stay in the freezer more than two weeks, double, or even triple wrap the meat product to prevent freezer-burn. Freezer-burned meat will be dried out, discolored and tough when cooked. The taste will commonly be bland.

Ground beef can be stored in the freezer, maintaining its quality, for three to four months. Beef cuts can be stored for up to twelve months. Protect your investment and your family with good management of your perishables.

Food Irradiation

Why does the term "irradiation" stimulate such an emotional response in us, as it commonly does? Is it because of the atomic bomb of WWII era? Irradiation used to treat some cancers? Seeing Geiger counters on television picking up sources of radiation?

There are a lot of good things that can be said about Americans; many, many good things. But, one of our weaknesses is that we tend to "overreact." As a people we are much like a giant pendulum. It takes a while for us as a whole to react; but, when we do, we generally go too far. There is and have been many examples that have occurred over the last fifty years regarding our overreaction. Today's "information age" probably exacerbates the issue.

Objectively it would appear that we do overreact to the term: irradiation. Yes, the term can conjure up negative images. Let us be smart enough to understand that there are also many, many positives associated with the term as well. Obviously, there are different kinds of radiation exposure. By definition, radiation is "the process by which energy is emitted as particles or waves—often transmitted through an intervening medium or space, and absorbed by another body." The term irradiation is "the state of being irradiated, or the use of x-rays or other sources of radiation for use in the medical, manufacturing, or transportation areas.

We come into contact with items that have been irradiated every day: medical supplies, medical procedures, plastic food wraps, tires, and presumably—the body scan at airports. Of course there are safety protocols in place; of course there is monitoring of the process; but, it is as every day as television news. Are you afraid of crossing the street? Are you afraid of going to the doctor? Are you afraid of taking or not taking, medicine? Sure some of us have anxieties. We all know the statistics, but some few of us are still afraid.

Would you not agree that better decisions generally come from having a foundation of knowledge? Poor decisions are most commonly the result of actions taken based on emotion. Knee jerk reactions to any source of stimuli are usually reactions of regret. Think it through. Irradiation is used in a vast array of activities that we are surrounded by daily. In these approved and monitored activities it is perfectly safe. People die from food-borne bacterial infections every year. All of which could have been avoided if that food had been irradiated, or at least that is my opinion.

Food irradiation involves treating a food item with energy from electrons and gamma rays to prevent food-borne illnesses, spoilage, and insect infestations. As healthy as spinach is, do you know how many microscopic bugs are present? Irradiation solves this problem. Food does not become radioactive when it is irradiated. The process is NOT a substitute for good sanitary practices. Food irradiation makes meat, and food of good quality, safer. It also increases shelf-life; because it destroys any presence of bacteria. It does not negatively affect the meat or leave any lingering aspect that would affect its quality. The American Medical Association and the World Health Organization have endorsed its use regarding food.

The FDA has approved irradiation of wheat and wheat flour to control insects, of white potatoes to control sprouting, of spices to kill insects, in pork to control trichinosis, in fruits, vegetables and grains to control insects, and growth and ripening. It has been approved in uncooked poultry to control bacteria, particularly Salmonella. Now, it is allowing the irradiation of red meats to control bacteria, which also extends shelf-life. Food irradiation makes meat and food of good quality, SAFER.

I like my hamburger meat cooked medium-rare. In better eating establishments, I am not concerned about their not having properly cared for the meat. Hamburger meat in particular should be irradiated because it is a pooled product from many individuals. It could be made safer. Please, irradiate my ground sirloin purchases. The question is why do you not feel the same way? If it is a judgment call, I win based on food safety; your defense is based on emotion. Yes, the FDA will require that the irradiated beef be labeled with a "green and white irradiation symbol." So what? The only reason it is not done even more widely, is because of you. We should all want the safest food possible. Irradiation allows that. When anyone is questioning the value of food irradiation, I would question the motives of the person speaking. Perhaps it is animal agriculture in general they want to see fail.

Food irradiation is safer than crossing the street in Matador, Texas—where an out of town vehicle can be identified a block away. Food irradiation is simply the next stop in food safety.

4

Your Personal Options Regarding Beef

Branded Cattle

Most of you upon reading this sub-title will think of hot-iron branding. So, while we are here, and before we explore the world of "branded beef," let us expose the topic of the hot-iron.

Branded cattle (proving ownership) were actually depicted on the walls of Egyptian tomb paintings 4000 years ago. The Spanish used brands for more than a century before it started in America. The oldest county records found under state government were along the Texas coast: Harris County (Houston) in 1836, Brazoria County in 1838, and Galveston County in 1839.

Branding did not gain in popularity until the 1870s and 1880s in other parts of Texas. Its popularity was principally due to the merging of herds (different owners) for the trip up one of the cattle trails leading to the railhead (usually in Kansas), or other market centers.

Today, most of the western states require branding as proof of ownership. In many of these states if you want to move cattle off your contiguous ranch acreages, a brand inspector (commonly a state employee) must have been notified, enabling their presence to write up necessary documentation prior to travel. As a part of their inspection process, every brand on every individual that is going to be moved will have been visually inspected.

Every brand within the state is properly recorded and maintained by the state. If you want or need a new brand, you must create one that is not otherwise recorded. Occasionally, one comes up for sale. These same brand "characters" are often seen at the entrance to the ranch, on the doors of their pickups, on their stationary, shirts, coats, and even on custom made boots. One's brand is without question a source of pride.

Many restaurants will have an entire wall or walls, dedicated to displaying the brands of the trade area. Most of the cowmen and women know all the brands in their area. When working cattle if a neighbor's branded animal is found, they are penned off separately and that neighbor is called to arrange a pick-up time. Yes, it is an honorable and trustworthy system. If anyone is caught doing otherwise, their standing in the community drops lower than the coldest night in the winter.

Bailey's boots and spurs.

This is Bailey—ranch raised and just got her RN degree.

Now, let us move on to the intended subject: "branded beef."

Initially, "branded beef" was the result of a producer led supply-chain bringing to the marketplace that specific beef desired by the marketplace. The many options could have included any one or combination, of the following: source-verified, no hormones, no antibiotics, humanely treated, limited or possibly no confined feeding periods, USDA grade, a geographical preference, breed or color preference, and/or an age requirement.

No antibiotics would simply mean that any sick cattle would be treated as necessary; but, lost qualification for this particular supply chain. Limited or no periods of confinement would simply mean that the cattle would be pasture-based, and the grain rations could simply be hauled to them by the feedyard trucks. Almost anything is doable, but is likely to cost more money to produce. If you are willing to pay for it; you can have anything you want, as long as the packer does not rain on our parade.

This branded beef carried with it a promise(s) to the consumer that was verifiable and auditable. The supply chain program was in effect at every location that these animals had spent time; each followed the same procedures and protocols necessary to maintain the integrity of the supply-chain.

These initial "branded" products were readily accepted by consumers and soon these "niche" markets were expanding throughout the consumer-base. The packers, never one to fail to involve themselves in anything that is economically promising, began to create their own "branded" product lines. These product lines generally did not have producer involvement as in a supply-chain. These are primarily marketing opportunities. Yet, they were also considered to be "branded" products. This marketing effort focuses on the emotions of the consumer and allows the perceptions of the consumer to aggrandize. The labels on these products might be called: Rancher's Choice, Silver Creek Ranch, Forman's Best, Prime Steak (having nothing to do with the USDA grading system), Timber-Line Beef, Texas' Best, Tender Cut, Billy Bob's Farm Raised, Three Sisters' Ranch, etc. You get the picture. You and I are sensitive to this type of marketing. We want to believe. The fact that it is very likely the very same beef they were producing before the label change, should come as no surprise. They are simply the result of good marketing. Pristine images and words that evoke environmentally clean and pretty locations, work. They do. It works to one degree or another on all of us.

However, all these different "branded beef" products lines do become somewhat confusing. You could easily desire to inquire as to which do and do not offer verifiable promises. How do you tell the difference? Good question. The easy answer is to assume that none of them do; because the vast majority will not. If seriously interested, go on-line and check out the name on the package. If still in doubt, ask your retailer for verification procedures. That information will be readily available if it is a producer-driven supply-chain.

Of recent times a new packer creation is now in the marketplace: "guaranteed tender." Fairly recently the packers have gained the ability of determining individual carcass tenderness with a 94% accuracy. For reasons already covered, our beef industry has had a problem with "inconsistency." So this is a timely product. On the one hand all of us appreciate the opportunity to buy beef that we can count on as being tender. On the other hand it strengthens the packer position of power; because, they now determine who does and does not receive the carcasses that did not do so well on the tenderness test. Bow-down, pay whatever price they decide, do not complain, and perhaps they will favor you (the beef purveyor) with the desired beef.

Until recently I had believed that a giant retailer still had clout with the packer; especially one who had bought one billion dollars-worth of beef the year before. I was proved wrong. I offered a beef supply chain (cattle raised and fed under the operational philosophy of "Genuine Care & Concern for the Individual"—a program fully verifiable and auditable) to a giant retailer. They wanted it. But, before we got down to the details, they contacted the three major packers that they dealt with, concerning obtaining the necessary slaughter-shifts that would be required. The typical response was: "We already have seventeen lines of our own branded beef product. If we give you want you want, it would cost us money." It is ironic to note that none of their current lines produced anything like what we wanted to create. It was obvious that they did not give "two hoots and a holler" about our effort to enhance the sense of wellbeing regarding cattle across the industry. This entire effort (creating the new production philosophy of "Genuine Care & Concern for the Individual") had to be economically driven by a giant-retailer willing to pay for the value-adding efforts of producers; efforts that would enable you to receive the kind of product they thought you would appreciate. All that was lacking was someone to harvest and fabricate the product in the necessary volume required.

If the packers can keep their work-shifts full, producing their own "branded" products, making more money than on commodity beef, it should not surprise us that their focus is purely on profitability. It is one of the reasons that I particularly appreciate such companies as COSTCO, TRADER JOE'S, and PUBLIX grocery stores; they are high-integrity companies that inherently want to do the right thing regarding socially sensitive issues like humane treatment. Needless to say that social consciousness is not found within the circle of the major packers.

The greed of the major packers may yet cause their own demise. Yes, they have squeezed and distorted the production aspects of our beef industry to the point that it is hardly recognizable. But, it may yet become their undoing. In their effort to control everything, they may have actually destroyed themselves. Mexico has plenty of cattle. They do not have the governmental constraints we do. They are utilizing American beef production experts and animal health consultants to establish production efficiencies. I predict that they will soon have modern, high-tech, slaughter facilities enabling them to send finished, fabricated beef into the United States. Remember that "COOL" (country of origin labeling) is soon to be in effect. This will certainly replace at least a portion of the need for slaughter and fabrication facilities domestically. By the way, Mexican beef will be USDA inspected just like it was in the U.S., prior to shipment into this country. The product will be wholesome and good. As much as I am distressed over the loss of the industry I love; I will be among the first to buy Mexican steaks knowing that its purchase is one less produced by the big three packers

Now let us explore the options available regarding commodity beef: conventionally-fed cattle, natural-fed cattle, and pasture-fed cattle.

Conventionally-Fed Cattle

These cattle do receive growth enhancing implants, most commonly administered under a conservative philosophy. This way, quality grade of the carcass created would be minimally affected. A more aggressive approach would certainly, negatively impact quality grade. Some of the cattle involved will also receive a late day, beta agonist type of product that minimizes marbling and increases lean meat percentages. Without question these products negatively affect grade. That does not mean that they do not yield a great beef eating experience—lean, tender and juicy—but it does mean less fat within the lean. (NOTE: as this text is being finalized, the beta-agonist products are losing favor; at least one packer has had enough negative feed-back, to stop buying cattle that have received them. We should anticipate the demise of their use.)

Conventionally fed cattle will finish (fewer days at the feedyard) quicker, and with enhanced performance parameters, compared to natural cattle. The duration of their stay (at the feedyard) is dependent upon their in-weight (weight upon arrival); the lighter the in-weight, the longer the stay. The average stay is likely around 160 days, but it varies from year to year and from feedyard to feedyard depending upon what class of cattle they like to feed.

Naturally Finished Cattle

These would be the same kind of cattle, but without any performance enhancers. All things being equal, they will take a little longer to finish, and commonly make a little less money for the owner. Those that are marketed through a supply chain as a branded "Natural" beef product, normally make up the dollars (performance) lost, through marketing incentives.

Natural is not the equivalent term to pasture. It does not mean they are not fed in a feedyard; it just means, no performance enhancers were utilized.

Grass-Fed Cattle

These cattle will have never been in a commercial feedyard. In theory, they will have never been fed grain-based feed supplements. They are pasture based their entire life. Days from birth to slaughter far exceed those of commercially fed cattle—three years of age (commonly) to reach the necessary slaughter weight.

These cattle are in a market "niche" that promotes emotional feelings from consumers that these cattle were left to roam the prairies. Remember: marketing is everything and everything is marketing.

If you like the idea that this grass-fed calf never had to experience fully prepared, high energy, balanced diets created by professional nutritional consultants; regularly cleaned water sources; living under professionally managed health programs; and monitored daily by experienced pen-riders; it is your choice.

Quality of the beef produced is a personal issue. If you will notice, grass-feds are not any cheaper—usually higher, when you find it at the grocery store. Grass fed producers do not spend the $550 (for example) per head to pay the feed bill at the feedyard. Yet, this beef costs, typically, more than grain fed beef. Grass-feds cannot even be grown in every state because it takes a grass (natural or planted forage) of very high quality to produce the desired end result.

Though other breeds are involved, Wagyu is the one most commonly talked about. Full-bloods (100% Wagyu) are very consistent as to their meat qualities. Half-bloods (50 % Wagyu) are to a very large degree what you find being offered in many of today's restaurants. This meat is different from typical American beef breeds in at least two ways. First, is how the fat is finely dispersed throughout the muscle; rather than having areas where there is significant fat. Second, it is more consistently tender than the domestic beef breeds if handled appropriately. Some few of these crosses, Jersey for example, produce a meat that appears "greasy." Those of us who like Holstein beef, would probably prefer the Wagyu-Holstein cross meat product. You don't see much fat, but it is there; and the product is very tender. Bottom-line: it is a very good but more expensive product. An environmentalist may not like the product because it has a significantly higher carbon footprint.

Our American beef product, when comparing one week's purchase to another, is not perfect. There is variability. But, no industry in the world works harder at making it better.

Organic Beef

We actually looked at producing organic beef on a volume basis a few years ago. If an operation were ideally located among farmers willing to grow all our feedstuffs locally, optimally, it would only double the cost of production. Commonly, much of what would be required would not be locally available. Given the questions and uncertainties involved, it would not be out of the question for the beef produced to be three times higher (costs) than conventionally fed beef.

Personally, I investigated some small, organic operations and was not comfortable with all I saw. Having to rely on natural fly control, natural internal parasite control, no antibiotics as might be necessary for sickness; and even the use of vaccines (preventing sickness) was questionable. Sanitation in the processing area look good, but having to rely on natural cleaners (for disinfecting work surfaces) was a personal concern. I actually like the idea of organic relative to the feedstuffs. But, I have issues with those things that could not be used that would elevate the health status of the animals involved.

You are the final authority relative to your own personal choices. Make your choice from a base of knowledge, not emotion. Do not let your ears (what you are being told) mislead you. Empower yourself with real information and facts, then make your own decisions. If you base a lot of your decisions on emotion, and are proud of it—you'll love this product. Many notable individuals are supporting the organic movement. I think we all like the perception of organic; but I would question the knowledge base of these notable individuals concerning the production specifics. Food safety is an issue that is much more common than most would assume; if you know the production practices specifically in place.

5

Your Beef Producers

There are cattle populations in every state of the union. Just as these cattle are often different from one owner to the next; and from one area (geographical area) to the next; so too are the individuals and families that raise them, different from each other. One might attempt to describe the type of person raising cattle in one geographical area, but that description would likely be vastly different relative to the people in another area.

There are a few things that each one of them will share. Every owner is going to go to the extreme, if necessary, to protect, nourish, and support those animals within their herd. An old axiom says that "you can't starve the profit out of a cow;" which means that if you do not take care of the cow; she cannot take care of you. For an individual cow to be productive, her nutritional needs as well as her sense of wellbeing must be maintained. Sure, they can handle some tough times for a while, but their productivity will begin to diminish as the stress factors accumulate and remain in their lives—much like people.

The vast majority of cattle raising locations across the U.S. are small operations—just a few head. These cattle might be present to keep the grass mowed down. They might be present to provide a little additional income each year. Perhaps their presence is to provide the family's beef needs for the year. Perhaps it is the milk, cream and associated byproducts that warrant their presence. But, for many of them, it is the intangibles associated with their presence that the owners enjoy the most. Who does not enjoy the sight of a brand-new calf? The interaction between individuals (of very young calves) can certainly bring a smile to the face. How about the "mooing" of a cow seeking her baby? Or, perhaps it is simply the herd grazing in the distance, providing a very picturesque setting. For most producers they do indeed provide quality of life issues separate and apart from income. Sure, there is work involved; but, there is work and effort involved in most productive activities.

Large cattle operations would certainly be tilted more toward the commercial (economic) side of the equation. That is not to say they do not equally enjoy the same intangibles; but their primary motive is very much focused on the reward for their efforts.

Though highly divergent individually, our people are our strength. Your cattle producers (men and women) are not distinguishable from each other by the size of their herd. The geographical area from which they come, does, however, create striking differences in the way they talk, and dress. By and large, your beef producers are an independent lot, unafraid of challenges. By and large, they are hard workers who find personal value in owning cattle. So, just because they look different, do not presume abilities as to management skills and financial stability, by the way they dress. Most do not dress for others; they dress for themselves. You may be able to guess which part of the country they are from, but determining who is and who is not a "mover of mountains" will not be determined by the way they dress. When a man shows up at your place wearing a dress shirt enabling what appears to be a few "hundred dollar bills" to show through the pocket of his shirt; and wearing what appears to be diamonds on his watch or rings; he is a man to stay away from. Conversely, if an elderly gentleman gets out of an old, rough looking pickup, wearing a hat with a lot of character, and walking with confidence; he can probably buy you out lock, stock, and barrel.

Their operations, regardless of size or location, are a reflection of themselves and their vision for the future; or, perhaps, an effort to hang on to the past. Each producer is unique as to his or her strengths, weaknesses, environmental influences, and operational savvy. Their ability to succeed depends upon several things: having grown up on a well managed cattle operation, education, financial resources, personal judgment, and work ethic. If you simply have access to a lot of money; or simply have a college degree; or simply want to own a ranch—you are going to cost someone a lot of money. If you have a lot of money, you can remain on the ranch a long time; but, you will not be successful by yourself. If you want to own a ranch, you must find someone with the managerial ability, and the chemistry to work with and for you, to succeed. Finding the right people for any specific operation is not an easy task.

Generally speaking, the men and women of the beef cattle industry today grew up around cattle. It is almost a necessity in order to possess the knowledge necessary on which to start. Most successful operators were a part of a family growing up that fought the battles, and met the challenges, enabling survival. They love what they do, and where they do it. They might wish it rained more; but they would be reluctant to change locations, at least very far.

You could drive through their home country and wonder "why in the world would anyone want to live around here? That question is not easily explained. Perhaps, it is the footprints and experiences of prior generations. Perhaps, it was just growing up there that creates strong bonds of attachment to the local environment. Many objects and locations might remind them of sentimental times and fond remembrances.

No matter where they live challenges are common. It is certainly not always easy to stay in the cow business; but when no longer involved there are parts of it we yearn for. Not the years of poor markets and drought, but the activities, the interactions with the people, and even the usual and routine chores that is as common as the school bus. Ranch life is never dull. There is always plenty to do. Every day is simply a choice of priorities—which project is more important to get done? Then there are those seasonal activities that are planned well in advance. And of course, there are those instances of individuals (cattle and horses) requiring immediate assistance. Sometimes this assistance is anticipated, and sometimes not.

Assisting in the delivery (birthing) of a calf is not very glamorous in bad weather or in the middle of the night; but it does warm the heart if both the cow and the calf do well. Even if the calf does not survive, it still makes one feel good about assisting a heifer (two-year old that has not calved before) through a difficult and stressful event that she may not have survived on her own.

When my dad was fifty-five years old, he had a heart attack. In those days it was thirty days of bed rest that the doctor prescribed. My brother and I were in the eighth and tenth grade, respectively. For just over a month we alternated missing school so one of us could stay with a group of heifers that dad had been calving out. Eighty percent of these heifers would calve on their own. The balance would need assistance—a little or a lot. We would pen (remove from the pasture and place in the corrals) those individuals that we thought would calve in the next day or two. Sometimes we were right, and sometimes we were wrong. Assisting a heifer in a corral was much easier that assisting her out in the pasture. In the pasture in order to get the restraint that we had to have, we would rope and hobble (tie one front foot to the opposite hind foot) the heifer as gently as possible. Some of them accepted the help rather well; others were now focused on doing us bodily harm, rather than having her mind on the calf. If my brother and I could have been there together it certainly would have been much easier. We survived and so did the heifers. We did lose a few calves, but not very many. No, there was no pay in it for Joe and me; but Dad did get to keep his job, and we were better for the experience. This experience and many others like it ingrained this way of life into our very souls. There was simply nothing else in life that we wanted to become, other than a cowboy—a good one.

Even though cattle are our commodity, the beef industry is a people business. Relationships and reputations are essentials regarding the successful management of cattle operations. There are three natural segments of our industry: cow/calf (location of origin), grow-operations, and finishing-operations (feedyards). Within the transference of cattle between these segments, one's reputation and word, enables the movement to be quick and efficient. Much of our business is done by phone. The buyer (a feedyard or order buyer) might come to your place a time or two; but if all goes well and the cattle met expectations, business is often done by phone after that. Once a set of producer calves have finished at the feedyard and close-out information is obtained, whoever bought the calves will now know exactly what this set of calves were really worth. Next year's price will be reflective (up or down) of this information. Two different sets of calves may look to be of the same quality and weight while still on the ranch; but that does not make them an equally good buy. One group may be better prepared (less sickness) for the high-exposure environment of a feedyard. One group may simply be more efficient feeders (converting pounds of feed into pounds of gain—increased weight—more efficiently). One group may hang up higher quality carcasses (higher percentage of choice carcasses, rather than select carcasses).

We had a set of calves come through (be fed at) one of the AzTx feedyards that hung up an unusually high number of high-choice carcasses. It took the company three months to back-track those cattle as to their origin. A company representative was sent to South Carolina (if memory serves me right) to find the location of the cowherd and visit with the owner. His marching orders from our boss were: "try to contract those calves for the next five years; if you cannot get that done, buy the cowherd." As it turned out the owner (of the cowherd) had dismissed the ranch manager and sold all the cows (dispersing them into the wind at the local sale-barn) because he did not think the manager knew what he was doing. The moral of this story is no matter how good or plain your cows might look, you do not know how good they are until their calf-crop has finished at the feedyard, and close-out information is obtained. The cowherd is often selected based on their projected ability to perform in a particular environment. The bull(s) is selected based on his projected influence on the quality of the calf-crop. These are broad generalizations but essentially true.

Are you beginning to appreciate that raising cattle is not as simple as it might seem from the highway, driving by? An individual producer with a good deal of experience with making bad decisions is usually in another profession pretty quick. You have to love what we do, and be pretty good at it, or you will not be around very long. There are too many ups and downs, winter storms, summer heat/drought, water issues, weed problems, fertility issues, governmental regulations, marketing challenges, and herd diseases that will drive you away if you do not love it.

The masses of our industry are likely third, fourth and fifth generation cattlemen; individuals who have plotted their course after that of their father and grandfather. With more and more women being involved, we can occasionally say, "after their mother and grandmother." It takes a half of a lifetime to absorb a decent knowledge base concerning our industry; and another half a lifetime to become truly experienced. By the second generation we are coping better with "external factors" (governmental issues and marketing in particular) affecting our operation. By the third generation expansion and diversification (new centers of income producing activities) are beginning to enter the picture.

Given the generation to generation knowledge and methodology that is passed down, it is no wonder that very traditional practices are created among producers. I experienced them myself and instinctively want to honor them. But, we are and should be responsive to "your" voice. We are and should try to produce the beef that "you" desire. Had I not gone through all the trials and effort at the feedyard proving to myself that elevating their (the cattle) sense of wellbeing (reducing stress at every level) absolutely enhanced performance parameters, I might argue myself about getting rid of some traditional practices. Without a doubt some modifications need to occur. We are now a consumer/retail-driven industry. We work for "you." It behooves us to produce what you desire. It also happens to make us more money (enhanced performance parameters). If we reduce all the necessary efforts down to its simplest description; it would be reducing stress at every level in their lives. Every source of stress should be evaluated and negated as much as is practically possible. As we then work through all the variables, a step at a time until we invariably arrive at our new philosophy: "Genuine Care and Concern for the Individual." The implementation of this new philosophy is measuring our efforts based on individuals, not on acceptable industry averages. "Your" beef producers have economic incentives to do just that.

The beef industry is one that I am proud to be a very small part of. I sincerely appreciate the people involved and their efforts. Our industry has undergone a tremendous transition over the last 100 years—unbelievable. It evolved out of need and desires to accomplish. At no point did most of us anticipate what the future held. When I entered the feedyard phase of my life, the environment was a distant planet compared to the ranch life I had experienced in my youth; but I quickly grew to love it.

I entered with no pre-conceived ideas relative to the subject of humane treatment, which most people in our industry might consider a "critic's topic." It is not an easy subject managed by most producers. It has too many connotations associated with our critics. Producers have had to withhold household funding during hard times to pay for cattle feed. They feel like they have often given up funding saved for a son or daughter's college education, to care for the cattle as needed. They have released blood, sweat and tears for the cattle under their care; and now our critics who know absolutely nothing about our industry, want to tell us how to do it.

A subject we can work with is that of "elevating their sense of wellbeing." Now we have something that is measurable. It is real. My personal quest began simply looking for ways to safely enhance performance parameters. I was lucky enough to be in a position where upper management gave me the leeway to try to prove some ideas. Within a few years it simply became "the right thing to do." We just happen to get rewarded by the animals involved for doing it.

"Your" beef producers—owners, managers, and cowboys—are great people. You will think so too when you get to know them. The industry needs your support. I think we can get that support by opening up the book about our industry, to you. I truly hope you will enjoy this book. It was written expressly for you—our much appreciated consumers.

6

The Business of Beef

There are many locations, many different breeds, many different owners, and many different philosophies under which calves are raised. Though the average size cow herd is forty head, it ranges from a few to in excess of forty-four-thousand mother cows. The cow herd at each of these operations is generally relatively static as to numbers. Significant deviations occur only when acreage is acquired or lost. A small yearly change does occur as older, and less productive (cull) cows are replaced with retained heifers. This turn-over rate would average about 8% per year.

Well managed operations will view each cow as an independent business. Thus, on this level playing field, each cow competes against the balance of the herd as to who gets to stay. The poorer performers, along with others that need to be culled for a variety of reasons (older cows, cripples, bad mammary systems, bad eyes, and the chronically under-weight), will all be removed from the cow herd at the appropriate time. An appropriate number of your best heifers would need to be retained, to replace the cows destined to be culled. These replacement heifers will likely be run as a separate cow herd the first year, and commonly even the second year, before they become part of the permanent cow herd. These second year, young cows are the hardest of all cattle to get bred-back, and commonly require additional nutritional support to be successful.

Breeding seasons are most commonly around 90 days in length. Bulls are then removed from the cow herd. Ninety days gives a cow the opportunity to cycle into heat three times. That is plenty for fertile cows. Very small operations may leave their bulls out year around. Their thought is that a late calf is better than no calf. These small operations generally sell their calves a small trailer load at a time utilizing the services of a local sale-barn. While larger operations generally sell their entire calf crop at one time. Obviously, uniformity is a major concern. In Florida, it is common to have six-month breeding seasons, but they manage it well. After the first calf is born, they wait until about one-third of the herd has calved or sixty days, whichever comes first. Then they ride out all the pairs (cows that have calved) and put them into separate pastures. These are now considered to be "slot one" cattle. When the next third of the cows have calved out, or another sixty days has passed, they again ride out the pairs—creating "slot two" cattle. This effectively yields the producer three distinct calf crops, with all calves in each slot being within sixty days of each other in age—assuring a uniform calf crop.

My hat is off to Florida cattlemen. They are open-minded and willing to give a new idea, an opportunity to prove itself. In Texas, except for a small minority, that is not the case. They simply do not like much in the way of change unless you can completely convince them it will positively affect their pocket-books. I can say that because I am one of them and know them well.

My hat is off to Kansas cattlemen as well. They are very progressive minded individuals and work closely with livestock extension people from their own home university, Kansas State, which is loaded with very talented people. This group does not allow their egos to get in the way when someone else shares a different opinion. They believe that having differences of opinion is healthy and ultimately leads to the better answer. That is not to say there are not other great individuals or groups of individuals at other state universities, there are. There are many strong agricultural programs at a variety of universities; the difference being the areas upon which they focus: animal science, meat science, food science, extension programs, beef and/or dairy production, nutrition, and food & health management, to name just some of the options.

In most well managed operations any cow that does not breed back is culled from the cow herd. The reasoning here is that it either cost too much to hold her over another year before seeing if she will breed the next year; or if she breeds a month or two later (after all the other cows were already found to be pregnant) she would be out of synch with the balance of the herd and her calf would not be marketable with the other calves. Genetics is also another consideration. You do not want to keep heifers from cows that do not quickly breed back every year.

Many factors come into play regarding just how many heifers should be kept and older cows culled in any given year. Moisture conditions and range forage availability is always a concern in the western U.S. in particular. Market conditions play a huge role as well. Many producers believe that when the market is weak (low prices), we should keep a higher percentage of heifers, and when markets are high, we should keep a lower percentage of heifers. Bankers also have influence over our determining how many heifers to keep. They often will not let you keep any heifers. They want the payment at the bank. Hell of a way to stay in the cow business when the banker won't let you keep any heifers. Some years, in fact, most years it is cheaper to actually buy appropriately sized heifers rather than retaining your own. True. But, for many of us, we want to keep a closed herd (bio-secure). We will not allow anything but virgin heifers and virgin bulls into our operation. It keeps most diseases out of our herds. If you have particularly good genetics (gene pool) in your cow herd, it makes sense to retain your own. However, in my own mind, the Seminoles in Florida have proved that you can get it done by simply focusing on the bulls. They focused on bringing in the best bulls they could find, and slowly upgrading their gene pool in this manner. Bull selection is hugely important to any successful operation for many reasons. First, that new bull must fit your country—must be able to make a living (maintain his flesh or condition) in the country you are going to put him into. It takes a much different bull to be successful in west Texas, New Mexico, Arizona or Utah, than it does in Mississippi, North Carolina or Ohio. Libido is also a huge factor. Just because a bull can pass the customary fertility test (that procedure alone), does not make him a good breeder. For this reason alone many operations do not keep any bull after his five year old breeding season. Many very bright producers buy yearling bulls instead of two-year old bulls for some very good reasons: better selection and usually cheaper, virgin bulls for sure (no disease), and it allows them a year to acclimate on your lands and in your environment, before depending on them during the breeding season.

Because of the enormous variations between ranches regarding available forage, moisture conditions and the area a cow must cover to find adequate grazing, it varies regarding how many bulls that are required to breed the cow herd. In one part of the country it could be as few as fifteen cows per bull, while another part of the country might be successful using one bull per 35 or even 40 cows. An average is likely one young bull for every fifteen to twenty cows and one adult bull for each twenty-five cows. It can be a real challenge to match up bull batteries (groups of bulls) for use together in a particular pasture. Fighting among the bulls is often an issue. It is very common for an older bull to fight off a young bull—keeping the younger bull away from the cows. Thus neither one of the bulls gets much business done. Also, smaller acreages in fertile ground (abundant forages) enable a bull to cover more cows, because they are not traveling very far between grazing activities and water.

Breed selection is as personal as what kind of hat you wear. Cattlemen with a lot of ego tend to focus on what we might be called the pretty breeds, and often buy them in spite of the fact that they do not fit the country they are being sent to. They tend to like big cows. You can do that in really good country—fertile lands with abundant forages. They would not last long in many of the western ranges. Breeds expressing a lot of black are currently popular because of some rather significant carcass premiums, if they grade high enough. Black cattle get "hotter" in the summer time. Sometimes hot enough to die—especially bulls. South Louisiana, among other places, is a poor place for black bulls.

Regardless of the breed that is chosen to put together a cow herd, ultimately, the report card will come in proving or disproving your selection. Perhaps it will be reflected in market price of the calf crop when they leave the ranch. It certainly will be reflected in your cost of production, if investigated. And, most certainly, everyone's cattle will be "exposed" at the feedyard. The feedyard industry is pure business. They know the numbers. It is a data-rich environment—anything and everything can be measured. The data is there if you are interested. Efficiency is a term that is often used when describing the kind of cattle that feed best. Cattle that arrive, well prepared for the environment, are a must. Health issues are often the difference in profit and loss concerning a group of cattle that go through the feedyard. Beyond that we need cattle that have good feed efficiencies. They convert feed into gain, economically. Cost-of-gain, rate-of-gain, low morbidity (sickness) and low out-cattle (culled for a variety of reasons) numbers, create pens of cattle that have real opportunity to be economically profitable. But, there is another huge factor that our feeding industry is just now becoming aware of. If we can enhance the quality of their lives—elevating their sense of wellbeing, we receive in return (from the cattle) elevated performance parameters.

Cattle are much more like people, than anyone might have thought. If they are well cared for, treated kindly and gently, and, all their requirements (including socialization issues) are met, they give us maximum performance. Not only is it the right thing to do for the animal, it also makes us money. Who can argue with that? The numbers speak for themselves. It creates a win/win scenario—making everyone happy. The cattle are happy, the owner is happy (enhanced performance of the cattle), the consumers are happy (confidence that their beef source animals are treated kindly), and the industry should be happy (sustainability issue).

The cow herd is impacted by the seasons of the year. This is likely true no matter which part of the country we are talking about. Cows in the far north may even be placed in shelters during at least parts of the winter months. Cows a little further south will be "hayed" (hay provided for proper rumen function and nutrition) during the winter months. A little further south yet, and you find protein supplements (usually cottonseed cake) fed during the winter time, particularly during winter storms. In the south, the winters will likely be the best part of the year for the cattle—grazing improved grasses (winter forage grasses like rye and oats). In the far south, the summer time is the hardest part of the year on cows and calves. The extreme heat prevents much in the way of weight gain during the summer months. Because of that, calves are often weaned early (taken off their mother) allowing the mother more time to restore her own body condition before her next calf. The young, weaned calf is supplementally fed, and will actually do better (as far as increased weight gain) than it would have, had he or she remained on their mother. Given the opportunity, these early weaned calves are often shipped out of state to more moderate climates where enhanced forage availability (that is appropriate for the calves) is an option. When these calves are moved early, it is always toward the feedyards and the packing house. For example, if these are south Florida calves, they might be shipped early to Texas for grazing because they are now that much closer to the feedyards. Freight (shipping costs) is expensive.

Generally speaking most ranchers would prefer their cows to calve just before or right after the beginning of the season when the best forages are available. It enables the cows to milk more (increased lactation) and hold, if not improve, their own body condition. A good momma will give herself up to feed the baby. This means that she will lose her own body condition to provide adequate lactation (milk) for her calf. Any cow that keeps herself fat at the expense of the baby (little to no milk) will certainly be culled for that reason alone. If she calves when grazing is good, she can often do both.

Cattle operations are normally family enterprises. It takes the whole family to make it work. This is not just a play on words; but a true statement regarding small and medium sized cattle operations. Sure, the big ranches have plenty of cowboys to handle the job. But, in reality, there are not that many big ranches left. There might be six or eight left in Texas. There would be fifteen or so in Florida. Arizona, Utah, Nevada, California, New Mexico, Oklahoma, western Nebraska, Kansas, Montana, Wyoming and the Dakotas, all have a few. But, except for these few, large outfits (which are usually family operations with a lot of permanent outside help), the vast majority are really family operations. The largest of which likely have grown children, often married with families themselves, who have stayed, or returned back to the operation enabling growth and sustainability. The smaller of these cattle ranches are generally a one family operation. But, just about everyone in the family has responsibilities, including young children. The level of responsibility would vary according to age and the time of year, pertinent to school. But having chores to do is as every day as mom's cooking. Most adults that grew up on these family operations have fond memories of their time spent there as a youth. It may not always have been fun at the time, however; because real work was involved, requiring real effort. But it was an excellent training ground for life, even for those that do not go back to the farm or ranch.

Most of these family operations were and continue to be, a financial struggle from time to time; if not most of the time. Cattle markets are not always good. It is a little like growing short-staple cotton, you may have to pause a moment just to remember that last really good year when you made all that money. At least it seemed at the time to be a lot of money. Mostly it allowed an opportunity to reduce some loans and perhaps to actually buy something fun for the family. Regarding recent times, markets have been good—particularly for the cow/calf operations. The problem is that our production costs have gone up as well. It was not that many years ago that corporate America would settle for an acceptable margin of profit. Now days, their pricing philosophy is more, one of "whatever the market will bear." It seems as though greed, short-sighted decision making, and promoting areas of self-interest (at the expense of others) is the norm for politicians and corporate America. Several years ago I would have said that agriculture was the exception to these practices. But, the pharmaceutical industry has led feed, fertilizer, and equipment companies to join the rest of corporate America.

Cattlemen do seem to be reluctant to change. They are resistant to leave their comfort zones; perhaps for good reason. They have been burnt more than a few times. Given the normally, narrow profit margins, they are reluctant to change too much unless they know it is economically advantageous. Due to the myriad of outside influences, it seems as though each year is a roll of the dice. Weather, markets, international trading agreements, government regulations and restrictions, soft economy and rising consumer goods, all affect our decision making process. No matter how good we are as managers of our livestock enterprises, rising production costs, force us to cut every corner we can. You, consumers, should know that we cannot cut corners regarding cattle care. The cattle and the lands, on which they reside, are our golden goose; their care level must be maintained at all costs. Our choice of options involving cutting corners, are family expenses beyond basic needs.

We have talked of how ranches, cattle operations in general, are very different from each other, particularly from state to state. Each must utilize what local assets are available within the confines of his or her cattle operation. In a sense the owner/manager might be described as a land manager, or perhaps a grass manager. Moisture and soil conditions dictate what grasses or other forages, can survive. Given an abundant rain fall (more than usual), particularly in the western U.S., new grasses may even appear. It is like having a wide variety of seeds present in the soil, and in any given year, depending upon moisture conditions (when and how much) primarily, a new combination may show itself. It is not at all unusual to have a few spring flowers to show up as well. After decent fall participation and a reasonably wet winter, usually involving snow, these bountiful springs can occur that give warmth to the heart. Cows start calving and milk like a dairy cow. It truly regenerates the spirit of life.

One of those glorious years when moisture conditions are ideal.

However, with different conditions the spring may bring trouble. Come spring, cattle are always craving "green" (anything in the way of plant life that is reasonably tender and green). Particularly so, after a fall and winter of harvesting forages (grasses) that have been dormant—usually brown and dry. So when some of the early weeds like "Loco" show up and they are the only green in the pasture, cattle will devour them. Loco weeds, among others, will cause a condition often referred to as "blind staggers." Most of this class of weeds has a fairly high death rate. They cannot be economically sprayed with a herbicide, so our options are to move them to pastures containing no weeds; or put them up into traps and provide hay or other roughage for a couple of weeks, until the return of green grass. It has been my personal observation that ranches that keep a good, high quality, loose mineral out for the cattle, year around, have much less trouble regarding these weeds. Each location across America has its own unique problems regarding toxic weeds and forages. Most have something to do with available moisture—too much or too little.

As land managers it behooves us all, to always be cognizant of opportunities to add income producing activities to that of harvesting grass for cattle operations. There are many possibilities. Some are available to one location and not to another. Cedar trees may be cut for cedar (fence) posts, and for fire wood. Rock of one sort or another can be an auxiliary source of income. Unique sources of water can produce opportunity. Historic sites could be basis of activities. Dude and guest ranches are possible. Exotic animals are commonly utilized to enhance income. Trail-rides and camping opportunities, with or without chuck-wagons, present opportunities. Hunting is a really substantial source of income. Food products like garden vegetables, dairy products, bread & pastries, sausages, jerky, and smoked meats can be options. Some few cattle operations actually market their own beef to the area or regional consumers. Currently a huge activity is to become part of a chain-supply, bringing to the marketplace a "branded beef" product that brings with it a guarantee to consumers: source-verified, no hormones, no antibiotics, humanely treated, or any number of other qualifying statements. For the producer these are value-adding activities. All require verifiable and documented protocols and procedures; but they add value and income to the operation.

Other additional activities might include bed and breakfast offerings, seminar retreats; or full-service conference centers with assorted side activities like cook-outs, horseback riding, trout fishing, and scenic tours. Additionally, many of these families have home-based businesses that produce auxiliary incomes as well. Lastly, a significant percentage of the spouses do maintain jobs in town or at some rural business closer to home.

From one generation to the next we see many changes. Some of these changes have been for the better. Some have not. We as an industry seem to be vulnerable to good salespeople. Our industry has a real weakness when it comes to chasing "silver bullets." These are typically presented as the latest and greatest solution to either "fix" our management ills; or give us a head-start on our competition. It may be a new software package, pharmaceuticals of one sort or another, technology or a developing science. We fixate on buying our way out of management weaknesses. In a year or two, the old "silver bullet" is gathering dust, and we're being presented a real opportunity to own a new one. This one really is the one we have been looking for to solve our problems. The level of the offerings, regarding these "silver bullets," has created a candy store effect upon our industry—we keep trying to buy our way out instead of working our way into solutions.

It is a real weakness affecting our industry. We seem to ignore the basics. It reminds me of a football coach after an embarrassing loss of Friday night. Come Monday, he is telling his players: "Boys, we're going back to the basics of blocking and tackling." At the feedyard level we have proven that going back to the basics is economically rewarding: Low-Stress, quiet and gentle cattle handling, Doing the Basics Perfectly (vaccine handling and administration), Selective Culling (identification and removal of immune-compromised animals), and Humane euthanasia (never allowing an animal to continue to suffer after active treatments have failed and there is no immediate salvage avenue available). There is nothing for a producer to buy. No "Silver Bullet" philosophy implied. All they need is an open-mind, elbow grease and a willingness to accept the new philosophy of "Genuine Care & Concern for the Individual."

In closing let us look briefly at the issues that affect all cattle producers and largely, all of agriculture.

GOVERNMENT: Who can argue that there is too much government? Regulatory agencies, for all their intended good uses, are counter-productive and often clearly focused on the wrong issues. Decision makers generally lack real knowledge and understanding of the subject material. They have risen through the ranks of government, experiencing only Washington mentality, and possess no real insight into the issues. But, they do have the power. Yes, there are a few exceptions;

a few great individuals in the USDA. These few exceptions are greatly appreciated.

TRADE ISSUES: Why is it that politicians think that food commodities are too important to be left in the hands of producers? Yet, every time they want something from another country, it is agriculture that they give up. Federal farm commodity payments, of one sort or another, largely exist only because our government officials gave up our marketplace—in a trade-off. These payments are a corrective action to the mess they created. Livestock producers are highly restricted in instigating international trade, because government wants to have all the control. I keep trying to think of "one thing" the government has done better than private enterprise, but I cannot think of it.

ECONOMICS: Not too many businesses buy all their equipment and source materials at "retail," yet sell all their production "wholesale"— except agriculture. Many of our more successful cattle companies today have figured out a way to cut out the middle-man, one or more. They are either bringing a finished beef product to the retailer, utilizing a small, independent, and meat-packer; or, they have created their own (small) processing plant; and will deliver a finished beef product to the marketplace, serving a local or regional area. Real success almost mandates that we go around the major packers. The major packers can and do limit what independent feedyards can make feeding cattle; artificially managing the price of feeder-calves (calves soon to enter the feedyards), and determining the fed-cattle (about to be harvested, post feedyard) price at the packer level.

As I write this, most of Texas and much of the central, mid-west, as well as California is in a serious drought; in many areas it is the driest in recorded history. Grass fires have caused devastation in the north-central part of Texas, in what some might describe as the best cow country in the world. Herds have been disseminated: sold off, partially sold off, and the balance removed to another state. Some producers have completely sold out; and many may never make it back into the cow business. Our industry cow numbers will be permanently reduced. This is not good news for you, our consumer. Production from our national cow herd has been going down for many years. These total cow numbers have been partially hidden by adding imported cattle (principally from Mexico and Canada) to our production numbers. All of this is currently being felt in the marketplace.

Our cattle numbers, calves in particular, are simply not there to meet demand. Fat cattle (finished cattle at the feedyard) have sold as high as a dollar, forty-one ($1.41) per pound, live weight. They are currently below that level. For many years they were in the eighties and nineties. All of this is somewhat meaningless without knowing the cost of production. If cattle are selling at ninety-two cents per pound, and break-even is eighty-two cents per pound, we will live to fight another day. If the selling price is $1.14, with break-evens at $1.12, or even $1.16 for that matter, we are about to be in a lot of trouble. I do not know of another business in the world that will accept our financial commitment and feel pretty good about breaking even. That is partially because the market changes quickly—hourly, daily and weekly; and, new pens of cattle come out of the feedyard every day. One pen may make $40 per head, and the next pen out (ninety days later) looses $40 per head.

When times get like they are now, with a lot of volatility, a lot of people have opportunity to go broke if a down market lasts very long at all. The last major disaster occurred in 1973, when fat cattle were sky-high (in the mid sixties), and cost of gain from 38 to 40 cents per pound (of feed). People were making a lot of money feeding cattle. Feeding clubs were established around Hereford, Texas, where anyone could own a percentage of a pen of cattle, for just a few hundred dollars. Then the bottom fell out of the market place. The price stabilized at thirty dollars (per hundred weights for finished, fat cattle). Grown men cried on every street corner in Hereford. Besides losing a lot of investor money, it broke a lot of serious cattlemen. The major packers who set the price of fed cattle, made above average profits. You, the consumer did not suffer. Now that we are part of a one-world economy, you may not fare as well as you did then. It is a new world today. Greed and corruption are everywhere. The prices are whatever the market will bear; and our politicians have given away the "farm."

I am proud of agriculture, and proud to be a part of it. We are not perfect; but, we very likely symbolically represent what is right about America. Our farm and ranch families raise good kids; kids that understand responsibility and know how to work. We still assist our neighbors in time of need. We still hold God and Country close. Our core values and proven, successful philosophies continue to be our guide-posts. But, we at the feedyard level operate under a monopolistic business frame-work.

FOOT NOTE: Though not an alumni, I always enjoy getting my CE from Kansas State University whenever possible. In my opinion, it is the current hub of information regarding cattle. If I were looking for a new, young veterinarian to help me in a bovine (cattle) veterinary practice; I would go to K-State to find them. A few months ago one of their students remarked that "at K-State it's *cool* to be from the farm." Consumers, perhaps we have come the full circle; perhaps, at least some, are ready to appreciate, if not go back to the farm. There you can become rich if measured in quality of life issues.

7

Life of a Calf

ife typically begins in a rural environment. The particular location could be in any one of dozens of vastly dissimilar locations. Perhaps the southern coastal areas of Florida, Louisiana, or even Texas; the high-country of Montana, Idaho or Colorado; the grass valleys of Wyoming, California, or Missouri; the plains of Kansas, Dakotas or Nebraska; the desert south-west of New Mexico, Arizona, or Nevada; the fertile grounds of Iowa, Indiana or Ohio; or, the hills of North Carolina, Tennessee or Virginia. Each location is noted for some unique climatic conditions: heat, humidity, altitude and snow, fine seasonal grazing, winds, severe winter storms, drought and scarce-water sources. Yes, these babies are born in every imaginable location from the harsh and unforgiving, to the most ideal your mind could visualize.

Given the wide variety of environments where cattle are located, adjusting to that environment is usually no great matter if nutritional needs are met; but weather related issues are often challenging.

Through good weather and bad, they are born typically, alone with their mother, and must quickly find a way to endure and survive. Except for heifers (first time calvers) assistance is rarely, readily available. It is a wonder of mother-nature how some survive even the first few hours, given some climatic conditions, but they do. The center of their world is mom and they try to stay close. Mom usually does not range very far for the first few days. But soon, she has to get to water. Here is another miracle of mother-nature. There exists a quiet, often unseen, social fabric between cows—some much more than others. These moms often trade off (within their own little group), regarding who is going to stay with the nursery (the group of new baby calves), and who is going to go, however far it might be, to water. Cattle usually drink every day; more often if it is handy. In the case of nursery cows, one may miss a day of watering to watch the babies, and drink the following day. The nursery cow(s) will not be standing over her charges, giving close attention, but she will certainly remain very handy should a need arise. Should a predator come close, she will become agitated, vocalize and become aggressive in her attitude. Within just a few days these new babies are getting around pretty well and begin to follow mom wherever she goes. Early on, the cow commonly stops frequently looking over her shoulder, making sure her baby is making appropriate progress.

Within a couple of weeks, the pair (momma and baby) is back to the normal grazing habits of the group. Country (the grazing territory of the involved cattle) can still be good, even if it is considered dry. Even if forage is a little scarce, it is usually strong (highly nutritious). In dry country cattle may have to graze two miles or more from water. In good years they can meet their nutritional needs without having to go more than a mile from water. The grass close to water gets grazed down, thus, they have little choice but to range farther. In better country it may only take a few acres (two or three) to run a cow on a so-called, year-a-round basis. Some of the best ranching country in the world may take twenty-five acres per cow. But, some of our drier areas (particularly in the south-west) will take a lot more. My brother bought some cows off a ranch in southern New Mexico, years ago. The owner told him that his best country would run two cows to the section (square mile, 640 acres), and that his worst country was two sections to the cow. True-story. My brother bought two loads (120 Hereford cows, averaging just about seven hundred and twenty-five pounds each—small cows). He shipped those cows to the Portales, New Mexico area and ran them on good grass (where they calved) until wheat pasture was ready. When they came off wheat in April, the calves were as tall as the cows. They were a great set of little cows. They were little because they were raised in that country, not because their genetics weren't good.

As young calves grow, they tend to graze on their own, not always at mother's side. Cattle have what is usually described as four stomachs. As a little baby, on milk only, only the fourth stomach (the abomasum) is developed. But as they begin to graze (consume grasses), they slowly develop their second stomach, the rumen. For adult animals this is where most of the work of digestion takes place. In a sense it is a fermentation vat where cellulose (grasses) products are broken down into utilizable food substrates. By the time a calf weighs six-hundred pounds his rumen function is pretty well developed.

An efficient and productive cow.

For most of the industry, the calf and it's mother have a quiet, peaceful time together until it is time for spring (or fall, as the case may be) branding to occur. In some parts of the country, it is referred to as marking and branding. At some point in their young lives, these calves will have to be "worked." Large ranches schedule these activities to occur when the last few calves will be at least a couple of weeks of age—making the oldest three months of age, or so. They tend to work pastures, one after another, until all calves have been done. This time frame is usually measured in weeks. Smaller ranches may get it done is a week or less. Some operations, for a variety of reasons, partially work the new-born calf. They generally want the birth-weight, and go ahead and castrate at that time.

The term "worked" simply refers to procedures that must be accomplished. There may be no perfect time to accomplish it, if all procedures are going to be done at the same time. Some we would like to do as soon as possible—castrate and dehorn. It is much easier (less stressful) on the very young calf, as opposed to an older calf. Other procedures are more efficacious if we wait until at least three months of age—vaccinations in particular. On larger outfits it is a major undertaking to arrange for all the necessary day help to accomplish gathering and working these calves, so from a practical sense, it is all done at the same time. Very small cattle operations often fail to even accept the responsibility of working their calves. They just haul them to the local auction barn. Thus older calves, five hundred pounds or more, now have to be castrated and dehorned, when it is much more stressful than would have been the case if accomplished while they were young. When the calves are sold, un-worked calves bring less money per pound. I would like to see that discount become even more substantial, bringing even greater pressure to bear on those producers who do not get it done while they are quite young. If you cannot accomplish this responsibility in an efficient manner that is easy on the calves, perhaps you should not be in the cow business. Let us now look more closely at the various procedures that have to be accomplished during marking and branding.

CASTRATION: With the exception of pure-bred breeders, that are raising prospective breeding bulls, all male calves need to be castrated as early as is practically, possible. The younger the individual, the easier it is on the calf. But it certainly should be done while under the nurturing care of their mother. To delay this procedure, because it is inconvenient for the owner, is irresponsible and completely insensitive to the wellbeing of the calf. If done properly and early, it is a non-event in the life of the calf. A necessary and vital component of a "humanely treated" chain-supply of beef source animals—is that this procedure be done as early as practically possible. Not to have this procedure done is losing touch with reality. Imagine the daily stress and crippling of the individuals involved, if all these calves were allowed to remain bulls, fighting and injuring each other daily. That is inhumane.

VACCINATIONS: Properly accomplished, administering vaccines substantially enhances the individual immune system's ability to fight-off disease. The industry's first vaccines were "killed" vaccines that were very durable and not neutralized by heat and direct sunlight. Modern vaccines for prevention of respiratory conditions are "modified-live" viral vaccines and are very fragile—neutralized rather quickly by heat and direct sunlight. Our industry has a history of doing a rather poor job of handling these vaccines. Based on a monitoring some 400,000 head of calves coming into feedyards from seventeen different states, as much as seventy percent of our producers do less than an optimal job of preparing calves for the high-exposure environment of a feedyard. At the feedyard level it is obvious which calves have and have not been properly prepared. A chain-supply is the only way to correct this weakness in the system. There, they have no choice but to follow established procedures and protocols, because they are all documented and auditable. Through our own chain-supply, we've already accomplished it, and reduced sickness at the feedyard dramatically. Perhaps here is a good place to mention a critically important fact: all the antibiotics in the world are a drop in the bucket, compared to what a properly prepared and fully functional immune system can do for itself.

DE-HORNING: Many, if not most, breeds have horns. As with castration, if good de-horning techniques, are utilized early on (at time of castration), this can be a minimally stressful event. The later it is delayed, the more stressful the procedure becomes. If de-horning is not accomplished, their "horns" become instruments to "bully" other individuals away from feed and water sources. Responsible owners will handle this issue early, using minimally invasive techniques—no deep de-horns. They don't have to be deep to be effective and are certainly less stressful, with reduced healing times. Only someone who is totally clueless, regarding fighting and injuring other animals would support NOT castrating and de-horning cattle. But, yes, it needs to be done early.

BRANDING: Yes, it hurts—no question about it. Yet, it is the law in many western states to prove ownership. Many states have brand inspectors, monitoring the movement of cattle off the current location (ranch). A written instrument is required before the cattle can be moved. Their ownership brands will have been individually inspected. Brands are more durable and harder to disguise than are ear-tags. Branding is stressful at any time in their life, but it seems to be of short duration. Slight soreness the next day and then it doesn't seem to bother them. I've seen a lot more instances where poorly applied ear tags, caused considerably more lingering discomfort, than a properly applied brand. At the feedyard level, there just is no substitute for ear-tags. They just serve too many vital functions to do without.

IMPLANTS: Yes, the word "hormone" is now going to be used. So, let us look at the issues. Why do we use them? Simply stated, they enhance feed efficiency. Meaning that they will grow more (increased weight gain), on the same amount of feed and/or pasture (roughage intake), than cattle that have not be implanted. Typically, we are talking about placing one or more pellets (dosing units) under the skin of the ear, above the cartilage. Here, these pellets dissolve at a pre-determined rate, leaving only slight scar tissue behind. The ear itself is not used in any human food product.

Why are they allowed to be used? The manufacturer has conducted all required trials and completed all safety requirements necessary to obtain approval from the FDA, principally, to make them available for sale to the cattle industry. The products are safe and effective—no question about it.

Are we (producers) all in agreement as to their use? No. A lot of us would actually prefer not to use them. But, it is hard to give up forty dollars (for example) per head by not using them. I think most of us would actually prefer to sell natural cattle, if that market would just let us break even, concerning the dollars we are giving up. If you use them, a philosophy must be ascribed to. A less aggressive attitude toward their use will cause little loss of "grade," yet yield enhanced performance parameters. An aggressive attitude regarding their use will certainly add more pounds (to sell), but will certainly reduce the grade (USDA quality grade of the carcass) of the cattle as a whole. Envision that target weights of any and every set of calves going through the feedyard, are pretty-well established well before sending them to the packer. Partially by the kind of cattle they are, and partially by packer desire. Also, the choice-select "spread" is always a part of every decision. If the spread is substantial (a significant difference between the market value of a choice graded carcass, over that of a select graded carcass), we are going to err on the side of finishing (putting on more fat or marbling, if you will) cattle a little more. If the spread is minimal, we are going to err on the side of cost-effective pounds—just focusing on getting the cattle into the "select" category. "Select" grade (less marbling) is the primary beef seen in the meat case at your grocery store. Most large, grocery stores have "choice" or even "prime" beef available; you just have to ask for it.

So, what is the bottom line regarding implants? To make the decision not to use implants (hormones), for most of us, requires that lost efficiency (dollars) to be made up (replaced) elsewhere. Typically, that means you (the consumer) are willing to pay a little more not to have hormone treated beef. The European Union is a great example to look at. They do not argue the issue of safety regarding the use of hormones. They just do not want it in their beef, period. They are willing to pay for what they want. We can give them what they want.

After branding and marking activities are complete, these young calves are returned to the pasture with their mothers. A lot of factors will determine just how much longer that will be the case—staying with their mothers. Their average weight, forage availability, commodity prices, market conditions, sale contracts that may be in existence at the time, weather issues and environmental stress issues are some of the factors that help us to decide when to wean the calves. A cow needs minimally two months, after a calf is weaned off of her, to prepare her own body condition to where it needs to be, before she calves again. Poor pasture conditions and environmental stresses, most commonly cause early weaning. Cows under this kind of stress need more than two months to regain necessary body condition. The calves themselves will actually do better, being fed supplementally or moved to improved pasture conditions elsewhere, than they would if left on the cow.

Many producers are too focused on weaning weights. They tend to use these as a measuring stick of how well they (themselves) have done. Sometimes, egos get in the way and they attain their target weights, at the expense of the cow. And, if they get her back into condition in time, they will have given up all they made on weaning weights, buying feed for the cowherd.

WEANING: Weaning is the next big occurrence in their lives. This separation from mom is an event of considerable stress. Interestingly enough, it also occurs in dairy calves that may have never actually nursed their mother. In that instance, it is the separation from the bucket, or bottle, with the nipple. Historically, when shipping time (selling the calf crop) occurs the cattle are penned, fairly early in the morning, and the calves are cut off (separated) from the mothers. The calves are then separated into steers and heifers, sorted and weighed, then loaded onto the trucks, where they are shipped to a grow operation or the feedyards. The longer the trip the more stress is involved. From the moment these cattle (pairs) are picked up in the morning, on the way to the pens, until they arrive at their ultimate destination, they are commonly without access to feed and water. That can be a long time—twenty hours or more. Proper aforethought and planning can minimize some of these negative effects. As rumen function begins to deteriorate (sustained periods of no feed intake), so too does immune function deteriorate, making them more susceptible to sickness.

It behooves everyone involved to make sure the transit, no matter how many miles, occurs as quickly and efficiently as is possible. Granted, they will be expected at the feedyard with arrival pens already prepared and waiting; but it may take several days (after arrival) for them to reestablish optimal immune function. As an industry we have been long guilty of rushing into processing (vaccinations in particular) at their new destination before they are fully restored, with fully functional immune systems. This compounds the problem because they cannot possibly respond to the challenge of the vaccine, building antibodies against future sickness, anywhere near normal. So, as mentioned, coordination needs to occur between the buyer and seller to minimize the effects of no access to feed and water during the trip, particularly before they (the cattle) are loaded into the trucks. We should remember that just separated calves are a lot more interested in where mom is, rather than eating and drinking.

If there is to be no weaning process at the point of origin, the sooner these cattle get to their new destination the better. We as an industry, tried to stop at some way-point and unload, feed, water and rest the cattle, but found that it only created more sickness. It did not really solve any issues; likely created even more. All of this is measurable. Every option can and has been measured (in lost performance and dollars). The real answer is to wean at home (point of origin), get them properly vaccinated there, and onto to some supplemental feed (accustomed to a feed-bunk). The weaning process is much less stressful there, rather than at their next destination.

There are a variety of ways to wean at home, some less stressful than others. Some more labor intensive on the owners. Some owners do not feel like they have the option to wean at home, perhaps lacking the facilities. Personally, I think it all about the money. Producers want to get paid to go to all the extra trouble. There is some validity to that. The value is there, and is known; so why can't we put a price premium that is adequate to receive compliance, on home-weaned calves—getting it done in that low-stress environment? Feedyards receive a lot of calves, commonly in excess of 100,000 per year. We know cattle. We know sickness. We have access to data you would not believe. It is quite easy to "see" which calves have been well prepared and which have not. Likely the real answer, is to buy all calves at market-price, and give set-aside premiums back to producers based on level (preferably very low) of sickness and carcass quality (percentage of choice carcasses produced). This way those that did a good job of properly preparing calves for the feedyard environment, get paid for it. Sickness (morbidity) is a critical issue in feeding cattle; and, can be largely avoided if a program called "Doing the Basics Perfectly" is followed. We started it at the feedyard level of production; and then began to get our source producers to adopt it as well. It really does work.

If a supply chain is in place (bring a branded beef product to the marketplace), then serious lines of communication between the producer and the feeder are in place. Required procedures and protocols, demand documentation and are auditable. Compliance will be there if they are to stay in the supply chain. This solves a lot of issues. The system demands integrity. Thus when you (the consumer) receive a branded beef product that meets your needs and/or desires (source-verified, no hormones or no antibiotics, humanely treated, etc.), you know that you are getting exactly what you should be.

STRESS: Even with cattle that are properly prepared, arrival at the feedyard causes a good deal of stress. They have arrived into a totally different environment. No longer in pastures, but intensive, confined feeding operations. Lights are on at night, feed trucks running everywhere, a grain-based ration rather than forage based ration, cowboys in each pen once or twice a day, and the bedding ground is now dirt rather than the grass turf they were used to in the past. So, yes, there are a lot of new changes relative to their environment. If they remain healthy (having been properly prepared), it does not take much time, if they are handled kindly and gently, for them to get acclimated to their new surroundings.

New arrivals at the feedyard.

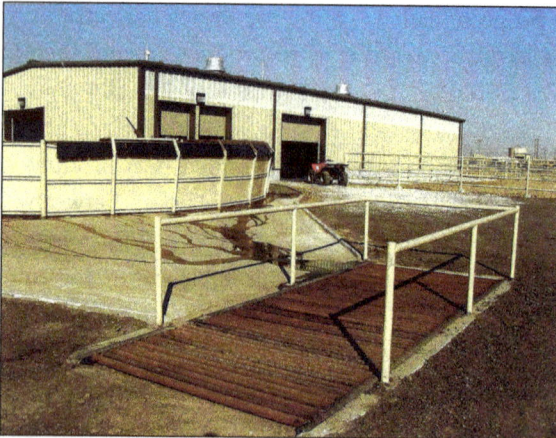

Feedyard Processing Barn.

View inside the processing barn.

Computerized record keeping at processing barn.

For many, it is actually a couple of steps up from what they were used to. Professionally created, warm rations are available twice a day. High quality hay is available initially for those who are not yet accustomed to eating out of a feed-bunk, and the water trough is cleaned regularly. As soon as they appear to be completely over the stress of shipment, they are processed (vaccinations, de-wormed, identification tags applied and scrutinized for other problems that may need attention). These new vaccinations are utilized to raise their protective titers (antibodies) that will hopefully enable them to remain healthy through the feeding period. When they are brought back to the chute at a later date for booster vaccinations or implants, they are again reevaluated. Computerized health and processing records are likely better than that in a human hospital. Why? Because we are extremely conscious concerning drug residues in particular, due to the fact that these animals are going to be providing beef for the table. Every product that is utilized for any reason (pharmaceuticals) is noted into the record with exacting protocols reflecting product used, dosage amounts, route of administration and when it was administered. The computer (software) will keep up with each individual record and bring it back up any time they are in the chute for evaluation.

When animals are determined to be immune-compromised, they need to leave the feedyard immediately. Due to pending residues (antibiotic residues in particular) they cannot simply be sent to the local auction-barn. They must be held until all residue issues have been met. Ideally, these cattle are simply removed to low-exposure environments (locally available pasture) and given time for their immune systems to improve. Historically, these cattle were kept on site in holding pens awaiting residue resolution. This was and is a bad choice. The death loss in these pens is high, and suffering is great. Following "Genuine Care & Concern for the Individual" guidelines, we offer: when active treatments have failed, and no immediate exit strategy exists, humane euthanasia is mandated.

I personally have become passionate about the issues of stress, critically supporting the immune system and supporting socialization requirements. These issues are real and they are measurable. A price (lost performance) is extracted every time we allow these items (stress—the number one enemy to good health, sickness due to lack of support for the immune system, and lost sense of wellbeing, due to lack of support for socialization issues) to negatively affect the animals involved. These negative effects are largely preventable if we are willing to accept the new philosophy, and are willing to make some immediate changes that will update our animal care level. These changes are cost-effective and practical. The only requirement is for producers to accept that it is your desire that we adopt the philosophy of "Genuine Care & Concern for the Individual." It is simply doing what we already know to be the right thing to do, just shedding the cloak of a few traditional practices. To know better and not do better is a reflection of our character.

The industry will provide you any particular beef product that you desire, when you make it clear to your retailer that you want it. I had visited with Walmart/SAMS, and then visited with Costco. Costco is a company all about doing the right thing. They wholeheartedly support the idea of humanely treated cattle. But, before we even attempted to work out the details, they contacted the three primary packers with whom they do business, to ascertain their willingness to give us the "shift-spots" we would need for these supply-chain cattle. Their answer "We have seventeen of our own lines of branded beef items. If we give you what you want, it would actually cost us money. We would have to cut back on our own lines of branded beef." Why am I not surprised? Originally, there were many, many packers serving a variety of locations and functions. Today, packer buy-outs have created consolidation down to a point that most people who know the packing industry would agree that it is a monopoly. Instead of serving America, they serve themselves.

THE FEEDYARD: For all the negative mental images that some of you may have regarding confining cattle during the finishing stage of production, let me share a personal perspective. I find great joy in being eminently involved in the beef cattle industry and particularly in the feedyards. Depending upon one's perspective, and certainly to those unfamiliar with confined feeding operations, one might be put off by all the activity and perhaps the smell as well. Personally, I find the feedyard to be a necessary and cost-effective way to fatten cattle. If well managed, a calf wants for nothing after they have become acclimated. It is kind of like sending your son or daughter off to college—there is an adjustment period.

The acclimation process likely takes three weeks, if they remain healthy, to become mentally at ease with their new environment and the rumen having had time to adjust its bacterial flora to match the new feed stuffs. All their nutritional needs will be professionally met. If we meet their other needs concerning socialization issues, pen, bunk, and water-trough space, quiet and gentle handing, and efforts to make bedding conditions as good as the environment will allow, these animals will be happy. Happy cattle perform well. They make everyone happy.

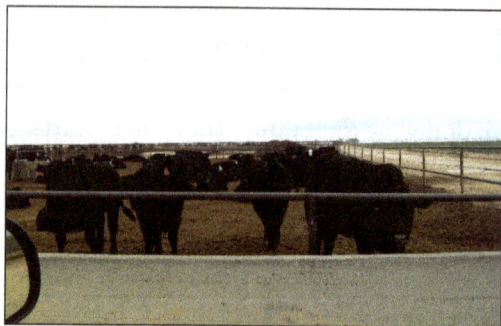

Short-Day Cattle
(Haven't Been There Too Long).

Once acclimated, the vast majority of these calves would not trade back, for their old pasture lands. They were going to be without mom regardless of their next location. Toxic weeds, predators, scarce grass, and dirty tank-water, they don't miss. They now get looked at and individually appraised for health issues every day. They get all they want to eat. Water is clean and plentiful. Sometimes, they do get a little bored, I'll not argue that. These cattle get fed and have access to clean water, every day, no matter what the climatic conditions. Blinding, white-out snow storms do not stop the feed-wagons. Ten below zero does not stop drinking water from flowing. Cattle are treated and doctored every day that it is necessary. Feedyards never stop making and delivering feed—twenty-four, seven. Christmas day, Thanksgiving, graduations, weddings, funerals, doctor appointments, doesn't matter, the feed trucks are going to run and the cattle are going to be monitored.

I love feedyards—at least well managed yards that truly have compassion for the animals under their care. In the old-days, we looked at industry averages regarding death loss, morbidity (sickness), and out-cattle (usually chronically ill and/or chronically crippled cattle). As long as our numbers were in line with industry averages, everything was OK. It is not OK, any longer. Today, we have "Genuine Care & Concern for the Individual." Every individual is important. Preventative health issues are a core interest. Every time we have to treat an animal for sickness, is like a small, personal failure of our preventative health program. Reducing stress is a core interest. Creating happy cattle (an elevated sense of wellbeing) is a core interest. Supporting socialization issues is a core interest.

The beauty of this philosophy is that it makes everybody a winner—a true win/win scenario. By keeping the cattle happy (elevated sense of wellbeing), they give us maximum performance. Great performance by their cattle makes the owners happy. Treating them kindly and gently makes you happy. Making you happy, gives our industry sustainability. The Industry is now happy.

Feedyards operating under this new philosophy are a great place. Calves are properly prepared for their arrival in this high-exposure environment. Because they are well prepared and well received, acclimation occurs rather quickly. No place within the entire industry can you find more professionals working in synchronized fashion to meet the needs of the cattle.

Feedyards come in all sizes, from a few hundred to well over 100,000 head. My own experience has been in yards with capacities from 45,000 up to 90,000 head. So, let us look at a typical day in the life of a calf in one of these high-plains feedyards.

12:01 am: The night-watchman drives the feed-alleys, closely monitoring activity in each pen of cattle. Most feedyards have night-lights that are very similar to street lights that enable visualization of the cattle. He also has an above-the-cab spotlight enabling improved visualization of individuals in the pens as might be necessary. In many instances, he also receives cattle (unloads the trucks) in the middle of the night. If they were expected and look as anticipated, he will place them into a prepared pen that was awaiting their arrival. Anything out of the ordinary, he will contact management. He is also head of security over the feedyard, until personnel begin to arrive around 5:30 am. He knows his responsibilities and whom to contact when the need arises.

6:30 am: Feed trucks are busy delivering warm, freshly mixed feed. Every pen is scheduled to receive feed at a specific time. Every truck has a set of built-in scales and a time clock associated with each feed delivery. It is all computerized. What was fed (which ration number), when it was fed, and how much was fed, is immediately accessible by administrative staff.

Feed truck delivering feed to new arrivals.

At large feedyards, the feedmills, never shut down. There is even a night-shift to oversee the steam-flaking of the corn. It is surprising how long this corn stays warm. Even after it is mixed with the other ingredients (as prescribed by the consulting nutritionist) the mixture is still warm when it is delivered to the cattle. In the winter time the cattle are anxiously awaiting their own delivery of feed.

Cattle awaiting their feed delivery.

The entire feeding schedule is synchronized so that any given pen is fed at the same times, every day. That truck will rarely be off more than five minutes. The cattle in that pen know when to expect their own delivery. When you look across a pen and see a lot of cattle lying down, chewing their cud (a part of the rumination process), you know it is nowhere close to when they will be fed. When cattle begin to stand up, stretch out, all looking toward the feed-bunk, it is getting close to time. When a third of the pen is standing at or near the feed-bunk, it is only moments away from their feeding time.

There is a shared philosophy, between management and the consulting nutritionist, regarding how long they want the cattle to be out of feed, before the next delivery of feed. It might be a few minutes or a couple of hours or more. There are good reasons for everything that is done. In the case of Holsteins, when they are fed out for beef, we never let them run out of feed. We want a small amount left in the bunk when their next delivery occurs. If we underestimated what they would eat during the period since they were last fed, that amount will be increased before being fed the next time. If they do run out, completely, and there are wet, lick marks still present, we are OK. No damage done. But, if the bunk is empty and dry, we should expect some GI (gastrointestinal) issues over the next several hours, and will be on guard for that event. Feed management is a critical component of a successfully feedyard.

9:30 am: Pen-riders (cowboy on horseback) go through each pen every day. We hope that every individual is appraised at each visit. At the AzTx feedyards we had to completely disallow them to carry cellphones, because it was just too easy for them to lose concentration. There is an old story involving an Indian who tells the cowboy: You look, but you no see. This is exactly what we are talking about to-day—everyday. These cattle must be seen and appraised, individually. Cattle lying down must be made to rise and take a step or two, making sure there is no lameness involved. Their primary focus is respiratory issues (pneumonia), but lameness, eye and ear problems, abscesses and bloat can occur.

A pen-rider at work.

This process of riding pens is usually completed by very early afternoon, at the latest. Usually the pen-riders then ride feed alleys, reevaluating each pen (that they had actually been in that same morning). They might see something that was missed earlier, or see something that is apparent now, that was not apparent this morning. It is just a second opportunity to monitor those cattle under their charge. Computerized records are kept enabling management to actually know just how good a job each cowboy is doing. It is a factual representation of their abilities. Good pen-riders attain incentives; poor pen-riders are soon working elsewhere.

Individual cattle that are "pulled" are left in the back-alley until that particular row of pens have been ridden, then they are gently moved to the hospital. In larger feedyards, every section of the feedyard has a treatment hospital. We do not like to move sick cattle any farther than we have to. In some instances, they are even hauled to the hospital.

10:15 am: the water trough man comes through the pen. This man's primary job is to clean water troughs. It takes about six to eight minutes to thoroughly clean the trough (usually stainless steel), and he is on to the next pen. When a set of cattle are moved (permanently) from a given pen, that trough is cleaned again before any new cattle are placed back in that pen. Otherwise, our goal is to regularly clean every trough (in the feedyard) every fifteen days. New cattle (fresh cattle) will have it cleaned even more often.

10:45 am: The whole pen is picked up by the cowboys and moved to the processing barn for a scheduled visit. It might be the initial processing, revaccination (usually occurring 17-21 days after arrival), implant, or perhaps an Endovac booster if pink-eye has flared up in the group. Every calf carries an individual, personalized eartag. Every time that anything is done to that calf, his or her individual record is brought up, and whatever is about to happen is documented into their record. Regardless of location, everything that is done to a calf is documented into the computer. It is really not a hassle to do so. What is going to be done to this pen of calves has already been entered into the computer by the "processing barn" manager. As they come through, each individual tag is scanned, verifying its presence and adding this action to its individual record. Records are always up to date and immediately accessible from many locations throughout the feedyard.

Calf displaying necessary eartags.

1:00 pm: A treated calf (pulled earlier that morning) is returned back to the home pen. Under "Genuine Care & Concern for the Individual" guidelines, if it was a respiratory condition that was treated, they are administered a long-lasting antibiotic, efficacious for 7 days, or more), identified with an eartag denoting date of treatment, and returned to the home pen as soon as possible. Recovery rates are substantially higher if allowed to return to their home-pen, as opposed to staying in hospital pens with other sick calves. Some feedyards even have a delivery vehicle (bobtail truck) with a hydraulic ramp that allows that truck to drive up in front of the designated pen, and deliver the calf, over the feed-bunk, right back home. The sooner we get them back home, the better they do.

"Animal Ambulance" is used to deliver pulled cattle back to their "home pen."

3:30 pm: Feed trucks are now delivering the afternoon feedings. A bunk reader (name of his job) will have already checked this pen at least once, monitoring consumption levels. If he or she adjusts the level of feed coming to this particular pen, they can do it electronically from their vehicle. The truck driver will see the change on his monitor in the truck even if it is just moments between the two, and deliver the adjusted amount of feed.

Interestingly enough, in the feedyard we all drive like we are in England—on the wrong side of the road. This allows the feed truck drivers to move around unimpeded. Delivery of feedstuffs occurs from the driver side of their truck, so the rest of us stay out of the way.

Fresh cattle (new arrivals) are commonly on #1 ration (higher in roughage percentage), and as their time (and weight) in the feedyard increases, they progressively move up to more concentrated rations. Commonly the last, finishing ration is #5.

Weather events will cause cattle to change their eating habits (the amount consumed and the time between feedings). This often causes an inadvertent change in the PH level of the rumen. GI (gastrointestinal) disturbances and/or bloat are a common end result. Bloat (gas accumulation in the rumen) in particular can be immediately life-threatening. Even, just more wind (higher velocity) than usual, can cause cattle to lie down for longer periods of time which will also cause the aforementioned PH changes. When a significant weather event is anticipated, we go to "storm rations" (higher roughage content), which helps to diminish GI disturbances. We give up a little performance during this time, but we reduce health issues. Holsteins are the exception to this rule, except in emergency situations.

Feed-wagons at work—more new cattle.

4:30 pm: We are preparing pens for late night and early morning arrivals (new cattle). If they are coming from a good ways off, we will have a large, round, metal water trough (usually 16 to 20 feet across) added to the pen and filled to capacity. This will allow for as many as possible to drink upon arrival. Plenty of fresh, high quality feed and hay are also commonly available. Our number one priority is to reestablish hydration and rumen function (of the newly arrived cattle) as quickly as possible after arrival. At bare minimum we want at least one-fourth of the cattle to be able to drink at the same time and every one of them to be able to easily access the feed and hay.

Their activity (processing) schedule is not started until they are completely over the stress of their travels. This may take one day or ten days. We have had some we waited three weeks on. It is a waste of time and money to vaccinate these cattle until rumen function and immune function, which go hand-in-hand, have been restored. Any cattle (individually) showing signs of sickness are quickly, quietly and efficiently medicated.

As management makes their last round of the day (up and

down feed-alleys), they always look at new arrivals and "problem" (higher sickness levels) pens of cattle. They often make several phone calls as they are looking, establishing tomorrow's priorities, and changes they desire, depending upon what they have just observed.

Larry Bilberry near end of day, establishing tomorrow's priorities.

Ultimately, management is responsible for everything that occurs, be it credit or blame. There is no replacement for good management. They have a huge job. Most, very good managers, surround themselves with good people. It is the only way you are going to be able to attend any of your son's little league games; or your daughter's volleyball games. For most feedyards, there are never enough good people.

Personnel issues are likely the greatest challenge of feedyard management. I believe that if we really knew the costs associated with lesser quality employees—the losses sustained because they failed to do what needed to be done, regardless of the time of day and who was or was not watching, we would hire only the very best and pay them whatever it took to make them happy. I believe it to be absolutely economically justified. But, most of the industry does not agree with me, so the people shuffle continues.

There are no days at the feedyard when cattle do not have to fed and cared for. That feedyard has to be fully staffed every day. If a cowboy and his horse falls down in a slick pen and breaks a leg, someone has got to be riding that pen tomorrow. A feedyard should actually be slightly over-staffed, but that is rarely the situation. A good manager will have a good assistant manager, a good office manager, a good cowboy boss and a good doctor (one who actually does the treatment of the animals as per the protocols of the consulting veterinarian). If he does not, he is going to miss a lot of little league games. The pressure is there: fighting packer buyers, explaining to owners why their cattle did not meet their expectations, keeping the office efficiently cranking out the paperwork, and putting out the fires of interpersonal relationships that smolder among employees at most feedyards. It is a hell of a job and you gotta love it.

HARVESTING the end product of all our extensive efforts finally comes to past. Yes, ultimately, every one of these big-eyed beauties will go to harvest. There are always a few individuals that we have created attachments to. Yes, I do hate to see them go. But, all the effort, energy, blood-sweat-and-tears, that we all have shed working to make them all they could be (like the marines), has been completed; their time has come. They are finished and ready to go to market, bringing you (the consumers) the finest, most wholesome and safest beef in the world. We are proud of our efforts. When I personally sit down to a good steak, I cannot but quietly say to myself, "good job buddy," for they became the best they could be. And I am talking about the big-eyed beauties, not the efforts of myself or other personnel at the feedyard. But, ultimately, it is only through all our efforts at elevating their sense of wellbeing throughout their lives—particularly at the feedyard, can we can enjoy their offering.

Fat cattle nearing harvest time.

So how does the harvesting process begin? Every week packer-buyers look at cattle on the show list at each of the feedyards. Some weeks these buyers have priorities as to the type of carcasses they are looking for. They have got to be able to look at the live cattle and know what kind (quality grade) of carcasses they will hang up (produce). They have each received their "marching orders" from packer management. This relationship between the packers and the feedyards has changed a lot in the last few years. There used to be room for at least, limited negotiations. That is no longer the case. The packer-buyer makes an offer for the various pens he is interested in. It really is a take it or leave it offer. You may like the guy, but he can only do what packer management tells him to do.

You are going to sell him the cattle—this week or next. He has all the power. The packers have a captive supply of over seventy percent. Yes, they own, directly or indirectly, the vast majority of the feeder cattle in the feedyards. As an independent feedyard you are going to take their offering; it's just a matter of when. Given the short buying session, you don't have much time. Next week, it could be up or down from today's offering.

So, they buy the cattle. Usually it is about two weeks before they will pick them up. Sometime before then, they will confirm the pickup date and the time. If the packer is running two shifts, there could be two different pick-up times (if very many loads of cattle are leaving that day). Early shipments start about 5:30 am. Cattle have been carefully and slowly brought to the load-out dock area. There, they are counted, weighed and placed into individual pens holding a truckload each. Afternoon shipments usually occur during or just after lunch, utilizing the same procedures. When the cattle cross the scales, they officially belong to the packer. The only thing you see in the eyes of these big, gorgeous things are: Where is the feed truck? They have been on a tight schedule for a long time. How long is that time? Heavier cattle coming in may only be there 160 days. Lighter weight cattle will be there longer. Holstein calves (arriving at three-hundred pounds, will be there a year. But, they will also leave there weighing 1,400 pounds. I happen to believe that a 1,440 pound Holstein is one of the prettiest things on earth. They are gorgeous.

From the time these cattle are picked up by the packer until they reach the "knock box" they are never alarmed. They have been in many chutes and many lead-ups before. They are not afraid of people. They are perfectly comfortable until they are very near the end—the knock box. Then they sense a smell that makes them uncomfortable. The side-walls of the lead-up are solid. They cannot see ahead. But, they don't like the smell. The cattle have been handled almost "ultra quiet" during their time behind the chute. There is no reluctance to moving forward into the knock box. I can positively assure you, that they never see it coming. They are immediately rendered unconscious from the "bolt gun" that drives a bolt into their head. It is instantaneous and effective. Videos are actually available. I do not find it pleasing to watch. I enjoy no part of it. But, I do feel that it is absolutely humanely accomplished. A much more humane ending than I see a lot of people go through.

Those of you, who may have grown up on the farm or ranch, may have experienced "butchering" a broke-legged calf or a milk-pen calf that was fed out for home consumption. It was as natural as catching the school bus. We also got to eat a lot better for a while.

Protein is a vital, required nutrient in our diets. To attempt to do without animal protein (in our diets), often leads to health issues. My own niece, the only vegetarian in seventy-five generations, actually broke her ankle, getting up from the toilet. Perhaps she was the exception, because a goodly number of people take a lot of vitamins and minerals and seem to do just fine, without beef. It is your choice. Just quietly allow those of us who do appreciate it, to enjoy our steak. Do not for a minute, hide behind "humane treatment issues" in your efforts to cause the demise of animal agriculture. These beef source animals are treated exceptionally well from the time they are born until harvest. Can we do better? Of course; we are not perfect. Even under the old philosophy of "Protecting our Investment," they got first dibs on family income. We had to take care of them first. Their basic needs were a higher priority than our own. We are now seriously elevating our game plan with "Genuine Care & Concern for the Individual." If you want to pick a fight concerning "humane treatment" in the beef industry, you better find someone else. You're gonna lose this one.

Is that to say that someone, somewhere, can't find an incident where someone (usually a new and/or untrained employee) has dropped the ball, exposing a weakness in our system? Of course you can and it has already been done, more than once. Are we embarrassed? Of course we are. We'd like to skin and hang every individual that failed to properly train the people that have been involved in those video clips. We have some cleaning up to do. Yes. Great pressure has been brought to bear on all of us. We can't just shoot the guilty parties.

Let me close with this. As a veterinarian with thirty-five plus years, more if you count my time as a youth on the ranch, of experience dealing with cow/calf, stocker and feeder operations, I am proud of the efforts of farm and ranch families who help to sustain the beef industry. They are good people who work hard at caring for their animal charges. They work long and hard to sustain their needs; to sustain their sense of wellbeing; and, to sustain production efficiencies, for without that, we cannot stay in business very long.

All our beef animals are ultimately going to be harvested for food. It is a fact of life—the young and the old. That cycle has never changed. I love the beef cattle industry and I particularly love the feedyard environment. I am as familiar with the birth to death cycle as anyone is. I have worked as hard as anyone in keeping them alive and productive. No one is any more focused on the wellbeing of the individual animal than I am. I'm there. I'm on their side. I want the best for them every day, every hour, every minute, but they are a food animal.

Yes, I hate to see those big eyed beauties go to the load-out dock. But, I will support what we do, I am even proud of what we do. No one in the world does it better. Their cycle from birth to death is just as natural as our own. Sleep well tonight and be not concerned about animal welfare in the beef cattle industry. Though we are not perfect we are always trying to upgrade our animal care level across the industry. "Genuine Care & Concern for the Individual" can become the new industry standard. But, everything works backwards from marketing. Tell your retailer that you want your beef source animals raised under the "Genuine Care & Concern for the Individual" philosophy. Tell Costco in particular—I'd love to supply it—we just may have to build our own packing house.

8

Humane Treatment

The term humane treatment could very well mean different things to different people. I dare say that most people could agree on what is, and is not humane treatment regarding dogs and cats. They are pets. They often live in our homes and become members of the family.

Regarding cattle, these same issues are not present. They are not pets. I freely grant that some few can express a personality with tendencies toward human interaction; but, almost without exception, these few would be limited to those that from birth interacted with people.

The specie as a whole has lived under a predator/prey relationship for millennia. Since becoming domesticated, they adjust to a given environment. In states where predators exist, generally focusing on the very young, the cattle residing there are certainly alert to their environment. In other cases they may be comfortably at ease.

Instinctively, this predator/prey survival reaction may appear in other circumstances when they are stressed; often as it relates to being penned and handled as necessary by humans in implementing health and management practices. The stress level associated with these human interactions varies tremendously between breeds, and even among individuals within a breed.

The ranch I lived on in my youth predominately had Hereford cattle. No one would have described their behavior as gentle. Those cattle were largely a product of their environment. They were gathered in the spring for branding activities, and again in the fall for weaning activities. This country had originally been a part of the historic Matador Ranch. The predator/prey relationship was a strong influence in their lives.

These survival instincts if you will, are still present in many cow herds, and can still surface from time to time. But largely, due to better handling techniques across the industry, we do not have so many wild cattle. As their environment softens around them, their own anxiety level will quieten as well.

In our harshest environments it takes a cross-bred (Brahman influenced) cow to be successful. These cows can be very gentle, and as easy to work as any of the rest. But, often they have a "hair-trigger." Meaning that if not handled in the way they are used to, things could become very dicey, quickly.

Florida cattle in their environment.

There was a very fancy set of young, Brangus type cows that arrived at Lubbock Stockyards, Lubbock, Texas. The old man in Brownwood who had raised these cows from calves, worked them using a feed sack. When he wanted to pen them, he walked out into the pasture, rustling a heavy, paper feed sack. The cows would follow him into the pen. He got a little help come branding time; but he always worked them gently.

Arriving in Lubbock they were already plenty "stirred up." Sale barn employees tried to work them gently, but they continued to be a challenge. They would come to you at the drop of a hat, ready to do battle. Two days later when they sold in smaller groups, they cleared the alleys wherever they went. I am sure that with time at their new location, they settled down. But, I dare say never to where they had been with the old man (who had passed away).

Cattle are largely a product of their environment and how they are handled. One bad (wild) cow can influence others. Fifty years ago our egos' would not let us sell a bad cow. We thought we were plenty cowboy enough to get it done, one way or another. Today, I would sell individual wild cattle in a heartbeat. I just do not want that negative influence on the others. I want them comfortable in their environment; and will do everything in my power to make it so.

As my professional career path moved me into the world of cattle feeding and feedyards, I gradually found myself focusing on individuals, rather than the herd. It took time to focus on new issues, new circumstances, and the new environment. Initially, my focus was on health problems, particularity pneumonia. Slowly but progressively, I came to realize that many other factors influenced health, and the wellbeing of the animals under my charge. Preventing health issues was a far wider scope than just a preventative health program. Aware that a feedyard is a data-rich environment, I began what has become a life-time search for ways to enhance their sense of wellbeing.

Initially, it began simply as a question. How do we enhance performance parameters safely? That simple question has become the cornerstone of my activities. The term "safely" might create different options from one person than it would for another, or for me.

I support conservative use of growth enhancers (implants). Unless we are going to get paid for "natural cattle," we cannot otherwise recoup lost performance dollars. Depending upon the implant philosophy, availability and pricing of feedstuffs, as well as management desires, the nutritional consultant can position performance parameters about anywhere desired. Too high and it causes me (consulting veterinarians) bloat and GI (gastrointestinal) problems in the cattle that we would all rather not have. Too low and no one is happy. Thus, it becomes an ongoing "fine-tuning" regarding performance parameters. With every visit of the nutritionist, a little adjustment may be made, depending upon health issues, commodity (feed ingredients) prices, and the desires of management.

Humane treatment is, in my mind, a composite of individual factors that influence the "sense of wellbeing" regarding the cattle in question. It would be human nature to attempt to extrapolate what we think we know involving dogs and cats, and apply them to cattle. Thinking like that is what has turned America from a nation of "haves" into a nation of trying to hang on to what we still "have." Though I grant you that I backed into the subject of humane treatment, while trying to find safe ways to enhance performance parameters; it has actually allowed the opportunity for the cattle to speak for themselves. Only in a data-rich environment could this be possible; but, we can literally measure their approval by monitoring performance parameters. At any given time in the feeding period, preferably after the transition period from the ranch to the feedyard is over; we can add or eliminate a factor and monitor performance levels. The change may only be a tenth, or two tenths of a pound of gain per day; but, it is a measurable response, and a repeatable response; an indication by the animals regarding their sense of wellbeing.

Holstein Grow Heifers.

Holstein cattle proved to be the perfect animal model. They have a very tight genepool, where what affects one, affects the others to more or less the same degree. Additionally, they (compared to beef cattle) have a higher sense of socialization. What we eventually learned from Holsteins (at the feedyard) does not apply equally well to colored cattle (beef breeds). We did not expect it to. Colored cattle are highly variable between individuals; their genepools are widely dissimilar. But, no one argues that it does not apply; just that it is much harder to see; harder to appreciate; and harder to measure. But, close scrutiny of "close-out" information convinced even the most skeptical.

By happenstance, four loads of same-source cattle came into the feedyard. On that given day we only had two pens available in the colored cattle (beef breeds) sections of the yard. We had several pens available in the Holstein section of the feedyard. So, we sent two loads into the colored cattle section and two loads into the Holstein section. These later two loads were handled and treated exactly as though they were Holstein cattle: quiet and gently, low-stress handling techniques, concerning their every activity and movement, which results in lowered stress-levels. The only difference being that they were fed typical of colored cattle—not as Holsteins.

Holstein feeder calves.

"Colored feeder cattle"—all the beef breeds and their crosses.

On a day to day basis there seemed little difference between the cattle in the two different sections of the feedyard. We may have had suspicions, but we did not know. Only at close-out, when all pertinent information was brought together, was it evident the cattle fed under the Holstein philosophy outperformed their source-mates. This began what turned out to be—a few years later—the one and only, operational philosophy that was adhered to throughout the feedyard: "Genuine Care & Concern for the Individual." The Holstein philosophy became the foundation on which we all operated.

Now let us look at the issues that appear to be most prominent, relative to humane treatment or "Genuine Care & Concern for the Individual," a term which is more practical and measurable. Basically, there are three distinctly different areas that are the foundation on which we base our philosophy, followed by four supporting, stand-alone programs.

Stress Reduction

This subject is the first of three foundation pillars on which we build our efforts toward enhancing the "sense of wellbeing" in the cattle under our care. In the past it seemed like we, the cattle industry, simply assumed that stress was just a normal part of cattle management. When any given aspect of stress was "highlighted" for whatever reason, we would of course concur that it was not beneficial; but, we seemed never to dwell on its effects. Today, we know better.

Stress is the number one enemy to good health. Its effects are measurable. Its effect costs us dollars (performance). Its effect causes a reduction of the cattle's sense of well being. Stress is also accumulative. Sometimes it is that last feather of stress that causes immune suppression. All the antibiotics in the world are a drop in the bucket, compared to what a properly functioning immune system can do for itself.

We received 3,500 Holstein "grow" heifers from north-eastern Illinois. These heifers were to be grown at a prescribed rate; bred at the appropriate time; and sent to Houston, where they would catch a boat for Russia. Prior to loading in Illinois a large group of heifers were commonly gone through, reading individual identification tags, to determine who went onto the truck, and who did not. This would take several hours (off of feed and water). Then they would begin what was estimated to be a 21 hour trip to Garden City, Kansas. Several different truck drivers were used. It soon became apparent that one of these drivers was very good; the others proved to be terrible. Meaning that the primary goal should always be to make the trip as efficiently as possible; stopping only for fuel and a quick bite while being fueled. No other stops except on the side of the road to check the cattle.

As these heifers began to arrive it was apparent that they had been stressed to the max. To our feedyards manager's credit, he sent people scurrying in every direction at once, to get additional sources of water (16 feet in diameter metal tubs) placed in the pens and filled with water. In a normal pen only a few cattle can drink at a time. Some of these heifers had been on the road 26 to 28 hours, in addition to the time on the ground being sorted, prior to loading. Most all of these heifers were less than 400 pounds. Due to the manager's quick action, all following loads had filled water tubs awaiting their arrival.

We initially waited ten days before processing. It was soon apparent that they were still not over the stress of shipment. On pen by pen basis, most of these heifers were not processed (initial vaccinations, primarily) for three weeks after arrival—allowing adequate time to fully restore metabolically, before receiving their initial vaccinations. This was only the second time that I could remember, in which immune suppression was so obvious and substantial.

Our nutritionist was told to grow these heifers at two pounds per day. Our first check weights were at 2.1 pounds per day. If you grow them too fast, they put fat into their udder, which significantly reduces their ability to milk later on. This particular owner wanted them grown a little faster, than is the industry standard of 1.7 to 1.8 pounds per day. Most grow heifers do not have a lot of "bloom," but these did. They were gorgeous.

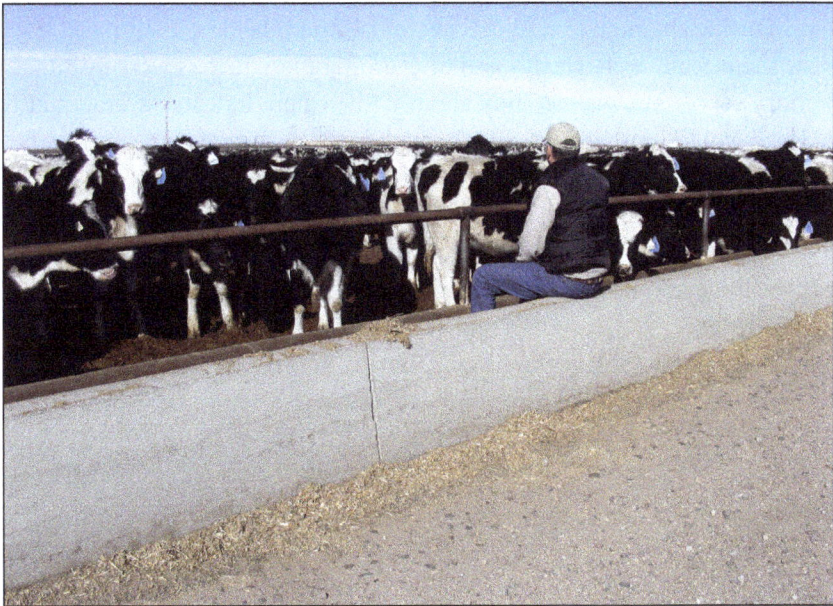

Holstein Grow Heifers—these ultimately destined for shipment to Russia.

More grow heifers.

Eventually, these heifers were bred and shipped to Houston for their trip to Russia. These heifers were to be spread out across Russia in small groups, enabling a regrowth of their dairy industry. This was a great project that most of us enjoyed immensely. But, it was vastly different from what we were normally used to, regarding feeder cattle.

During the many months that we had these heifers, I felt that I got to know them really well. Health issues regarding these heifers were minimal. If memory serves me, we lost only about 0.5%; where industry averages at the feedyard would more likely be 1.5% death loss. This is only an estimate, but I believe that 6-8% of these heifers never returned to fully-functional immune status, due to the stress associated with the way their transit was handled prior to arrival; it was more of a feeling, rather than substantiated fact. Immune suppression could not have been totally prevented, but it could have certainly been lessened.

Let us now look at the more common sources of stress as they might occur in the life of a calf, beginning just prior to leaving the ranch or other place of birth.

Weaning

Every operation is unique as to when and exactly how their calves are marketed. Small operations simply separate the calves from their mothers, load them into a trailer, and haul them to the local sale barn. Larger operations, usually with prearranged agreement (with the buyer), pen the herd, cut-off the calves (separate them from the cows), sort heifers from the steers, and then weigh all the heifers (getting a good head count), and finally weighing the steers. Now they know exactly how many pounds that have to be paid for. Steers usually sell for 7 to 10 cents more per pound.

The optimal method is to wean the calves off their mothers, at least thirty days (forty-five is better) ahead of time, and keep them there at the ranch, pending vaccination protocols; getting them used to pelleted or grain-based rations; and becoming used to not having mom around. Accomplishing this weaning process there at the point of origin, is much less stressful, and is accomplished in a low-exposure environment. Sickness is usually not much of an issue at all. Properly managed, weight gain can occur during this time, just about paying for the extra time, effort and expense. That aspect, however, pales in comparison to the benefits received by the calf. That calf—or calf crop, more accurately—can now arrive at the feedyards, prepared and ready for his/her new environment.

The transition time to adjustment is appreciably shortened if everything was done correctly. Less sickness and enhanced performance by this set of calves, now makes next year's calf crop from the same place, worth more money. It is a slam dunk. It is as obvious as apple pie. Yet, many producers find excuses for not doing it. Mostly, "no one is paying me to do it." Sounds a little weak, does it not? It is so shortsighted that it would almost be humorous, except that it is the calves that are paying the price. The other aspect is that very often, there are middle men involved between the seller and the feedyard, which strictly limits lines of communication. At every opportunity I encourage producers to create relationships with feedyards. It ultimately makes for a better beef product for you.

Shipping and Transit

The process must become better managed across the board. Weaning the calves at home, prior to shipping, accomplishes most of the issues. It enables steers and heifers which are already separated, to simply be weighed and loaded.

Trucks (trailers actually) have to be clean, or should not be loaded. Drivers have to be well rested, or the trailer should not be loaded. Let him take a nap now, while the calves are still on feed and water, before loading the trailer. Good instructions and good contact information should be placed in their hands, along with the "window of opportunity" (when the cattle should arrive at the feedyard) clearly understood by all concerned.

My younger brother used to haul light (250 to 350 pounds) calves from far south Texas (the valley area) to Brawley, California. He had to be in the valley (of Texas) by 5:00 pm in order to get loaded. He then had a two hour window to unload the calves, 36 hours later. I made that trip with him a few times. We stopped twice for fuel (El Paso, Texas, and Shady Grove Truck-Stop near the New Mexico-Arizona line). Other than stopping along the interstate to check the cattle from time to time, these were the only two times we stopped. We also had a quick meal while we were being fueled. After unloading in California (between 5:00 and 7:00 am), I had thought it would be a leisurely trip back. That was not the case. We had to make it back in 30 hours in order to be in San Antonio by noon, which would allow us to be back in the valley by 5:00 pm. Hell of a way to make a living. I truly believe that my brother suffered as much as the cattle; but no one took better care of the cattle than he did. By the way, if you missed that window of opportunity to unload in California, the feedyard did not have to take the cattle.

Those little crossbred calves that came out of south Texas did well, and looked great when they weighed 1,150 pounds. By the way, it took a crossbred (Brahman cross) to tolerate the heat of southern California. We would be short a whole lot of beef today were it not for crossbreds. Black cattle may get the headlines, but crossbreds carry much of the load.

Receiving Cattle at the Feedyard

At every feedyard I have been a part of, there is a separate alley (sometimes, two alleys, each composed of many, identical pens, set side by side) where new cattle are going to be placed. They will usually stay there thirty to sixty days, depending upon whether or not they will receive the official revacc processing, necessary for cattle of unknown background. After this required stay, they will be moved to their permanent home pen.

These new cattle "receiving pens" are fully prepared ahead of time, awaiting the arrival of cattle. Usually a pen or two will be made up (feed ration in the bunk and high quality loose hay spread on the bunk pad) and ready, even if no cattle are expected that night. Fairly often, unexpected loads do show up.

Having the ability to quickly enable all the cattle to drink their fill of water is unbelievably important. The weaker cattle in particular, that cannot muscle their way through the group to reach feed and water, will simply go lay down to rest. That is the last thing in the world that calf needs to do—another 6 to 8 hours without feed and water. If they are under my charge, someone is going to quietly walk those cattle about thirty minutes after arrival to make sure we do not have any "little guys" laying around that have not eat and drank. All of them will have good opportunity to eat; it is the water source that will get crowded for a little while. In fact we want at least 25% of them to be able to access water at the same time.

Feedstuffs (hay and grain-based rations) will be of high quality, nutrient dense and the best we can find. Palatability (how much they like it) is a huge factor as we select these feedstuffs. Right now (upon arrival) these babies are just trying to live over the stress of transit. They may not feel much like eating. I want their "options" to be so good, they cannot pass them up. If when they do lie down, they are full and rehydrated, then when they get up six to eight hours later, rumen function will have been reestablished and immune function level should not be too far behind.

New arrivals at the feedyard.

Handling

The way we handle our cattle is the one area that we as an industry, have been most resistant to change. It is a deeper issue than just habit. It's almost as if we express ourselves to others, by our traditional cattle handling practices. The things I do, and say, and use, generally reflect what others did as I was learning. Thus our expectations from the cattle involved are much the same. We have all allowed our anxiety levels to rise while complaining about how dumb the cattle were.

I find it only modestly humorous to recognize today, that we all should have been looking in a mirror when we used the word, dumb. This is one of those things in life that you can only appreciate, after you have learned a better way. Then it becomes modestly embarrassing when we think back to how we used to do it. The interesting thing is that I (or we, if I speak for the industry) would never have appreciated advanced (quiet & gentle, low-stress) handling techniques had it not been from someone whom we all had great respect for—showing us a new way. But when Dr. Tom Noffsinger, a feedyard consultant from Benkelman, Nebraska, demonstrated it for us at our feedyard, it was inspiring to say the least.

For me personally, you have to show me the numbers. Meaning, show me proof that your way is real; your way creates measurable differences in performance. If it is real it is measurable. It is; it was; and now I am a believer. Without question, learning and implementing the details of handling cattle in a quiet and gentle, low-stress manner improves sense of wellbeing and performance of everyone involved—cattle and people.

"Heidi"—Many of these Holstein Grow Heifers were bottle fed as calves, and enjoy human contact.

Today, I look back and am modestly embarrassed at how we used to handle cattle. We are not stupid people. We were just riding the coattails of our traditional heritage. It is unbelievable how much more stress was involved regarding the cattle and the people, doing it the old way. If you use these new cattle handling techniques, starting from the moment you enter their pen (at the feedyard), you can finish with them in the same manner.

Stress is the enemy. There are no positives associated with stress. Anyone can learn these new techniques. Personally, I would not feed cattle anywhere that did not utilize these techniques. They make that much difference in the performance of the cattle. Knowledge and efficient compassion is the order of the day. You want your beef source animals to have been kindly treated; we want the same thing; it enhances performance which makes us money. Personal compassion is icing on the cake.

Processing

Processing is the handling and management of cattle through a "processing facility" allowing for the administration of vaccines, ear tags (ownership and individual identification), and deworming agents (anthelminics), most commonly. If done properly, using quiet and gentle, low-stress handling, it is a simple, practical and efficient process. Cattle walk out of the chute. They are not big-eyed and scared to death. Coupled with the same handling techniques all the way back to their home pen, it may be more than a nonevent, but is certainly not a serious event in their lives.

Just like with American travelers abroad, it is always good to get back home. Their "home pen" is their comfort zone. They are back to eating and drinking with their buddy. On a couple of future opportunities, they will actually enjoy going somewhere in the alley-ways of the feedyard again; but, when they "jump and kick" as they reenter their home pen, they are happy to be home.

Upgrading processing techniques takes leadership, knowledge, and persistence. I know the feedyard manager (where it all began), a personal friend as well, on more than a few occasions, thought I was a "little overboard" regarding our efforts. But, to his credit, he made it clear to all, that this was the new standard; their continued employment was contingent upon acceptance of the new philosophy "Genuine Care & Concern for the Individual." I add my thanks to Larry Bilberry, Garden City, Kansas, for his friendship and his leadership.

Is the entire feedyard industry up to speed on this philosophy? No. But, we are gaining one at a time. The economic incentives are there; the care and concern is there. You are our new boss; I think I know what you want; and you shall get it.

Critical Support of the Immune System

This is the second of the three foundation pillars on which we build our program regarding elevating our cattle's "sense of wellbeing." Most sickness can be prevented. If prevented, that animal's sense of wellbeing is appreciably higher. Elevating and then sustaining this sense of wellbeing is a significant part of a successful humane treatment program.

COLOSTRUM: Let us begin with our attention on the source producer (where the calf was born). As many years as the subject of colostrum (that first milk produced by the mother) has been discussed, it still does not receive the importance, regarding our efforts, as it should. There is a twelve hour window for the proper volume of high quality colostrum to be received by the calf. Usually producers are not involved in the calving process. But when they are, if there is any doubt in their minds concerning that baby's ability to nurse within an appropriate time span, they should take care of it while they are there. Failure to receive proper quality and quantity in the allotted time, negatively affects them reproductively and performance wise, for the rest of their lives. Fact.

PLANNING AHEAD: Stockmen should plan ahead for possible eventualities that would add stress to the lives of the cattle involved. Stress can limit the immune systems functionality. Examples would include winter storms, drought, loss of a primary water source, and disease coming into the cow herd from a neighbor's herd. There may be no real solutions, but at least management options as they exist, can be utilized more quickly.

MINERAL DEFICIENCIES OF THE SOIL, AND MINERAL EXCESSES INVOLVING THE WATER: This is a huge category that is not taken as seriously as it should be. Know your soil. Have appropriate mineral supplements available—preferably loose. Provide these calves all they need to have strong immune systems. Mineral excesses in the water are often even more profound relative to limiting the immune system's ability to respond to vaccines.

Where I was raised we had "gyp water." Shipped in cattle would not even drink it. It was many years later before I knew why our cattle had more sickness at the feedyard. The high sulfate levels severely limited the immune system's ability to respond to vaccines. Prioritizing vaccines became essential. Getting them onto good water for thirty days commonly enables the immune system to perform normally.

CHRONIC HERD DISEASE: Some herd diseases are low-grade and seem not to have too much effect on the herd. If that is remotely true—it is only in regards to the adults. A chronic inflammatory response is often associated with this disease in the young. It has a negative effect on the development of young immune systems.

CHRONIC PARASITISM: Internal parasites, uncontrolled, often causes anemia. Anemia in the young certainly limits their immune system's development and functionality. If anemia is not involved, these parasites are stealing nutrition that would otherwise be available for metabolism and good health.

POOR VACCINE MANAGEMENT AND ADMINISTRATION: This has long been a problem—improperly handling and administering modified-live viral vaccines, in particular. These are fragile vaccines. They begin to deteriorate from the moment they are reconstituted (mixing the liquid with the powder). Heat and direct sunlight enhances this deterioration. Clean equipment and sharp needles are also vitally important.

POOR VACCINE SELECTION: All vaccines are not created equal. Some cell-lines are simply a lot better than others. They all seem to work in low-exposure (pasture) environments. Many will not protect adequately in a high-exposure environment. Marketing is everything and everything is marketing. Reading the label on the product and talking to the salesperson, does not give you real information.

These are the primary areas that our industry often fails to handle properly, regarding supporting the immune systems of their calfcrop. If they (producers) do their job well, it is quickly evident at the feedyard. A report card is created on every set of calves that go through the feedyard. Everyone's cattle are "exposed" for what they are. The bottom-line to you, our consumer, is simply that sickness (often due to weak immune systems) and stress negatively affect the marbling aspects of the carcass. Fact. And, they both significantly diminish the sense of wellbeing in the affected calves.

Every immune system is inherently unique. Some are so strong that they could probably get through the feeding period without vaccinations. Some are so weak that they simply cannot be successful at the feedyard. Most are somewhere in between. Not in the middle, but incrementally at some point in between the two extremes. An average immune system is perfectly capable of accepting the challenge of vaccines and producing protective titers (antibodies). Weakened immune systems from any of the above issues, will present additional challenges that normal immune systems do not have to endure.

Socialization Issues

This is the third and last of the foundation pillars involving their sense of wellbeing. Holsteins set the standard. What we know of these issues has come from Holstein calves in the feedyard. I have for a long time, said: "Colored cattle are simply the lucky recipients of the Holstein philosophy." Colored cattle (the beef breeds) simply do not have the level of socialization requirement that Holsteins do. But, on an individual basis, many have absolutely as much a requirement as Holsteins.

Holstein feeder calves—these have been here 86 days.

Holsteins seem to require other Holsteins to meet this requirement. They can make do with other dairy breeds, if they have to. Beef cattle can make do with horses, sheep or even goats, if they have to. I am familiar with an incident involving a broke-legged steer that could not be shipped in the fall with the other cattle. That steer spent the winter with the brood mares. He ate with, watered with, and bedded down each night with the brood mares. He never uttered a vocalization. I wish I understood all that I actually saw involving that calf.

SUPPORTING SOCIALIZATION: Most people in our industry could not tell you, if asked, what the socialization issues even consist of. I would not know if it were not for Dr. John Lynch and the fact that we fed a lot of Holstein steer calves. It took Dr. Lynch two years to teach me the Holstein Philosophy. Once you understand them, you love to feed Holsteins. They are very predictable compared to colored calves. Holsteins are the perfect animal model because of their tight genepool; whereas the genepool of colored calves is highly variable. So, we proved our theories using Holstein calves as our model. Their very tight genepool allowed for consistent performance parameter deviations, given a particular insult or stress factor.

Then the question becomes, does it apply to colored cattle as well? No one would argue that it does not. But, given the highly variable nature of colored calves, results were and are, harder to see, and harder to appreciate. But, it is on "close-out" information that even the skeptics are converted.

The socialization issues are real; real being a result, measurable in performance parameters (dollars). Let us look at some of the factors. Do not be too quick to jump to conclusions.

BUDDIES: Holsteins have a best buddy. Sometimes they have two best buddies. That two-some fits into a group of six to eight, most commonly. That group fits into the pen as a whole. The buddy is a very tight relationship. The small group is not tight, just comfortable. The relationship with the pen is not very important. In fact if you replaced the two buddies, into another pen, it would cause no great consequence; just do not separate the buddy system.

Buddies lying next to each other at the feedyard.

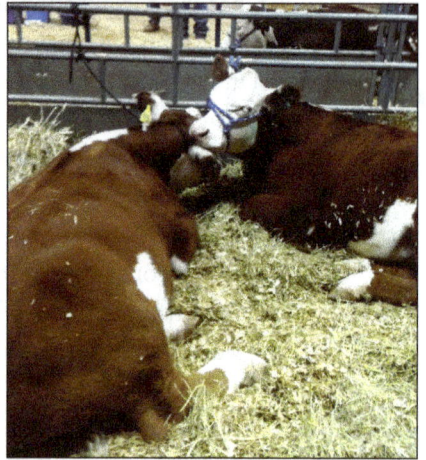

Buddies at a livestock show.

Buddies in the pasture (grazing rye grass with their mothers).

Dr. Noffsinger once showed a picture (on a large screen during a meeting) of an eight-weight black, steer standing at the back-alley gate in about a foot of mud. The steer was gaunt (dehydrated and not eating) and looked terrible. Dr. Noffsinger's question to the audience was: "Is this calf sick?" The answer turned out to be that his "buddy" had been pulled and taken to the hospital two and a half days before. This steer was waiting, at the gate where his buddy had gone out, for his return—refusing to eat or drink in the meantime. Even the most skeptical individuals in the room had to concede this socialization issue. Buddies are most important. This is one of the reasons that at the feedyard, we never split up groups of cattle after the transition period. And, very importantly, if they got sick, they were treated with a long-day antibiotic and sent back home (home pen) to recover.

PEN-SPACE: An animal needs 200 square feet of pen space. This has largely to do with socialization issues. Those buddies often want to get off to themselves, at least a little off to themselves. If we support this space requirement, they give us enhanced performance. If we do not, it cost us performance (gain) every day. The difference can be from two-tenths of a pound, up to a pound of gain a day if severely overcrowded. This is huge.

BUNK-SPACE: Bunk-space is probably the least critical factor, but it is still a factor. Every animal in the pen at any given moment that wants to eat should be able to comfortably get to the feed bunk. If the manager thinks otherwise, it is costing him some degree of gain (performance) every day. Even a tenth of a pound of gain a day, across the feedyard, is a lot of lost performance dollars—wasted.

HIGH TEA: For lack of a better term this one works. This may only apply to Holsteins. A group of six to eight (commonly two or three sets of buddies), go hang out at the water trough. Yes, I am sure that they taste, perhaps even drink while they are there, but that is not "why" they are there. This is a social occasion. I don't know what they do; I'd guess that they tell wild-west stories; but it is meaningful time to them. They need an adequate sized concrete pad for this to occur. Don't think it's real? The pens that cannot accommodate; the pens that have problem surfaces around some of the water troughs; and the pens that have pads too small to accommodate; will all have diminished performance values compared to the pens that do accommodate. May just be a tenth to two-tenths of a pound per day, but it is there.

HOLSTEIN NEXT TO HOLSTEIN: Holsteins like to be around other Holsteins. For that reason we put all the Holsteins together in a section of the feedyard. If a pen of Holsteins is not surrounded by other Holsteins, they are giving up one to two-tenths of a pound a day, and often more. The Holsteins at the very end of an alley, give up some performance. The Holsteins that have a pen of colored cattle in the adjacent pen, give up performance.

I love to go to the very end of an alley holding Holsteins, and monitor the distribution of the individuals within each pen of that alley. Whatever it may be at that part of the day, it will be very close to the same in every other pen. If it is not; if one pen looks distinctly different from the others, you had better go check it out. Something is wrong in that pen.

CONSUMERS: I truly hope that you are getting some idea of how much attention these cattle actually receive in the feedyard environment. Many of you have assumed that they were crammed into pens and largely ignored. Nothing could be farther from the truth.

If I were a calf, get me to the feedyard at the earliest convenient time. Let me be well prepared on arrival. Let that arrival occur in mid-September. By the time bad weather arrives I will have sufficient cover (fat) to handle the weather just fine. I will be gone before the heat of the summer returns. We all have to go some time. I will take mine at a high-plains feedyard—southwest Kansas, if I get to pick.

FOUR STAND-ALONE SUPPORTING PROGRAMS: These four programs support the three larger foundation pillars: reducing stress, critically supporting the immune system, and socialization that we just discussed.

> 1. "Quiet & Gentle, Low-stress Handling" is likely the single most important change we have made regarding our new philosophy of "Genuine Care & Concern for the Individual." Once compliance is gained and results are obvious; there are no detractors. However, in the beginning, there are lots of issues with pen-riders, the processing crew, and the doctoring crew. Persistence, strong persistence is the key.

> 2. "Selective Culling" is a program designed to identify the immune-compromised animal(s) and promptly remove them from

the feedyard. This is more art than science. Looking at old records involving "chronics and cripples" helps enormously. Most of these individuals fit a history. Many can be identified fairly quickly. Most of the rest are identified between day 31 and 70. Early and quick removal allows the animal to be successful in a low-exposure environment, and stops the economic bloodbath that is likely to be in their future. To err on the side of culling too many, costs the owner a few dollars. To err on the side to culling too few, costs the owner many dollars.

3. "Doing the Basics Perfectly" is a program created to significantly upgrade handling and administering vaccines in particular. Its goal is to deliver a cool, 100% efficacious vaccine dose into every calf; I repeat "every" calf.

4. "Euthanasia Program" is one that is long overdue. Simply put, when "active" treatments have failed, and no immediate exit strategy is in place and available, properly euthanize the individual. No longer do we hold them, pending antibiotic reside issues to be resolved, before selling them for a few dollars. We will not let them suffer from this point forward.

9

Nutritive Value of Beef

Beef has been described as nature's best tasting multivitamin. Calorie-for-calorie, beef is often considered to be one of the most naturally nutrient-rich foods. When properly prepared it satisfies like few other food items are capable of. Even when poorly cooked, it provides the dense nutrient base required for sustained, physical activity that few other food items are capable of. Beef has a long history of being greatly appreciated by consumers. Only in recent times have its critics seemed to go out of their way to place blame on the product and its consumption.

Compounds called amino-acids are the basic building blocks necessary to form proteins. There are essential and non-essential amino-acids. Essential amino-acids cannot be made in adequate quantities by the body, and must be supplied through the diet. Meat, eggs and milk supply all the essential amino acids, making them complete, high quality protein sources.

We should also be aware that all fats are not created equal—regardless of what the advertising on the label may say. Some are a whole lot healthier than others. Butter (preferably raw), extra-virgin olive oil, and coconut oil happen to be my personal favorites. Fat is an essential nutrient. It provides for the absorption of fat-soluble vitamins, and the formation of hormones, and it can be used as an energy source. The goal is to balance low-fat with high-fat options over time.

Half the fatty acids in beef are monounsaturated, the same kind of fatty acids found in olive oil, and championed for their heart-healthy properties. In addition, approximately one-third of the saturated fat in beef is "stearic acid." Studies have shown that stearic acid does not raise blood cholesterol levels like other saturated fatty-acids do.

Beef is not bad for you. The middle meats, rib-eyes for example, do have a lot of fat. Eat in moderation. Do not have a rib-eye three times a week. As much as I like beef, I will not have a rib-eye three times a month; but, I sure do enjoy one occasionally. Personally, I am a fan of sirloin steak. I believe it to be the most flavorful part of the carcass. It is not as tender as a T-Bone, rib-eye, filet mignon, strip steak, or tenderloin, but when properly prepared—delicious. Roast beef cooked long and slow, a great hamburger, BBQ, and even an occasional chicken-fried steak are all great entrees that provide meaningful beef eating experiences. But, like with KOBE BEEF, eat in moderation—regarding amount and frequency. That way you can enjoy any and every aspect, regarding what beef can bring to the table.

Lean beef fits easily into low-fat meal plans designed to decrease blood cholesterol levels. Research shows that Americans can eat six ounces of lean red meat five days a week as a part of a cholesterol lowering diet. Further, both red and white meat produces the same favorable changes in blood cholesterol levels. Lean beef is just as effective as skinless chicken in lowering blood cholesterol levels.

Calories are another big issue. All calories are not created equal. Good calories we need; bad calories we do not need. If you eat right—you can have a lot. Processed sugar and corn syrup that our food processors and food manufactures are so proud of (they must be, they put them into almost everything), are terrible. They are hollow and unhealthy calories. Investigate a product called Stevia; it is a natural extract that sweetens without calories. I believe that the day will come when we will all find out that artificial sweeteners with all the chemicals, hydrogenated oils, processed foods, high-fructose corn syrup, as well as sugar in general are responsible for many, if not most, of our health issues associated with being over-weight and unhealthy.

The term moderation is well understood by most people who are successful in life's various activities. I believe the term is a foundation principal regarding eating. Change your lifestyle, change your eating philosophy, change your eating locations, but do not simply starve yourself to reach target weights. Cravings are going to occur. Yield to them in moderation from time to time. You can afford to do so, if you have developed a healthy eating life style.

Interestingly, the protein group is the only food group Americans currently eat within USDA Dietary Guidelines recommendations. The surprising fact is that Americans, on average, eat 1.7 ounces of beef every day, well within recommendations for a healthy diet. Research shows that beef is a vital source of protein, iron and many other important nutrients that sustain a healthy diet. Let us now look at what science says about some of the nutrients that are found in beef's naturally nutrient rich package.

MUSCLE:

Sarcopenia, the slow loss of muscle mass, and endurance which begins in a person's mid-40s, is associated with a three to four fold increased likelihood of disability, and cost the United States healthcare system $18.5 billion in 2000. A body of evidence reviewed by leading protein researchers concludes that protein intakes greater than current Dietary Reference Intake of 0.8g/kg/body weight may enhance muscle protein development and reduce progressive loss of muscle with age.

(Paddon-Jones, Short, Campbell, Volpi, and Wolfe: "Role of Dietary Protein in the Sarcopenia of Aging;" *American Journal of Clinical Nutrition*; 2008.87

This research study examined the role of beef in stimulating muscle growth in older Americans, which is critical in helping people avoid bone fractures, and live well and independently as they age. The study found that consuming four ounces of lean beef protein each day can help enhance muscle development by 50%. These results suggest that consuming an adequate amount of lean protein can lead to an improved ability to increase or maintain muscle mass, and as a result, may delay the onset of sarcopenia or loss of muscle.

(Symons, Schutzler, Cocke, Chinkes, Wolfe, and Paddon-Jones: "Aging Does Not Impair the Anabolic Response to a Protein-Rich Meal;" *American Journal of Clinical Nutrition*; 2007.86

This research review indicated that increasing daily high-quality protein intake may optimize muscle strength and metabolism, and ultimately improve overall health. A growing body of evidence suggests muscle metabolism may also play a role in the prevention of many chronic diseases, such as type2 diabetes and osteoporosis. Eating at least 15 grams of essential amino acids at each meal, equivalent to four ounces of a high quality protein like lean meat may help maintain muscle mass, and provide strength to lead an active lifestyle.

(Wolf, R: "The Underappreciated Role of Muscle in Health and Disease"); *American Journal of Clinical Nutrition*; 2006.84

WEIGHT MANAGEMENT:

A body of research discussed by 52 international protein researchers suggests protein may play a key role in several aspects of weight management. Evidence suggests that a moderate increase in dietary protein in association with physical activity and a calorie-controlled diet may aid with weight management by increasing thermoneogenesis, which influences satiety and augments energy expenditure, helping maintain lean muscle mass and improve metabolic profile.

(Paddon-Jones, Westman, Mattes, Wolfe, Astrup, and Westerterp-Plantega: "Protein, Weight Management and Satiety"); *American Journal of Clinical Nutrition*; 2008.87

Numerous studies have shown that dietary protein is more satiating than carbohydrates and fat. This particular study showed that protein intake below the Recommended Dietary Allowance can lead to increased hunger and desire to eat among men.

(Apolzan, Carnell, Mattes, and Campbell: "Inadequate Dietary Protein Increases Hunger and Desire to Eat in Younger and Older Men"); *Journal of Nutrition*; 2007.137

Research shows that exercise is more effective when coupled with a moderately high-protein diet. This study demonstrated that a protein-rich diet with reduced carbohydrates, combined with exercise additively improved body composition during weight loss, reduced triglyceride levels and maintained higher HDL (good) cholesterol levels. Researchers concluded that the protein rich diet is successful in maintaining muscle mass while burning fat because high quality protein foods, like beef, contain high levels of the amino acid leucine, which works with insulin to promote muscle growth.

(Layman, Evans, Baum, Seyler, Erickson, and Boleau: "Dietary Protein and Exercise have Additive Effects on Body Composition during Weight Loss in Adult Women"); *Journal of Nutrition*; 2005.135

This clinical trial examined the effects of protein on body composition, cardiovascular disease risk, nutritional status, bone turnover, and kidney function in 100 obese women. Researchers found that people on the higher protein diet lost more fat mass and achieved nutritional benefits either equal to or greater than those on the higher carbohydrate diet. In particular the higher protein diet is associated with greater reduction in triglyceride concentration and improvements in hemoglobin and vitamin B-12 status. There was no evidence of adverse effects on bone health or kidney function.

(Noakes, Keogh, Foster, and Clifton: "Effect of an Energy-Restricted, High-Protein, Low-Fat Diet on Weight Loss, Body Composition, Nutritional Status, and Markers of Cardiovascular Health in Obese Women"); *American Journal of Clinical Nutrition*; 2005.81

Abdominal obesity or "belly fat" is significantly related to morbidity and mortality. This study gave insight into how to avoid this condition. A cross-sectional study found that those who had the highest proportion of energy intake (or calories) from protein also had the lowest waist-hip ratio. Thus, replacing protein for carbohydrates may help to reduced stomach fat.

(Merchant, Anand, Vuksan, Jacobs, Davis, Teo, and Yusuf: "Protein Intake is Inversely Associated with Abdominal Obesity in a Multi-Ethnic Population"); *Journal of Nutrition*; 2005.135

This study tested a higher protein, low-fat diet compared with a higher carbohydrate, low-fat diet, and found equally favorable results. Both diets reduced cholesterol levels, body weight, and body mass equally. However, those on the higher-protein diet did not complain of hunger and were much more satisfied than those on the higher carbohydrate diet.

(Johnston, Tionn, and Swan: "High-Protein, Low-Fat Diets are Effective for Weight Loss and Favorably Alter Biomarkers in Healthy Adults"); *Journal of Nutrition*; 2004.134

This research shed light on why moderately high protein diets may be beneficial for weight loss and muscle maintenance. The study theorizes that, due to the amino acid leucine found in protein rich foods such as beef, increasing the proportion of protein to carbohydrates in the diets of adult women may have positive effects on body composition, blood lipids, glucose homeostasis and satiety during weight loss.

(Layman, Boileau, Erickson, Painter, Shiue, Sather, and Christou: "A Reduced Ratio of Dietary Carbohydrate to Protein Improves Body Composition and Blood Lipid Profiles during Weight Loss in Adult Women"); *Journal of Nutrition*; 2003.133

BONE STRENGTH:

Protein and calcium intake interact positively to affect bone health, and intakes of both must be adequate enough to fully realize the benefit of each nutrient on bone. Optimal protein intake for bone health is likely higher than current recommended intakes, particularly for the elderly. Some studies found meat as a protein source is associated with higher blood levels of insulin like growth factor 1 (IGF-1) which is associated with increased bone mineralization and fewer fractures.

(Heaney and Layman: "Amount and Type of Protein Influences Bone Health"); *American Journal of Clinical Nutrition*; 2008.87

This study confirms that middle-aged people who eat more protein rich foods, such as beef, have fewer hip fractures resulting from osteoporosis. These findings support the hypothesis that adequate dietary protein is important for optimal bone health which can have a significant impact on overall health and independence.

(Wengreen, Munger, Cutler, Corcoran, Zhang, and Sassano: "Dietary Protein Intake and Risk of Osteoporosis Hip Fracture in Elderly Residents of Utah"); *Journal of Bone and Mineral Research*; 2004.19

HEART HEALTH:

Studies evaluating health risks across the range of protein intakes found individuals with the highest protein intake had the lowest risk for coronary heart disease (CHD) and the highest quality diets. Leading researchers conclude that earlier associations of dietary protein or protein foods with CHD may have been due to coincidental relationships with other modern lifestyle factors, such as total energy intake, daily physical activity, stress, inconsistent meal patterns and convenience foods.

(Layman, Clifton, Gannon, Krauss, and Nuttal: "Protein in Optimal Health: Heart Disease and Type 2 Diabetes"); *American Journal of Clinical Nutrition*; 2008.87

OPTIMAL HEALTH:

This research report found protein quality is as important as adequate quantity to achieve optimal health. Animal protein foods such as beef, pork, eggs, fish, poultry and dairy products are essential sources of high quality protein. There is strong emerging evidence of a positive role for high quality protein in promoting optimal health at intakes beyond the RDA of 0.8g/kg/day.

(Millward, Layman, Tome, and Schaafsma: "Protein Quality Assessment: Impact of Expanding Understanding of Protein and Amino Acid Needs for Optimal Health"); *American Journal of Clinical Nutrition*; 2008.87

NUTRIENT-RICH PACKAGE:

A study, which examined the health benefits of dietary patterns that follow current dietary guidelines and includes multiple nutrients, suggests women who follow diets including fruits, vegetables, whole grains, low-fat dairy and lean meats or other naturally nutrient-rich foods, have a lower risk of mortality.

(Kant, Schatzkin, Graubard, and Schairer: "A Prospective Study of Diet Quality and Mortality in Women"); *Journal of the American Medical Association*; 2000.283

LEAN BEEF AND HEART HEALTH:

A review of 54 studies provides substantial evidence that lean red meat, trimmed of visible fat, does not raise total blood cholesterol or LDL (bad) cholesterol levels. When consumed as a part of a diet low in saturated fat, lean, trimmed beef does not increase cardiovascular risk factors (plasma cholesterol levels or thrombotic risk factors).

(Li, Siriamornpun, Wahlqvist, Mann, and Sinclair: "Lean Meat and Heart Health"); *Asia Pacific Journal of Clinical Nutrition*; 2005.14

B-VITAMINS:

Seniors with low vitamin B-12 status but high serum folate were more likely to experience anemia and cognitive impairment. When vitamin B-12 status was normal, however, high serum folate was associated with protection against cognitive impairment.

(Morris, Jacques, Rosenberg, and Selhub: "Folate and Vitamin B-12 Status in Relation to Anemia, Macrocytosis, and Cognitive Impairment in Older Americans in the age of Folic Acid Fortification"); *American Journal of Clinical Nutrition*; 2007.85

The Framingham Osteoporosis Study examined the relationship between vitamin B-12 blood levels and indicators of bone health in 2,576 men and women, aged 30-87. Researchers found that those with vitamin B-12 levels below 148 picomoles per liter had significantly lower average bone mineral density—at the hip in men and the spine in women—than those with higher concentrations of the nutrient.

(Tucker, Hannan, Qiao, Jacques, Selhub, Cuppies, and Kiel: "Low Plasma Vitamin B-12 is Associated with Lower BMD"); The Framingham Osteoporosis Study; *Journal of Bone and Mineral Research*; 2005.20

Pregnant women who followed a vegetarian diet that included eggs and dairy products, but no meat, had an increased risk of vitamin B-12 deficiency, which is a risk factor for neural tube defects. In addition, breast-fed infants of a vitamin B-12 deficient mother are at greater risk for developmental abnormalities, impaired growth and anemia.

(Koebnick, Hoffman, Kagnelie, Heins, Wickramasinghe, Patnayaka, Gruendek, Lindemans, and Leitzmannn: "Long-Term Ovo-Lacto Vegetarian Diet Impairs Vitamin B-12 Status in Pregnant Women"); *Journal of Nutrition*; 2004.134

While vitamin B-12 and folate have been shown to have positive effects of dementia, research found that people consuming more than 22.4 milligrams of niacin or vitamin B-3, from food daily were 80% less likely to suffer Alzheimer's disease and age-related cognitive decline than their counterparts.

(Morris, Evans, Bienias, Scherr, Tangney, Hebert, Bennett, Wilson, and Aggarwal: "Dietary Niacin and the Risk of Incident Alzheimer's Disease and of Cognitive Decline"); *Journal of Neurology Neurosurgery and Psychiatry*; 2004.75

CONJUGATED LINOLEIC ACID:

Beef is a natural source of conjugated linoleic acid (CLA), a polyunsaturated fatty acid. While research on CLA is still evolving, a body of evidence suggests this compound may have cancer fighting properties, as well as positive effects on cardiovascular disease, body composition, insulin resistance, immune function, and bone health.

(Bhattacharya, Banu, and Rahman: "Biological Effects of Conjugated Linoleic acid in Health and Disease"); *Journal of Nutritional Biochemistry*; 2006.17

ZINC:

Seventh graders who consumed an additional 20 milligrams of zinc, beyond their normal diet, each school day for 10 weeks scored better on visual memory and word recognition tasks, as well as functions requiring sustained attention and vigilance, than their counterparts who consumed less zinc.

(Penland, Lukaski, and Gray: "Zinc Affects Cognition and Psychosocial Function of Middle School Children"); Abstract presented at the American Society of Nutritional Sciences, Experimental Biology 2005 Conference, April 4, 2005; San Diego.

Among healthy school age children, increasing zinc intake has been demonstrated to improve cognitive performance. In fact, research suggests zinc has a role in improving recall skills, reasoning, psychomotor function and attention.

(Sandstead, Penland, Alcock, Dayal, Chen, Li, Zhao, and Yang: "Effects of Repletion with Zinc and Other micronutrients on Neuropsychological Performance and Growth of Chinese Children"); *American Journal of Clinical Nutrition*; 1998.68

IRON:

These studies found that overweight 1 to 3 year olds, who are not in daycare, are at higher risk for iron deficiency. Researchers think this may be due to extended breast-feeding without introduction of iron rich foods, or inadequate intake of iron rich foods once the child is weaned. This is an important public issue as 4 million U.S. children are iron deficient, and childhood iron deficiency anemia is associated with behavioral and cognitive delays.

(Brotanek, Gosz, Weitzman, and Flores: "Iron Deficiency in Early Childhood in the United States: risk factors and racial/ethnic disparities"); *Pediatrics*; 2007.120

This research review found that iron and zinc rich meats are important first foods for breast-fed infants to provide essential micronutrients. In addition, the American academy of Pediatrics, the World Health Organization and The Centers for Disease Control and Prevention all recommend meat as a complementary food to ensure that breast-fed infants consume adequate amounts of these important nutrients.

(Krebs: "Food Choices to Meet Nutritional Needs of Breast-fed Infants and Toddlers on Mixed Diets"); *Journal of Nutrition*; 2007. February.

Researchers found that, even though children received iron therapy in infancy which corrected their iron deficiency anemia in all cases, iron deficient children had lower motor scores than their iron sufficient counterparts when tested in infancy, at age 5, and in early adolescence. The difference in motor scores remained constant throughout these life stages.

(Shafir, Angulo-Barroso, Calatroni, Jimenez, and Lozoff: "Effects of Iron Deficiency in Infancy on Patterns of Motor Development Over Time"); *Human Movement in Science*; 2006.

Iron deficiencies may impair crucial mother-baby interactions. Researchers found mildly iron deficient mothers were less sensitive to their babies' cues, were less likely to give their babies the chances to lead interactions, often interrupted play at inappropriate times, and appeared bored or distant more frequently than mothers with adequate iron levels.

(Corapci, Radan, and Lozoff: "Iron Deficiency in Infancy and Mother-Child Interaction at 5 Years"); *Journal of Behavioral and Developmental Pediatrics*; October 2007.27

Postpartum stress and depression are estimated to affect 40% of U.S. pregnancies each year. Researchers found that anemic new mothers taking iron supplements experienced a 25% reduction in depression and stress.

(Brard, Hendricks, Perez, Murray-Kolb, Berg, Vernon-Feagans, Iriam, Issacs, Sive, and Tomlinson: "Maternal Iron Deficiency Anemia Affects Postpartum Emotions and Cognition"); *Journal of Nutrition*; 2005.135

This report shares that 84% of children studied who had Attention Deficit Hyperactivity Disorder (ADHD) also had abnormal iron stores. In addition, researchers found the children with the lowest iron stores had the most severe ADHD symptoms. Researchers suggest these children could benefit from additional iron intake.

(Konofal, Lecendreux, Arnulf, and Mouren: "Iron Deficiency in Children with Attention-Deficit/Hyperactivity Disorder"); *Pediatric and Adolescent Medicine*; 2004.158

Diets rich in lean beef can help teenagers maintain their levels of useable iron, teach important balanced eating habits and dispel misperceptions that healthy diets cannot taste good.

(Snetselaar, Stumbo, Chenard, Ahrens, Smith, and Zimmerman: "Adolescents Eating Diets Rich in Either Lean Beef or Lean Poultry and Fish, Reduced Fat and Saturated Fat Intakie and Those Eating Beef Maintained Serum Ferritin Status"); *Journal of American Dietetic Association*; 2004.104

The website www.Explorebeef.org (active at the time of the publication of this book) shares these interesting nutrition facts:

1. There are 29 cuts of beef that meet governmental guidelines for lean,

including consumer favorites like Tenderloin, T-Bone and 95% lean ground-beef.
2. USDA defines "lean" as less than 10 grams of total fat per 3 ounce serving.
3. Lean cuts of beef have 4.5 grams or less of saturated fat and less than 95 grams of cholesterol per 3 ounce serving.
4. 20 of the 29 lean beef cuts have, on average, only 1 more gram of saturated fat than a skinless chicken breast per 3 ounce serving.
5. Beef is a naturally nutrient-rich food, helping you get more nutrition from the calories you take in.
6. Beef has 8 times more vitamin B-12, 6 times more zinc and 2.5 times more iron than a skinless chicken breast.
7. A three ounce serving of lean beef contributes less than 10% of the calories in a 2,000 calorie/day diet.
8. A substantial body of evidence shows protein can help in maintaining a healthy weight, building muscle and fueling physical activity—all of which play an important role in a healthy lifestyle and disease prevention.
9. The cut of beef with the lowest amount of calories, saturated fat and total fat, is the eye round roast and steak, with only 144 calories, 1.4 grams of saturated fat and 4 total grams of fat in a three ounce serving.

Meat in general and beef in particular is an excellent source of many nutrients, especially protein, B vitamins, iron and zinc. As a nutrient dense food item, beef provides significant contributions to our diets relative to the calories it contains. A three ounce cooked portion of lean beef containing 195 calories would provide 25 grams of protein, 9 grams of fat, over one-third of your daily requirement for zinc, and fifteen percent of your daily iron needs. To get the same amount of zinc from salmon, you would have to consume 2,363 calories. To get the same amount of vitamin B-12 from chicken breast, you would have to consume 1,050 calories. To get the same amount of riboflavin from white tuna would yield 491 calories.

I have reached a point in life where I do want to eat healthy, and have little interest in "fads." So, here is my personal form of natural eating. I want to focus on foods that are single item entrees—carrots, broccoli, spinach, corn, beans, sweet potatoes, beef, pork, chicken, etc. What I do not want to eat are any prepared, processed, or manufactured foods. I want no chemicals, no preservatives, no by-products, no dyes, no flavor enhancers, no synthetic anything, in my food. I want Mother Nature's products, including milk, meat, eggs, fish, wild game, and garden vegetables. Sure, I want seasonings and butter.

Life style, eating habits, exercise, personal health issues, your gene-pool, and making poor choices in general, very likely have at least as much to do with our weight and lifespan, as what and how we eat. Focus on these external issues and minimize what you can in order to optimize your life. Then, be smart; recognize the problem foods, and problem food groups. Choose your fats and oils carefully; stay away (as much as possible) from processed foods. Eat single item foods and entrees. It is amazing how beneficial making good food choices and a little exercise can be, regarding your health and your weight. No magic, no programs, no meetings—just thinking about avoiding foods that do you harm. Have moderation in life's choices. Let me share one last example—the lowly "Twinkie." It used to be made with sugar, milk, vanilla, flour and eggs. Look at the label today. The ingredients are chemicals, preservatives, flavor enhancers, bi-products and who knows what. If you must have a sweet, pick one laden with mother-nature's best: Blue Bell Ice Cream, for example. Wholesome products are used as ingredients; that is the key to selections.

10

Health Issue Involving Beef–The Harvard Study

L et us begin with a quick discussion about the media; especially since we live in a world of instantaneous news gathering services. The days of simply reporting the news (concerning beef or any other subject), as much of the story as possible, including all known facts, are long gone. Today, news two hours old is old news. There is enormous competition to single out oneself or one's news gathering service, in regards to sharing news to the world. There exists a zeal for speed. The full story can be someone else's responsibility. For now, let us just break the story.

The media lives and dies on ratings. Everyone wants to be number one—at least some of the time. How do you get to the position of having the largest viewing or listening audience? The quickest way to stardom is to collect the facts that can be associated with "hot-button" issues; and, then hit as many emotional "hot-spots" as possible, in reporting your abbreviated version of the story. Stimulating "emotional" responses is the short version of gathering in an audience. Thus, your story is short, sweet and highly reactive. And, as in the days of old, regarding newspapers, any corrections can follow in a few days on page 6. *"Get the story, that will get the audience, that will get the necessary response," seems to be the order of the day.*

To make the issue(s) a little more complex, today it seems necessary, when and where possible, to slant the story to match your or your service's point of view; the inherent philosophical position, if you will, of the hierarchy involved. If you are a liberal, it is tilted favorably in that direction. If you are in business, it is tilted favorably toward supporting capitalism. If you are vested in inequality, it is tilted toward supporting personal feelings.

So, when a story does come out in the news concerning beef, we in the industry are all riveted in on the story. In the past most of these stories have focused upon topics involving beef recall due to some contamination at the packing house or fabrication facility. Rarely have they involved the production segment of our industry; with the exception of some YouTube videos depicting untrained, unsupervised and inexperienced employees involvement with cattle. Yes, management must accept the blame; they were the responsible party without question. These episodes have embarrassed us all to no small level. But, they are very, very isolated incidences.

When a significant story concerning beef does break from a major news service that puts beef consumption in a bad light, our industry becomes a bedlam of activity desiring to understand the who, what, how, and why concerning the incident. That was the case when Harvard Medical School released a report on beef that captivated everyone: "Consumption of Red Meat and Processed Meat Increases Risks of Mortality." For the most part, scare tactics do work—stimulating emotional responses from the consumer base. Most of them you do get back as consumers; some few we do not get back. It does not matter that it was a poorly conceived study. Let me now share a synopsis of a response made on the website www.MeatIssues.org (active at the time of publication of this book).

There are several methods that might be utilized when drafting the architecture of a planned medical study. The most commonly used is one known as the "scientific method" The "scientific method" involves asking a question, designing a well-controlled study to reduce statistical error, and drawing conclusions based ONLY on observations from the study. In an "epidemiological study" (which was used in this instance) observations are collected over a period of time from people who may be at risk or have contracted a health issue. The researchers look at trends from this population and draw conclusions. Thus, the population is appraised, common factors are denoted that may be related to the issue of concern, and then conclusions are drawn. Yes, it is effective, but it leaves plenty of room for error.

While the report indicated a direct causation of red meat intake to mortality, it did not indicate factors that may have been involved. Along with segregating responses into who did and how much (or who did not) into 5 different quintiles, subjects also listed other health and lifestyle factors in the study, including body mass index, level of physical activity, alcohol consumption, servings of fruits and vegetables, as well as whole grains per day.

When looking at the data, the 5th quintile (highest red meat consumption) versus the 1st (the lowest red meat consumption) the 5th also had:

Higher BMI (body mass index)
Lower physical activity
More likely to smoke
Higher alcohol consumption

Higher caloric intake
Consumed less fruits, and whole grains
Used less multivitamins

What it really tells us is that this 5th quintile was composed of people that have high red meat intake AND probably were not very healthy people overall. Yet, they are drawing conclusions that eating more red meat increases their risk of dying. Their statistical analysis used covariates to reduce statistical noise. When controlling for covariates it does not eliminate the material from the data, but rather it pulls the variable to a centralized mean. For example, if average smoking for all people (in the study) was five cigarettes per day, it drags everyone into that central mean, including those that smoke two packs a day. Though accounting for the data (smoking), it is artificially skewing the data, when in fact a coviate is used to normalize data sets. When you have a variable in a study looking at death rates, can we really exclude their smoking status out of the analysis? The main point being that an "unhealthy lifestyle and diet" increases your risk of mortality."

Beef plays an integral role in a healthy diet, especially for growing children. While the science of food may be hard to understand and appreciate, this particular study was unfair and was simply bad reporting on the researchers part to imply causation that beef was responsible for higher mortality. It is not accurate or fair to draw parallels with skewed food reporting, confounding variables, and say that a single factor does without question, increase your risk to die. Its causing unnecessary fear among consumers was even worse. My personal thanks go to MeatIssues.org. regarding their insightful and candid response.

Harvard Medical should have caught and reevaluated this report before being released. Was this particular report completely blamed on the lead investigator who also created the architecture of the trial; or did Harvard Medical spread the blame around? That, largely, turned out to be an internal action. They certainly were not as proactive in taking corrective action through the media as those of us in the beef industry might have desired. Perhaps oversight of research projects at Harvard will improve, just as oversight of employees will improve in the beef cattle industry.

By happenstance, I have been a part of a long-term study (involving allied medical professions), as a regularly surveyed individual, instigated by Harvard Medical. I have received regular questionnaires since the 1980s, when

I became involved. On some occasions they have wanted blood and urine, in addition to filling out the questionnaire. Each questionnaire is lengthy and takes several minutes to fill out. Each question directs you to find an answer between none, a little or a lot. Though the range of options is wide, my answers always tended to stay in the same general range as I viewed down the list—perhaps just left of or just right of center. My issue was remembering how many helpings of spinach I had eaten in the last year (for example). I suspect that it was an issue for most people surveyed. I never felt really comfortable with the accuracy of the information being obtained. It just never seemed personalized; or perhaps it was simply too generalized. How would you respond to the question of how many helpings of spinach have you had over the last year?

Obviously there have been other sources and stories attempting to present beef consumption as something horrible. When our "usual" critics are involved it is apparent what they are up to. The Harvard study was a shock, principally because it was from Harvard, and on previous occasions they had actually supported the consumption of beef, with some moderation—just as I do.

Conclusions:

Just because it appears in print, even by notable individuals, do not presume that everything is fact. We as a people at this place in time, sometimes seem incapable of expressing information without incasing the substance of the story through our own political or philosophical view points.

Just as I am skeptical of every new veterinary product that comes out into the marketplace (given the marketing strategies of today); so too should you be skeptical. Growing up I remember reading articles in magazines (Western Horseman, perhaps) about horses, and aspects of their training that just did not sound right. Dad's response was typical: "Anyone can write a book or an article."

Our detractors are going to make as much negative noise about the beef cattle industry, and animal agriculture in general, as possible. Think for yourself. Be not too quick to make judgments until all the facts are in.

Our industry is still evolving from being producer-driven to that of a consumer/retail-driven industry. Our growing focus is on producing the specific kind of beef that you desire. No obstacle so big or mountain so high that we (producers and consumers) cannot overcome, if we have open lines of communication that yield you a knowledgeable platform from which to make decisions concerning the beef cattle industry.

Environmental Issues

D o we have environmental issues in the beef cattle industry? Of course we do. Methane gas is deserving of an earnest discussion which we shall have. But, regarding most environmental issues, our problem lies more with the people having "oversight" of our industry, without knowledge about our industry, than the issues themselves.

Let us begin with the subject of sustainability, a current topic of the international community. Though not a subject producers talk much about, there seems to be general concerns in two specific areas. The two subjects that appear at or near the top of most involved groups list are "humane treatment" and "low environmental impact." Humane treatment was covered in Chapter 8 of this book. Environmental impact is a broadfaced subject that we will try to separate into some fractional issues, enabling better understanding.

GRASS LANDS MANAGEMENT:

Ranchers, stockmen, and stock-farmers, all necessarily have to be good stewards of the land. In many ways the land is the "golden goose." We must take care of the land in order for it to take care of us. This over-simplification is at the heart of all we do. We can run only as many cows as the land will allow. A stockman is in many ways, a grass farmer. A wide variety of grazing plans and systems have evolved over the years to maximize forage production, with keen interest in not overgrazing. For example, if our cows stay on a particular pasture long enough to remove 60-65% of the grass; and then are moved off the pasture, it will stimulate new production. If we overgraze we stunt the forage crop/grasses and two things happen. Weeds begin to come up and grass regrowth is slow. Neither one of which aids our production practices.

Most of the lands we graze cattle on are not suitable for row crops (farming). The poorer the quality of the land, the more fragile the ecosystem (that is present) is, and must be carefully managed. Grazing mistakes (overgrazing in particular) can prove to be very costly for a number of years. These kinds of mistakes have put many operators out of business. Management of our ranch lands is critical. Quality of life issues of the family diminish as grass availability diminishes. We as an industry are always working with extension personnel from state universities to learn new techniques to improve forage grazing opportunities. It is subject matter that we take seriously.

As a grass manager we have to know our soil. In many, perhaps most, parts of the United States, various areas are deficient in this mineral(s) or that mineral(s). Sometimes we can make applications to correct. More commonly, we cannot. So, depending upon the soil analysis, we offer a mineral package to the cattle grazing these pastures. Most commonly this is in the form of mineral blocks placed near water, across the ranch. Better managed operations often choose a good, high quality, loose mineral. We have to know our soil and its weaknesses; then do our best to take corrective actions.

Every area of the country seems unique in its own way. In some areas owners are constantly expending energy and money to control, if not eliminate, emerging noxious weed or brush issues. Some of these plants are toxic to the animals. Some just steal subsurface water away from grass production. Every chemical used can only be obtained by individuals who have "qualified" themselves through product education training. When to apply, rate of application, how it is applied, under what weather conditions it should be applied, proper protective clothing issues, and how long cattle might have to be removed from the pastures, are all issues addressed and followed by the applicator. These are weighty issues, requiring detailed instruction, and follow through. These chemicals are, for the most part, very expensive. We cannot afford to do it incorrectly.

Another issue might involve that of trash. In town you have a landfill. In the country we have traditionally dug a hole or pit, and dumped our household trash. At some point, either incrementally or when almost full, we would cover it up, level it out, and allow grass to regrow over the top. These procedures are already coming under discussion on a state by state basis, involving new oversight and/or regulations. The bottom line is that each state has rules, regulations and/or limitations that are followed—period.

Discarded materials other than household trash, including chemicals of one sort or another, most commonly have printed instructions on the label of the product giving explicit instructions as to how this particular product should be disposed of. Extension people and state government personnel assist in this matter as might be necessary to find solutions to properly accomplish the disposal.

WATER ISSUES:

Without question water issues of one sort or another affect most areas of cattle operations. Usually it has to do with the scarcity of water and its preservation. Some areas it is the reverse—too much water. Either way, if you have cattle they need water. That water may come from lakes and ponds, rivers and streams, snow runoff, windmills, pipe lines, deep irrigation wells, or springs of one sort or another. Water quality is just as variable as are the sources. Some areas have great water. Many areas have less than ideal water quality.

Where I grew up we had "gyp water." Cattle new to the area would not drink it. It was many years later that I found the answers as to why our cattle (from gyp water sources) had more health issues at the feedyard. The high sulfate levels minimized the immune system's ability to respond to the challenge of vaccines. Additionally, these "limited" immune systems could quickly become overwhelmed if too many vaccines were used at once. Prioritization of these vaccines is absolutely critical. Send them to town (on good water) for thirty days, then, they could respond properly to vaccines. Water issues and in particular, the scarcity of water in the western states is a real problem. This is nothing new, but perhaps exacerbated by the dry weather cycle we seem to be in. These are problems that have to be managed; rarely are there real solutions. An area of ranchland in eastern New Mexico that I am familiar with is watered by a pipeline that originates sixty miles away. Another area west of Albuquerque has a semi-load of water hauled every day to the highest point (elevation wise) of the ranch where it is gravity-flowed to the various watering tanks located across the ranch. Water has always been a key element in cattle grazing operations, and no one in their right mind would do anything to contaminate or diminish a water supply, knowingly. It is a vital and cherished commodity.

MANURE:

How about the lowly subject of *manure?* Manure at the ranch level of production is likely more of a blessing than a problem. It is at least, modest fertilization. However, in confined feeding operations, as well as the dairy shed (commercial milking operations), manure is an issue. For many, many years, we have had "oversight" from government officials regarding runoff issues at the feedyard. Particularly focused upon would be: lagoons or pits to hold runoff water pending evaporation and percolation, treatment facilities of one sort or another, and a vast array of other things that were tried over the years. The focus continues to be: do not allow this manure-tainted water to drain toward water ways, including dry creek bottoms, and certainly not onto your neighbor. Containment is a key objective.

Dairies are beginning to adopt procedures where they haul their manure to "recycle centers," where the methane gas produced is actually captured.

At the feedyard level it has been stockpiled and when composted, spread onto farm land to help fertilize the soil. Depending upon the state involved, this avenue for removal is proving to be less than a long term solution. The water runoff from these feedyards, after a certain amount of settling has occurred, has occasionally been pumped onto farm land through specially modified, circular sprinklers.

We are and have been for a while, looking for new ways to dispose of manure that does not have possible repercussions down the road. The two more viable options include putting it onto pasture land, not farmland, and truly composting it to a point where it can be bagged and sold as composted plant and garden material. Both of these options are growing in popularity each year.

One Texas ethanol plant developed the technology to take dried, feedyard manure and grind it (pulverize it actually), then sprinkle it into a very hot incinerator type device that burned the manure. This process provided 80% of the necessary "heat" to produce ethanol.

GOVERNMENTAL OVERSIGHT:

Our issues regarding manure disposal are commonly more with federal officials, who do not have any real knowledge of our industry, than with the problem itself. No one wants to pollute. We do not want our kids and grandkids negatively affected, any more than you want yours affected. We are not running and hiding from the issues. We will find long-term solutions. Solutions will come from within our industry and within our universities—not the government. Let me share a case in point.

In north Texas there was a small grow-yard where a wide assortment of cattle were brought in truckload lots, to get "straightened out" and prepared for the high-exposure environment of a feedyard setting. Any sick cattle were properly treated and all cattle fed under the supervision of a consulting nutritionist. It was a good, well managed "grow yard." Was, is the key term.

The manager knew he had a problem with runoff after a rain (manure tainted water running off into a dry creek-bed located on the same property). Over a period of several months he created a plan to correct the problem; accumulated set-aside monies; and gained access to some grant money that would have corrected the problem. Then he initiated the process to get his plan approved by the appropriate governmental agencies. This soon became a story of "if it could go wrong, it did." The major problems were two-fold: the EPA representative who spoke limited English, knew nothing of the industry, and simply wanted to punish rather than find solution; and a lack of communication between two different sections (with the same boss) of the EPA in Washington. In the representative's zeal to punish he immediately had a court ordered injunction put in place, shutting down the grow-yard. Then he had area newspapers run negative stories concerning the embattled grow-yard. The manager and his attorney ultimately did arrange a meeting in Washington with the administrator of these two segments of the agency. After being made aware of all that had transpired and the associated lack of internal communication, he approved the manager's original plan of action. However, the set aside funds had now been used to pay the attorneys. The representative was transferred "elsewhere," and the fourth largest employer in the county (the grow-yard) has never reopened; and the problem never corrected.

Another story involved the same agency, the EPA, not understanding why Lubbock, Texas could not meet "air particulate matter" standards. They had on several occasions made prior trips to Lubbock trying to understand the problem. Lubbock did not appear to have enough industry to produce particulate levels that had been measured. Even though the EPA had been repeatedly told of dust storms that frequented the area (particularly in the spring)—that just did not make sense to them. On one and final occasion, as far as I know, they arrived in town and were bused down into the Plains and Seminole area (southwest of Lubbock perhaps 75 miles away) in an effort to show these Washingtonians residual evidence of past blowing dust storms that often left debris in the Lubbock area. I have actually seen it down there when maintainers (road graders) were needed to reopen the highways so traffic could resume—several feet of sand in spots.

On this particular occasion one of those black storms, the area was known for, blew in. The town folks on that bus got a real education. Actually experiencing the magnitude of Mother Nature's wrath, struggling to breathe and not being able to see ten feet, proved to be a clarifying experience. I am pretty sure that when they left Lubbock the next day, they did not anticipate a return trip. But, they did find the causal agent as to the "air particulate matter." It came from the southwest and was just passing through Lubbock.

URBAN SPRAWL:

Last but not least, particularly around fast growing suburban areas (like south Florida where retirement communities are stacking up like tailgate party participants), is the problem of building or desiring to build homes that will "interact with agricultural establishments." Developers do not seem to care where they build homes as long as someone buys them. Suddenly, at least it seems that way, there is an outcry from neighbors around sale-barns (livestock auctions), feedyards, pre-conditioning yards, packing houses, and even cattle ranches, because they do not like the smell, or the dust, or the noise or the truck traffic, or the railroad having to make more stops than it used to. These business operations were there long before the houses were built. Who wins? Regardless of who wins, it leaves someone unhappy.

This is happening in most areas of the country where fast growing metropolitan areas need to expand. People want to live and/or work there, so the population growth continues. Generally, it is agriculture that has to move or go out of business. Smell, manure and proximity that are offensive to encroaching populations invariably cause the displacement. Some of these displaced operations survive; many simply close out operations. The general population seems to have no concept of what the future holds as agriculture is consistently losing position, power and influence in America. As our world population expands and the quest for animal protein grows, an awaking is going to occur as the loss of the scope of agriculture becomes evident to all. Agriculture is shrinking without question. Only through greater production efficiencies have we kept our lost production acreages from directly affecting you, the consumer. The day will come when our ability to provide for all the desires of consumers, will become an obvious challenge; perhaps involving beef more than most other segments of agriculture. Regarding this shrinking scope of agriculture, as it is lost there will be no getting it back. Urban sprawl is growing, water scarcity issues are growing (regarding pasture lands), government land ownership is growing, and expense (costs) of beef production in particular, is growing. Beef production operations are holding on (economically) because of good management and improved efficiencies (like growth hormones we use in finishing our cattle). With no relief in sight, we will begin to lose operations purely from economic challenges, further exacerbating the challenges of a diminishing national cowherd (total numbers of cows in production).

If you are ever in the Texas panhandle, drive through Hereford, Texas—Wall Street of the cattle feeding industry. When you drive through Hereford, and you are not from around there, your olfactory senses will light-up. Locals hardly notice. There is not a business in town that could survive if the feedyards all closed down. Cattle and cattle feedyards are king. Ninety cents of every dollar involves or was just involved with cattle. Yes, there is a smell. Mostly it has to do with the manure and the feed-mills, in full operation. Largely, we simply do not think about it. It is just a fact of life within our daily operations.

Let me share an example of how we live with it. As a large-animal veterinarian I practiced a lot of years in eastern New Mexico. I rectally palpated a lot of cows over the years, to determine their pregnancy status. I often arrived home in the evenings with a fair amount of evidence on me. When my sons were very young, I came in one evening, and the youngest asked what it was that I had all over me? "Cadillac paint" I responded. For many years we enjoyed the humor involved regarding one who earned a living with one arm up the rectum of a cow, several thousand times a year. Never did get the Cadillac.

A few years later when the same son entered the first grade, the teacher asked each child what they had done that summer. My son remarked: "I had my arm up a cow's butt and felt the baby." The teacher, who had never before lived in a rural environment, called the principal, ready to have social services put on my case. Luckily, the principal had been a farm boy, and found great humor in the story. The teacher left at the end of her first year, and moved to Albuquerque. Apparently, our social graces were not up to her standards.

Yes, agriculture has rules to follow just like most industries in America. If they are rules created for us, we may not like them, but we can follow them. But, many, many times, that is not the case. How can government officials in particular, who know so little of our industry, be responsible for enforcing policy, especially when the policy is vague as it pertains to us? It was likely written for an industrial setting, and its application in a rural environment is unclear.

LOVE OF THE LAND:

Rural dwellers have a great appreciation for our environment, and recognize that it is the "golden goose." Ours may not be as pretty as a lot of others'; may not receive the rain that others get. But, we respect and appreciate what we do have. If they knew; if they had spent real time; if they visited our environs more often; those unfamiliar with our lands would see how valued and cherished our lands are.

Good, soaking rains, regularly, would solve most or our real environmental issues. Anyone can pass legislation, or have a "plan of action" for the future that sounds good—even reasonable. But, as much as we care for, and try to serve our environment; it can be mighty, brutish, and forceful in its own right. At times our environment seems to have all the power it needs to enforce its own will. As kind and gorgeous as it can be, its ferociousness can and has, sent us scurrying as mice.

Sounds simple, keep it covered in vegetation and it will not blow off. It has to be the right vegetation or the cows will not eat it; otherwise, the land has lost its value. The good vegetation that cattle will eat needs a little rain occasionally. Therein lies the conflict.

Someone else's country may be covered in snow for a few months of the year. Grass is great for a few months; but, it is a little tough on cows when the grass is buried under a foot or so of snow. Some other location has bottom-country that will grow anything. The river comes up twenty feet, and they've lost their "bottom."

I have to believe that somewhere across our nation is the perfect place. Cows in knee-deep, high-quality grass; plenty of good water and no storms, droughts, or encroaching populous that is about to drive that producer over the hill. No government officials enforcing regulations on situations that they do not fit, and no politicians who care only about themselves; and, school systems that really work.

Ours is not a perfect world. Ours is not a perfect industry. But, nowhere in the world will you find producers willing to work harder for you than in the beef cattle industry.

GLOBAL WARMING:

We are now going to immerse ourselves into a subject that not even the experts, can always agree on. It is a subject that involves our cattle; a subject that creates a good deal of emotion; and, one that our vocal critics love. Bear with me as I try to present subject material that is not always easy to read or understand.

The bulk of this material will involve greenhouse gases (GHG). But first, let us examine the Greenhouse Effect. It is so named by an analogy to the greenhouses we are familiar with. The difference is the mechanism by which heat is retained. A greenhouse works by preventing absorbed heat from escaping the structure. If it gets too hot, open a roof window to allow circulation.

The Greenhouse Effect acts to warm the earth by re-radiating some of the energy back towards the surface of the Earth. A process by which thermal radiation, from a planetary source (the sun), is absorbed by atmospheric greenhouse gases, and is re-radiated in all directions. Since part of this re-radiation is directed back towards the surface, and the lower atmosphere; it results in the elevation of the average surface temperature above what it would be in the absence of the gases.

Earth's natural greenhouse effect makes life as we know it, possible. This process has been going on for billions of years. Ice core sampling provides evidence for variation in greenhouse concentrations over the past 800,000 years. Direct data does not exist for earlier periods. However, various proxies and modeling scenarios, suggest much larger variations in prior periods—six, ten and fifteen times higher than today. These variations were of course from natural sources.

There are also natural mechanisms to reduce the levels of the gases creating this greenhouse effect. But, it takes a very, very, very long time to bring it back to what some describe as equilibrium.

Since 1750 (the birth of man's industrial revolution) human activity has increased the concentrations of the greenhouse gases. Measured atmospheric concentrations of carbon dioxide are currently 100 times higher than pre-industrial levels. Between the period of 1970 and 2004 greenhouse gas emissions have increased 1.6% per year, with carbon dioxide emissions growing at the rate of 1.9% per year. Emissions of methane and nitrous oxide have also gone up.

Without question, carbon dioxide, methane, nitrous oxide, and the group of man-made fluorinated gases (sufurhexafloride, hydroflurocarbons and perfluocarbons) are the major anthropogenic (due to human activities) causal agents regarding our problem.

CARBON DIOXIDE comes from several sources including the burning of fossil fuels (petroleum in motor transport), coal burning activities for electrical generation, and deforestation (principally in the tropics), and account for up to one-third of total anthropogenic emissions.

METHANE has even more sources: livestock enteric fermentation and manure management, paddy-rice farming, land use and wetlands changes, pipeline losses (leaks), covered and vented landfill emissions, and the newer style, fully vented, septic systems that enhance and target the fermentation process. They all raise atmospheric methane.

NITROUS OXIDE is emitted by bacteria in our soils and oceans and has thus been a part of the earth's atmosphere for millennia. This source alone accounts for about 70% of its presence in the atmosphere. Anthropogenic (from man) sources account for about thirty percent (30%) of its current level. Agricultural farming activities including the use of fertilizers, lead to higher nitrous oxide concentrations. Many manufacturing and industrial activities are also involved, and each is a part of the problem.

Additionally, nitrous oxide gives rise to nitric oxide (laughing gas) on reaction with oxygen. This nitric oxide in turn reacts with OZONE. It is the main naturally occurring regulator of stratospheric ozone.

OZONE is formed from dioxygen by ultraviolet light, and atmospheric electrical discharges. The peculiar smell after lightning storms is that of ozone. It is a potent respiratory hazard and pollutant near ground level. As a part of the greenhouse gases, it is of great benefit, preventing damaging ultraviolet light levels from reaching the earth's surface, to the benefit to us all, including plants and animals.

THE GREENHOUSE GAS MIXTURE includes:

WATER VAPOR (36-72%) and has a lifespan of 9 days, and has no GWP (global warming potential). Clouds are water droplets or ice crystals suspended in the atmosphere. It is the major contributor to the earth's greenhouse effect. Clouds also absorb and emit infrared radiation, and thus have an effect on radiative properties of Greenhouse Gases.

CARBON DIOXIDE (9-26%), and has a lifespan of 30-95 years. It has a GWP of 1, throughout its lifespan.

METHANE (4-9%), and has a lifespan of 9-15 years. It has a GWP of 72 at 20 years; 25 at 100 years; and 7.6 at 500 years.

NITROUS OXIDE (3-7%), and has a lifespan of 114 years. It has a GWP of 289 at 20 years; 298 at 100 years; and 153 at 500 years.

OZONE (3-7%)

There are other greenhouse gases present but only in very small quantities. That does not mean they are not important; just not as important relative to the "Greenhouse Effect." Carbon monoxide is a non-greenhouse gas; but has an indirect radiative effect by elevating concentrations of methane and tropospheric ozone, through scavenging the hydroxyl radical (OH) that would otherwise destroy them. Carbon monoxide is created when fossil fuels are incompletely burned.

Among these other gases present in low levels, are the fluorinated gases that do cause very significant problems. Their contribution is not with global warming; but rather, with depletion of the OZONE LAYER. These two processes are often confused in the media.

SULFUHEXAFLUORIDE has a lifespan of 3,200 years; a GWP of 16,300 at 20 years; 22,800 at 100 years; and 32,600 at 500 years.

HEXAFLUROETHANE has a lifespan of 10,000 years; a GWP of 8,630 at 20 years; 12,200 at 100 years; and 18,200 at 500 years.

One of the early offenders (of fluorinated gasses), CFC-12 (a chloro-flurocarbon used in refrigeration systems) is no longer available after having been completely pulled from the market. Most of the others in this class of offenders are being phased out as quickly as possible—the last, as late as 2030.

As these greenhouse gas levels continue to rise, more and more thermal radiation is redirected back to Earth. The result is that average temperature gradually begins to rise; seemingly not much, just a little at a time. What most of us non-scientists do not realize is that just a couple of degrees can result in rather large changes. Imagine ice in the freezer at 31 degrees Fahrenheit. Imagine that same ice at 33 degrees Fahrenheit. As I understand it, our current average temperature of the Earth is 57 degrees Fahrenheit. So, what happens at 59 degrees Fahrenheit?

The critical areas would seemingly be the outer edges of the "north and south poles." Ice is going to melt. How much? Good question. How much would it take to raise sea levels a foot, two feet, or four feet? Everyone would be affected, no matter where you live. How could that be the case? A little thing called the "Hydrologic Cycle."

Water vapor (clouds) in the form of water droplets or ice crystals, make up, as previously discussed, a significant portion of GHG volume. It obviously gets replaced regularly, having a lifespan of 9 days. The "Hydrologic Cycle" describes the pilgrimage of water, as water molecules make their way from the

Earth's surface to the atmosphere and back again. This gigantic system, powered by the energy of the sun, is a continuous exchange of moisture between the oceans, the atmosphere, and the land.

As water travels through the water cycle, some water will become part of the GLOBAL CONVEYER BELT. It represents in a simple way how ocean currents carry warm surface waters from the equator toward the "poles" and moderate global climates. Thus in many ways we all share temperature changes.

I hope through this narrative you have come to appreciate that most greenhouse gases have both natural and human caused sources. The 2007 Forth Assessment Report concluded that "anthropogenic concentrations are very likely to have caused most (greater than 50%) of the increases in global warming temperatures since the mid 20th century. The contribution of each gas to the GHG mixture is affected by the characteristics of the gas, its abundance, and any "indirect" effect it may cause.

This is obviously a vast and complex issue. People quick to react will invariably focus on one company, or one industry, and try to lay blame. Sure, some sources are certainly more noticeable. Our industry, the beef cattle industry, finds that our political critics (Humane Society of the United States, and People for the Ethical Treatment of Animals) want to direct as much attention as possible to the portion that our industry contributes to GHG levels. Consumers, please, make the effort to become informed. Make your decisions based on fact. Do not be used by our critics.

Our worldwide population is growing, rather quickly. Future nutritional needs, regarding this increased population, are going to push us to our limits with today's knowledge and technology. If you enjoy the futuristic thought of us all eating "green tinted gruel," support our critics. Otherwise, appreciate the efforts that have been and will continue to be made by our beef industry to reduce our carbon footprint. Yes, the fermentation process (stomach activity of ruminants) of our beef, and dairy, and goat and sheep animals, does make methane gas. No question about it. But, as you will soon see from Judith L. Capper's material, our carbon footprint has been getting smaller since 1944. The world needs our beef and we are already working hard to reduce any negative impact on GHG emissions. Look at the sources of increasingly larger carbon footprints. We are not one of those sources.

OUR CARBON FOOTPRINT:

We can find experts in many fields of study that are brilliant in their own field. But when they expand their horizons into agriculture, and attempt to make assumptions concerning agriculture, things begin to fall apart quickly. The Union of Concerned Scientists believes that beef is an insufficient protein. They have shouted to the world that beef production uses 60% of the world's agricultural land, but produces only 5% of the protein, and 2% of the calories required to feed a global population. It is obvious that no one in the Union of Concerned Scientists knows the first thing about agriculture. Their basic premise is wrong. They should have realized that their academic credentials only give them credibility within their own field of expertise.

The vast majority of all lands used for cattle production purposes are unsuitable for crop-farming. Were it not for cattle, sheep, and goats and wild-game harvesting available forage, producing pounds of protein, these lands would be waste-lands. Sure, there are cattle on some good lands, lying next to farm ground. But, most commonly the cattle are on location to help clean up, graze out, or otherwise keep residual farm crops from going to waste. Cattle can make a pretty good living on crop leftovers, after the harvest is completed. But, during the grow season, the cattle are left to graze unlevel and bottom country, or acreages that the farmer does not have a use for—at the moment, or even this year. It tends to always come down to economics. What makes the most money on this particular piece of ground? That is where cattle fit in regarding fertile lands.

But, by and large, the lands on which cattle are permanently placed, have little, if any, use otherwise. I would like for a group of "Union of Concerned Scientists," to walk some of the western lands where the cattle have to make a living. They would be a whole lot smarter after a few miles. These lands are only listed as "agricultural" because of the cattle, sheep and goats that are there.

Environmental Impact of Conventional, Natural, and Grass-Fed Production Systems—Judith L. Capper, PhD

So, how do you get good scientific information concerning the beef industry? You go to an expert within the industry. Dr. Judith L. Capper, Department of Animal Science, Washington State University, has published

"The Environmental Impact of Beef Production in the United States: 1977 compared to 2007"; and "Is the Grass Always Greener? Comparing the Environmental Impact of Conventional, Natural and Grass-Fed Beef Production Systems." She is a brilliant academician and is focused on the environmental issues of the cattle industry. The balance of this chapter will be her words and her works. Please, read it carefully. This material is at the very heart of the "outcry" against beef from the vocal few who simply desire the demise of animal agriculture. She has also categorically stated that she has no bias. Here's what she says:

The global population is predicted to grow to 9.5 billion people in the year 2050, with a widespread increase in milk, and meat requirements per capita conferred by increased affluence. The Food and Agriculture Organization of the United Nations suggest that food production will have to increase by 70% to fulfill the caloric and nutritional needs associated with this population increase. Existing competition for energy, land, and water supplies is likely to continue as urban development encroaches upon agricultural land. United States livestock producers therefore face the challenge of producing sufficient safe, affordable beef to meet consumer demand, using a finite resource base.

An environmentally sustainable food supply can only be achieved through the adoption of systems and practices that make the most efficient use of available resources and reduce environmental impact per unit of food (Capper et. al., 2008, 2009). However, understanding the relationship between environmental sustainability and efficiency requires a certain amount of conceptual change to occur. The role of efficiency in improving US beef system sustainability has been called into question by individuals and agencies promoting a social or political agenda opposed to animal agriculture (Nierenberg, 2005; Koneswaran and Nierenberg, 2008). Nevertheless, improved production efficiency (resource use per unit of food output) considerably reduced the environmental impact of a unit of milk produced by the US dairy industry between 1944 and 2007 (Capper et. al., 2009). To analyze the effects of efficiency changes in the US beef industry over the past 30 years, a deterministic whole system model based on ruminant nutrition and metabolism was used to evaluate the comparative environmental impact (defined in this paper as resource use, waste outputs, and greenhouse gas emissions) of the US beef industry in 1977 and 2007.

Consumers often perceive that the modern beef production system has an environmental impact far greater than that of historical systems, with improved efficiency being achieved at the expense of greenhouse gas emissions. The objective of this study was to compare the environmental impact of modern (2007) US beef production with production practices characteristic of the US beef system in 1977.

Modern beef production requires considerably fewer resources than the equivalent system in 1977, with 69.9% of animals, 81.4% of feedstuffs, 87.9% of the water, and only 67.0% of the land required to produce 1 Billion kg of beef.

Waste and outputs were similarly reduced with modern beef systems producing 81.9% of the manure, 82.3% methane, and 88.0% nitrous oxide per billion kilograms of beef compared with production systems in 1977. The C footprint per billion kilograms of beef produced in 2007 was reduced by 16.3%, compared with equivalent beef production in 1977.

As the US population increases, it is crucial to continue the improvements in efficiency demonstrated over the past 30 years to supply the market demand for safe, affordable beef while reducing resource use and mitigating environmental impact.

A recent FAO (2006) report concluded that livestock production contributes 18% of total global GHG (greenhouse gases). Despite a subsequent public admission that comparisons between GHG emissions from livestock production and transport were flawed after in-depth scientific review by independent scientists (Pitesky et al., 2009), the report is often used to support claims that animal agriculture should be abolished (Deutsch, 2007; Humane Society of the US, 2009), despite the obvious and inadmissibility of using global data to represent the environmental impact of regional production systems. Improved production efficiency (resource input per unit of food output) is a major factor effecting variability in GHG emissions per unit of food. Gains in productive efficiency allows increases in food production to be achieved concurrently with reductions in environmental impact.

US dairy industry, which produced 59% more milk, using 64% fewer cows in 2007 than in 1944, with a consequent 41% decrease in GHG emissions from the dairy industry (Capper et. al.2009).

Nonetheless, improved efficiency is often perceived by the consumer as being achieved at the expense of animal health and welfare (Singer and Mason, 2006).

Within the beef industry this may be defined as a population-wide "reduction and dilution of maintenance," which encompasses the individual effects and interaction between meat yield per animal, daily maintenance requirement, and time period from birth to slaughter.

Although the total daily energy requirement is increased in the 2007 animal, a combination of reduced time from birth to slaughter and increased BW (body weight) at slaughter decreases total energy use per kilogram of beef produced.

Carbon is the fundamental unit of energy within animal systems; thus differences in total maintenance energy can be considered to be a proxy for both resource use and GHG emissions. It is biochemically impossible to maintain a system with a greater net C output than input, for example, forage-based extensive systems (grass-feds) with characteristically low growth rates have increased land, energy, and water use and GHG output per unit of beef produced.

FEEDSTUFFS AND LAND USE

An intrinsic link exists between the quantity and quality of feed required for beef production and the area of land required to support this system. As the global population continues to increase, the land area devoted to animal agriculture, specifically ruminant livestock is likely to continue to be an issue of major debate.

Several authors claim that world hunger could be abrogated if meat consumption decreased considerably (Pimentel and Pimentel, 2003), (Millward and Garnett, 2010) because the quantity of land currently used to raise livestock could instead be used for human food crop production.

There are several implicit flaws contained within the theory, including the assumption that a vegetarian or vegan diet would be acceptable to the global population, which is negated by the predictions of increased global milk and meat requirements by the FAO (2009), and the false assumption that crop production could be maintained for a wholly vegan population without an increasing reliance on fossil fuel-based fertilizers (Fairlie, 2010).

Aside from these issues, the major point of contention is the supposition that land currently used to graze livestock could equally be used to grow corn, soy beans, or other human food crops.

As the study shows, between 1977 and 2007, cropland use was reduced substantially to produce 1 billion kg of beef. Pasture land had a proportionally greater decrease resulting from the smaller number of beef cows (for whom pastureland is the main dietary component) required for beef production in 2007. The quantity of both cropland and pasture land available for agricultural use in the US has continually decreased since 1945 (Lubowski et. al., 2006). The cropping land released from the beef system could be used to grow other human food, yet pastureland used for ranching operations is generally unsuited for growing other crops due to climatic, topographic, or soil limitations. Indeed, data from the Economic Research Service of the USDA (Lubowski et al., 2006) indicates that only 8% of US grazed land is sufficiently productive to be classified as cropland pasture, yet it may remain marginal for crop use and be used for pasture for long periods of time.

Given that forage is the major dietary component for animals within the cow-calf and stocker system and that 50-70% of the lifespan of a beef animal finished in a feedlot is spent grazing forage crops, the supposition that ruminants compete with humans for nutrient resources is unfounded. Nonetheless, increasing competition for land resources between food production, industrial, and social uses is an inevitable consequence of population growth.

WATER USE

At a superficial level, water appears to be an entirely renewable resource within the beef production system, with an ongoing cycle of water use from the atmosphere, through plant material into the animal, and then back into the atmosphere.

However, fresh water supplies are increasingly scarce due to a combination of excessive withdrawals, contamination, and loss of wetlands. All food production has an embedded water cost, but livestock production is often cited as a major consumer.

Estimates of water use for beef production range from 3,682 L per kg of boneless beef (Beckett and Oltjen, 1993) to 20, 555 L per kg of beef originating from the animal rights group PETA; the greater values often being used to promote the suggestion that livestock production is too resource intensive to be environmentally sustainable. The Water Footprint Network has published the most often-quoted figure for water consumption at 15, 500 L per kg of beef, which is a means to compare beef with other food products. By contrast, the thorough analysis of water consumption within beef production published by Beckett and Oltjen (1973) with system boundaries extending from feed production to processing, reports the aforementioned water-use figure of 3,682 L per kg of boneless beef. Our results demonstrate that water used as modeled within the current study is equivalent to 1,763 L per kilogram of beef in 2007, a decrease of 12.1% compared with the corresponding resource used in 1977. As demonstrated by other resource use metrics within the current study, improved animal productivity was the main factor affecting the reduced water use of beef in 2007 compared with 1977, yet crop productivity also played an important role.

NUTRIENT EXCRETION

Livestock production industries within the US have undergone considerable consolidation since the end of WWII, and the number of operations has declined as production has become increasingly specialized and region-specific.

The quality of knowledge and modern computational resources relating to animal nutrient requirements and ration formulation are far superior to those available in 1977. In combination with previously discussed improvements in productivity, manure output has been significantly reduced per unit of beef: nitrogen excretion by 12.3%; and phosphorus excretion by 10.3% (between 1977 and 2007). This represents a critical move forward in US beef industry sustainability, which must continue to improve in the future.

GHG EMISSIONS AND FOSSIL FUEL USE

The C footprint of livestock production is one of the most widely discussed environmental issues within the current agricultural arena because of its association with nonrenewable resource consumption and climate change.

Historical analysis always carry a certain burden of uncertainty based on the data available; however, the current study suggests that the shift toward agricultural intensification between 1977 and 2007 reduced fossil fuel use per billion kilograms of beef by 8%. This is notable given that corn production is one of the major contributors to fossil fuel use.

The C footprint per billion kilograms of beef within the current study was 17,945 X 10 to the 6th power kilograms CO_2 (Carbon dioxide) equivalents in 2007 compared with 21,445 X 10 to the 6th power kg equivalents in 1977. This 16.3% reduction resulting from improved efficiency and productivity that reduced C emissions from crop production, enteric fermentation, manure and fossil fuel combustion.

Reduced GHG emissions resulting from a decrease in feed and animal transportation are often claimed as an environmental advantage of "local" or extensive production systems (Nicholson et al. 2011). Within the current study, the contribution of transportation to the total C footprint of a billion kg of beef constituted less than 1% (0.71%) in 1977 and 0.75% in 2007), with the majority of GHG emissions resulting from enteric fermentation and manure. These data suggest that potential opportunity to mitigate the environmental impact of beef production through transportation efficiency is limited.

CONCLUSIONS

It is clear that improving productivity is key to reducing the environmental impact of beef production, yet anecdotal evidence from the current beef industry suggests that beef yield per animal has reached a plateau. The processing/packing industry infrastructure is not currently equipped to deal with animals weighing considerably more than 600 kg (1,320 lbs.), and consumers are unlikely to demand greater portion sizes in the future.

Further investigations into the contributions made by improved growth rates, fertility, morbidity, mortality, and forage management are therefore essential to better understand and apply the management practices by which the industry can continue to provide sufficient animal protein to satisfy the market while continuing to reduce resource use and waste output per unit of beef.

ENVIRONMENTAL IMPACT OF CONVENTIONAL, NATURAL, AND GRASS-FED BEEF PRODUCTION SYSTEMS / SIMPLY SUMMARY

The environmental impact of three beef systems was assessed using a deterministic model. Conventional beef production (finished in feedlot with growth-enhancing technology) required the fewest animals, and least land, water and fossil fuels to produce a set quantity of beef. The carbon footprint of conventional beef production was lower than that of either natural (feedlot finished with no growth-enhancing technology), or grass-fed (forage fed, no growth-enhancing technology) systems.

All beef production systems are potentially sustainable; yet the environmental impacts of differing systems should be communicated to consumers to allow a scientific basis for dietary choices.

Conventional, natural and grass-fed beef production systems were compared relative to producing 1 billion kilograms of beef.

The conventional system required 56.3% of the animals, 24.8% of the water, 55.3% of the land, and 71.4% of the fossil fuel energy required to that of 1 billion kg of beef compared to the grass-fed system of production.

The C footprint per 1 billion kg of beef was the lowest in the conventional system (15,989 X 10 to the third power, t), intermediate in the natural system (18,772 X 10 to the third power, t), and highest in the grass-fed system (26,785 X 10 to the third power, t). The challenge now becomes to communicate differences in system environmental impacts, to facilitate informed dietary choices.

RESULTS—PRODUCING 1 BILLION KG OF BEEF

Animals within the conventional system had an average slaughter weight of 569 kg (1,252 lbs.) and took 444 days to raise from birth to slaughter. Their supporting population (the cow herd producing the calves) was 5,539. Required land was 5,457 ha X 10 to the third power. Water was 485,698 L X 10 to the sixth power. Fossil fuel energy was 8,773 MJ X 10 to the sixth power. Manure output was 36,976 t. Nitrous oxide was 7,532 t. Carbon footprint was 15,989 (t CO2-sq X 10 to the third power).

Animals within the natural system had an average slaughter weight of 519 kg (1142 lbs.) and took 464 days to raise from birth to slaughter. Their supporting population was 6,265. Required land was 6,678 ha X 10 to the third power. Water was 572,477 L X 10 to the sixth power. Fossil fuel energy was 10,304 MJ X 10 to the sixth power. Manure output was 45,431 t X 10 to the third power. Regarding greenhouse gases: methane was 586,729 t, nitrous oxide was 9,078 t. Carbon footprint was 18,772 (t CO2-sq X 10 to the third power).

Animals within the grass-fed system had an average slaughter weight of 486 kg (1,069 lbs.), and took 679 days (minimum) to raise from birth to slaughter. Their supporting population was 8,482. Required land use 9,868 ha X 10 to the third power. Water was 1,957,224 L X 10 to the sixth power. Fossil fuel energy was 12,290 MJ X 10 to the sixth power. Manure output was 74,392 t X 10 to the third power. Regarding greenhouse gases: methane was 854,561 t, and nitrous oxide was 13,833 t. Carbon footprint was 26,785 (t CO2-sq X 10 to the third power).

If the total US beef produced in 2010 (11.8 x 10 to the ninth power kg) was produced by a grass-fed system, the increase in land required compared to conventional production would be 52.2 X 10 to the sixth power hectares, equivalent to 75% of the land area of Texas.

Increased growth rate and slaughter weight in the conventional system reduces water consumption to 17.9% less than that required by natural cattle, and 302% less than grass-fed cattle. However, irrigation water is the major contributor to total water consumption, thus the magnitude of the difference in water use between the conventional and grass-fed systems is due to the assumption within the model that 50% of the grassland used to finish cattle in the grass-fed system is irrigated. This is an area of uncertainty compared to the irrigation data for the feed-crop (corn, soy, or alfalfa) components of the model. If we change the original assumption (50%) and run the model with 25%, 15%, or 5% of land being irrigated, the total quantity of water used by the grass-fed system declines quickly. Thus, the model is sensitive to irrigation water use to the extent that if greater than 9.7% of land used to finish beef is irrigated, the grass-fed system is less environmentally-friendly than the conventional system.

The carbon footprint of livestock production systems is one of the most debated issues relating to environmental impact. This is exemplified by a report from the Environmental Working Group that states. "Meat, eggs, and dairy products that are organic, humane and/or grass-fed are generally the least environmentally damaging." Within the current study the grass-fed system had a carbon footprint that was 67.5% larger, compared to the conventional system. The increase was primarily affected by the increase in population size and time elapsed from birth to slaughter in the grass-fed system. However, provision of a forage-based diet also increased methane emissions per animal as noted by Johnson and Johnson, and Pinares-Patino et al.

CONCLUSIONS

The US beef industry faces a clear challenge in supplying the needs of the increasing population, while reducing environmental impact. Uses of technologies that improve animal productivity in combination with intensive feedlot finishing systems demonstrably reduce both resource use and GHG emissions per unit of beef. The beef industry is then well placed to continue its tradition of environmental stewardship, yet it faces considerable opposition in terms of consumer perceptions of intensive production systems that may have a negative impact upon social sustainability. Demonization of specific segments in favor of niche markets that intuitively appear to have a smaller carbon footprint further propagate the idea that large-scale production systems are undesirable, yet all systems that fulfill the three facets of sustainability have a place with the industry.

CONFLICT OF INTEREST: Dr. Judith L. Capper declares no conflict of interest.

FOOT NOTE:

Yes, we (agriculture in general and the beef cattle industry in particular) are guilty. We have contributed to the issue of greenhouse gases, and we are responsible for a carbon footprint. We are part of the industrialized enemy. But we are not nearly as guilty as many of you have been led to believe.

I mentioned that my last developmental editor is very bright, very well educated, very sensitive to environmental issues and very engaging in her efforts to attain information relative to just how bad our industry has treated the environment in particular. She still wanted to believe that something was still hidden. She could not but think that our industry has short-changed the environment through greed. Dr. Capper's material, largely, won her over; but she still wants enlargement ("flesh out more substance") of the critical issues. If you, like her, want to preview the entire works of Dr. Capper's articles, please refer to: "Is the Grass Always Greener? Comparing the Environmental Impact of Conventional, Natural, and Grass-Fed Beef Production Systems" found at OPEN ACCESS, ISSN 2076-2615; www.mdpi.com/journal/animals (active at the time of the publication of this book); or "The Environmental Impact of Beef Production in the United States: 1977 compared with 2007" at *Journal of Animal Science* 2011, 89:4249-4261; doi:10.2527/*Journal of Animal Science*.2010-3784.

The only greed in our industry is within the realm of the packers. Everyone else (producers) is just trying to find economic stability; and continue a way of life that sustains our needs and desires. Believe me when I tell you that the land is our "golden goose." Our God, our family, and our land are the supporting pillars of our life. We live in the same environment that you do. We enjoy good food as you do. We recognize that an emerging world population will affect both of us. World climatic changes will affect both of us.

Is global warming real? Some would say that it is only the latest of many cyclic changes that have involved planet earth over the millennia. That may well be true; but also true is the clear evidence of anthropogenic (caused by humans) contributions relative to global warming. Can the two coexist, independent of each other? Sure. The one we have no control over; the other we do. Would not any reasonable person want to diminish anthropogenic contribution though it may not be the single cause of global warming? I think so. But we must do so with wisdom and understanding of the issues involved. Let us not stop agricultural food production simply because it is a contributor. Agriculture is sensitive to its part of the problem. Aggressive and ongoing efforts are actively being pursued that will allow our part of the problem to be permanently reduced. Can we go to zero? No. Quality of life issues would deteriorate quickly without the food stuffs made available from farm animals. Serious efforts to reduce our carbon footprint even more, will continue.

I do not want to eat "green-tinted gruel" while the wealthy segments of the world, eat beef. You must recognize that we (cattle producers) are not the enemy. You, unknowingly, have believed our critic's statements about our industry. Their voice is the only voice you have heard. Many of them (those with endowed financial foundations) simply desire the demise of animal agriculture. From this point forward, if you support the consumption of "green-tinted gruel," believe them. Donate to their causes.

If on the other hand you believe that I am not selling snake oil; but rather trying diligently to share a truthful and honest in-depth look within our industry for your evaluation; you have made gigantic inroads toward educating yourself. From this beginning you now have a wide variety of university contacts that you can visit with concerning any additional questions that you might have. If the contact list I have included does not contain "your university," contact them. They will refer you to an appropriate department, extension service, or individuals that can be of service. Many state extension services have "Ask an Expert"—an email service available to consumers enabling you to ask your questions.

Look back in history at some of the staggering collapses of caring for our fellowman. Just because they were red, yellow, brown or of a particular religious persuasion, does not make them bad. Yet society was misled by a few, and we all allowed great loss of humanity. Think for yourself. Educate yourself to the issues of today. Do not be misled by a few who are self-centered on hidden agendas. Be like my developmental editor; have a voice; have a yearning to discern the truth. Be not afraid of walking toward enlightenment. It is easy to be lazy. It is easy to be misinformed.

We, the beef cattle industry, have no hidden agendas. Our only agenda is the desire to continue our way of life; and being flexible and adaptive enough to bring to the marketplace that specific type of beef that you desire. It sounds simple. It is simple; and it is the truth.

Within a short time after publication I anticipate having a website that will enable your continuing search for information regarding our industry. I expect it to have dozens of pictures, and the ability for you to be able to directly converse with a variety of producers. This is my all out effort to build bridges of communication with you. Make the effort and take the opportunity to inform yourself. Know where your beef comes from. Get to know our industry. Get to know our people. In many parts of the country the beef cattle industry is in dire straits. It is not doing well economically. The packers and their feedyards are the only ones doing well in the feeder cattle industry. The independent feeder cattle industry is dying a slow death masterfully crafted by the major packers. The death knell is tolling as we speak.

For now I shall continue to share "Genuine Care and Concern for the Individual" in hopes of enabling this new philosophy to grow and expand across the industry. It would have been much easier had the giant-retailer been able to gain packer concessions. Then the effort could have been economically driven. For the moment you will continue to get the beef the packers want you to have. I still have hopes of seeing a new, state of the art, beef-packing facility being built that is owned by beef purveyors, and beef producers. That will not happen quickly if at all. I will personally continue to work for you, and for the individual cattle that populate our industry.

12

Consumer Evolution

You live in a changing world. Your role within the family group may very well have changed, from that of your parent's role. Time spent in the kitchen on a daily basis, is often greatly reduced. You still want healthy, nutritious meals, but your time, and sometimes your desire, at the end of the day, may dictate the meal you and your family will enjoy that evening.

The major options might include going out, ordering in, and preparing in. Concerning the latter, options abound given the "Heat N Serve" beef entrees, as well as portion-controlled convenience entrees that require little preparation time, and yield a very pleasurable beef eating experience. How about back-yard grilling, while interacting with the family? And yes, on those special days, when the pace has moderated, you can produce your parent's kind of meal, made from scratch. Most of us find that it takes all combinations, of the above, to soften the challenges of simply getting it done on a daily basis.

Your beef industry understands, and is going to great lengths, to provide beef designed, and prepared, to meet the needs and desires of your family; fresh, wholesome and yielding a consistently high quality, beef eating experience. You are in the driver's seat; you can have almost anything you want. If it comes down to simple economics, you have a question to answer: "What am I willing to pay for exactly what I want?" In a nutshell that is where we are today; creating beef, and beef products, in an effort to determine your needs, your desires, and what you are willing to pay, if you get exactly what you want. Today's beef industry is here to meet those needs and desires, in providing for your family; but we need your feedback.

You have changed. You are certainly not the consumer of old. But, then again, who is? Our world has changed us all. Those of us in it must evolve as we try to adjust to new circumstances. Pause for a moment and remember how it used to be. Pick any subject matter that comes to mind. Compare today to a period twenty, thirty, or even forty years ago. Whether you appreciate the change or not, notice how it affects our daily lives. I find myself amazed at how far we have come in some areas, and how much ground we have lost in others. Considering the amount of money we throw at education, how can we be happy with the public school, educational system? Just throwing money at any problem is rarely the answer. Look at the sheer size of our government. Almost one in three (people) work for the government. Yes, most every aspect of enlarging individual government powers could be largely justified. Yet, when all these hundreds of new governmental activity centers that all require funding, are collectively melded together; we have created a monster, gobbling up operational funding without showing any efficiency of effort.

In our zeal to help others, to accommodate, to rectify "wrongs," we have unquestionably become fragmented, and largely ineffectual. In our zeal to make government more responsive, we created a bloated giant that we cannot afford. In our efforts to protect ourselves from terrorist threat, we created a virtual police state. In our zeal to help the down-trodden, we created a society that is never satisfied with their level of assistance. Much of our society has lost its zeal for productivity; we languish and we complain. We have empowered our politicians (knowingly or unknowingly) to become corrupt, robbing Peter to pay Paul (and a little for themselves) because we wanted more, and more, and more. We wanted so many things at the same time, and we got our wish.

It is no wonder that you are not the consumer of old; our nation and our world has changed. We have all changed. Through this vast evolution you (the consumer) and I (the beef cattle industry) have lost contact with each other. What can we in the beef industry do to better enable you to become a more knowledgeable consumer regarding beef? The answer must begin with the restoration of two-way lines of communication. You must have real access to our industry. Sure, web-sites are great sources of information; but, your questions need direct attention. Utilize the noted individuals and sources at the back of the book. They are there for you. Treat them as you would like to be treated. Know your questions ahead of time. Be nice. If you are in search of knowledge, you will be rewarded.

Most state universities have agricultural departments. The scope of these programs is vastly wider than was the case even twenty years ago. The subject of food in general is broken down into a wide array of activity centers. Most of the staff at these universities is interested in receiving your sincere questions; certainly the extension aspect of these universities, interact with the public every day. Some few of these universities do not make contact information available to the public, concerning their staff. All these universities are state supported. As a state resident you do support them with your tax dollars. But, if you cannot get satisfactory answers from there, contact another university in another state if necessary. A part of us (including some universities) have become a nation in hiding, afraid of the world in general. If you are nice and respectful, you may enable them to once again interact in the sunshine of humanity. You will make them feel better and you will gain the information you desire.

Yes, ours is a changing world. So, as we rekindle our interactive efforts, perhaps we should all begin to rekindle "Americanism." Ask first, what is best for America, before asking what is best for me. No one can be happy with our political systems; they only represent the system—not the individuals they are supposed to represent. Change begins within us. So, as you and I (the agricultural industry) begin to interact, perhaps we all (individually) need to reexamine our position? Are we hiding from society? Are we happy with our current state of affairs? Agriculture is doing a lot of things right. It is very largely composed of people you would enjoy knowing—honest and trustworthy. You could have a friend in agriculture—a best friend. Perhaps you and I (the beef industry specifically) can take the first step in the restoration of "Americanism." The pyramids began with a plan; colonization (initial habitation) is the beginnings of a nation; the first aero plane was the beginning of inter-planetary exploration. We can restore and rekindle the American spirit and its integrity. We can do it one person, one household, one town at a time. A simple thought process is at the core of all decision making: not what is best for me, but rather, what is best for the country. I see it as no dream to be one of 9.5 billion people inhabiting this earth. I want to dream of what made our country great. That is a dream worthy of restorative effort. It begins with individual commitment, then two, two hundred, two million, and then a nation. I am sure that in many other countries the residents feel much the same regarding lost sovereignty as the world decision makers try to make us all a common denominator.

This book has been a joy to create. My driving force was that few know the industry as I do. I had a story and a philosophy "Genuine Care & Concern for the Individual" that needed to be shared. You are very much the key to our (the beef industry) success or failure. Let us not hide from each other; there is already far too much of that today. Join us, will you not, as we attempt to preserve what is right about America. Thank you from all of us, as we attempt to "do the right thing" regarding the cattle under our care.

Closing

From the 1870s until the 1950s chuck-wagons were a common part of cattle working activities. Early on they provided a way to feed the cowboys on the long drive to the railheads in Kansas and Nebraska. In later days they continued to be used on the larger ranches because the location of cattle activities was simply so distant from the ranch headquarters. To give you some perspective of size and distances, let me share some specifics concerning the ranch I primarily grew up on. That ranch (42,000 acres) had been created (largely) from a portion of one pasture of the now defunct (historic) Matador Ranch. That original pasture (Turtle Hole Pasture) was in excess of 90,000 acres (141 square miles). The nearest fence line of Turtle Hole would have been approximately 12 miles (as the crow flies) north-east of the ranch headquarters. Now I think you can appreciate why the "wagon" (as the cowboys referred to it) saved a lot of arduous travel back and forth to cattle working sites. On the larger ranches it was not unusual for the "wagon" to stay out on a year-around basis. Either freight wagons or in later years, the pick-up truck, were used to resupply the wagon as necessary.

For reasons still unclear, my granddad took my dad (as a three year old) out to the wagon where he was working. This particular wagon was out on a year-around basis. I believe that location to have been the Waggoner Ranch, south of Vernon, Texas. How a three year old survives in that environment (sleeping in a bed-roll on the ground with no shelter at all), I do not know. It must have taken every cowboy and the cook to help look out for him. He stayed out there with the wagon until he was seven years old; when his dad took him back to town to go to school.

I know that Dad was back at the wagon (same ranch) when he was seventeen. Though he was not one to relate very many personal stories; he did relate one that involved that location and time. On voting day all the men old enough to vote were hauled into town for that purpose; and were allowed to spend the night. The next morning with only one other young man (also not old enough to vote) present, they began to cook breakfast. He said: "we must have gone through three dozen eggs before we found enough (that were not already spoiled) to cook for breakfast." The following morning when all the cowboys and the cook were again present; the cook threw "nary" an egg away as he prepared much the same breakfast. Dad simply commented that he and his friend "laid off" the eggs until they were resupplied.

Meal time for two panhandle (Texas) range crews.

JA Ranch cook making biscuits, circa 1891.

Modern transportation and decent roads have now put the regular use of chuck-wagons into the category of nostalgia. Today their use is more to keep a little bit of the past, alive and well. Their use simply brightens the embers of one's memory.

My younger brother (Joe), tending the skillets (chicken-fried steaks) and I doing some cooking on the Running Creek Ranch, Elizabeth, CO., that involved our own chuckwagon.

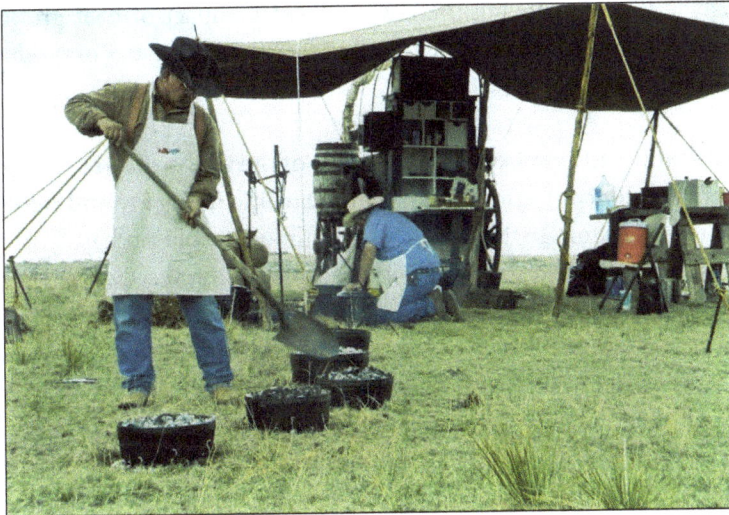

Cousin Ricky tending the Dutch ovens (yeast rolls and cobblers), and brother Joe checking the beans and potatoes.

Times do change. Which brings us back to you. I told you in the opening of this book that we would attempt to answer some serious questions near the end of the book. We have arrived. These questions were saved until now to allow you the opportunity to upgrade your knowledge concerning our industry. Serious questions often do not have simple answers. Now, you are ready.

#1. "What is the environmental impact of industrial-scale beef production?"

The methane gas produced as a result of any ruminant animal is roughly equivalent regardless of location—confined at the feedyard or spread out in the pastures.

The fact that feedyards are commonly centralized near corn production simply makes fossil fuel usage better for some and worse for others; but certainly reduces the cost of shipping grain. If you spread out the feedyards, fuel usage would go up; you would have to haul them a lot further to the packers. You would still have the issue of getting the fresh meat from the packer to urban centers for redistributing.

Dr. Capper clearly pointed out that "transportation" was less than 1% (0.75 %) of the total carbon footprint of a billion kg of beef. Thus the ability to mitigate the environmental impact of beef production through transportation efficiency is obviously limited. Her conclusion stated that improving productivity is the key to reducing the environmental impact of beef production. Spreading the animals out would actually exacerbate the issues of productivity (efficiency of production).

#2. "What about the environmental impact of the feedyard itself, concerning issues of high concentrations of animal waste, including ground water?"

Great question. I will share personal thoughts, but perhaps you should contact some of the listed experts within the extension services of the universities for additional comments.

The major issue by far is surface runoff. Rain and melting snow do carry fecal contamination away from the immediate area if not properly managed. Every feedyard must abide by regulations, the Environmental Protection Agency in particular. Beyond approving containment options, initially, state/federal officials monitor feedyard operations through continued surveillance. The receiving vessels that were created to hold this runoff are usually referred to as pits, ponds, or lagoons. Here the runoff is allowed to slowly evaporate, and percolate into the soil; which gets us to the issue of ground water.

Deep wells and aquifers of one sort or another are unaffected for a variety of reasons. Some of which we will now go into. Shallow wells (drinking water) do require protection. Just like with a "septic system" of a rural home; that septic system must be a minimum number of feet from the nearest well (source of water). The concern is not so much with lateral (horizontal) spread of contaminates, but rather vertical aspects of its movement. Just how many feet of soil and sub-soil must it percolate though before it becomes benign, I do not know. Ask the experts. I suspect that it is determined by the type and depth of the various layers present; and I am sure this requirement would vary from one area to the next. Never have I experienced any instance where subsoil was damaged; on the contrary, life in these subterranean cultures seems to flourish. Remember too that we are not talking about manufacturing or chemical residues, but rather organic residues.

#3. "What is the impact of industrial-scale beef production on the local economy?"

FIRST: Without question the number of small beef producing operations is shrinking. Knowing the specifics involving east-Texas, where a lot of cattle used to reside; it has more to do with evolving lifestyles, rather than economics. The newer generations do not want the hassle of raising a few cattle. They would rather have timber companies plant trees to be harvested in 14-18 years.

SECOND: Production efficiency is always at the heart of any operation. If you just have a few cows, you still have to have livestock handling facilities, including the ability to restrain an animal as might be needed in providing assistance (necessary for proper management). The expense and upkeep of these facilities is harder to justify with just a few cows. In earlier times (a more agrarian culture) these expenses were more justifiable.

THIRD: Larger operations can spread these cattle working expenses over a much larger numbers of cattle. Let me share an example. A friend of mine used to own a 30,000 head feedyard in north-west Texas. He replaced his hydraulic chute every one-million head that it handled. Remember that a feedyard is a data-rich environment. He could project ahead and tell you just about to the day when that event would happen. The new chute would already have been ordered. Production efficiencies drive our industry. Yes, it does cause the loss of a few smaller operations. The smaller operations that prosper are the ones that developed new marketing alternatives. However, this same production efficiency (review Dr. Capper's material if necessary) actually reduces our carbon footprint.

FOURTH: As to the effect on the local economy, go to any locality with a sizeable feedyard presence, and compare that economy to a similar sized community located in other parts of the same general agricultural area; you will find thriving economies, compared to dying economies. Look at Hereford, Texas and Garden City, Kansas. Without cattle feeding operations they would not exist as the economic success they are today. They grow while small towns away from this activity shrink in size. Small towns in west Texas in general are dying. The same is true over much of the arid and semi-arid areas in the southwestern United States.

Feedyards provide jobs. Ancillary services gain jobs. Packing-houses require a large number of employees. These communities are growing. Ranches (cow/calf producers) are largely unaffected. They might have to drive further to buy groceries. The kids might have to ride the school bus further to go to school. Home schooled kids for the most part enjoy not having to ride the school bus sixty miles (one way) to attend public school.

In production agriculture we are used to adapting as necessary to fit into new constraints. We are used to the mental challenges of having to become flexible and adaptive, as related to environmental, financial, and governmental issues that affect our lives. Our world is not one for the weak of heart.

#4. "What exactly is beef sustainability?"

In its simplest form it is the capacity to endure. Sustainability creates and maintains the conditions under which humans and nature can exist in productive harmony that allows for the requirements of present and future generations to be met. This holistic and balanced approach would necessarily be focused on environmental, economic, and social aspects of production—beef cattle production.

The subject of sustainability may be the hottest topic on the planet. Everyone wants to be involved—no knowledge needed, just an opinion: corporate America, environmentalists, animal rights activists, consumers, producers, educators, and a few assorted crazies. Obviously a consensus supported by all will not happen anytime soon. But, two reasonably objective groups have, independently, identified the same, six target areas to be focused upon regarding the subject of beef sustainability.

Air—greenhouse gas, dust and particulate matter.
Animal health and welfare.
Contribution to GNP, trade and wealth.
Contribution to rural economy and rural communities.
Land use, productivity and biodiversity.
Water usage, availability and quality.

I find it interesting (in retrospect) that we have, during the course of this book, focused on at least five of the six targeted subjects.

In a subliminal way sustainability has long been involved in management's decisions. Any business owner wants to stay in business. The ones, who have practiced the basic components of sustainability by definition, have survived. Granted, modifications and changes did occur over the years. The decision makers were sensitive to what consumers were thinking (relative to our environment in particular), and modified practices accordingly. I am sure that greed also played a part in prolonging some of those more obvious decisions that needed to be made.

I mentioned early on in this book that the beef cattle industry is now a consumer/retail-driven industry. You are our ultimate decision maker. From my own perspective, you have already greatly influenced the direction and methodologies of our industry. More is to come; I am sure. We, largely, have no problem with that. If your personal sensitivities extend to fragile ecosystems, water issues, performance enhancing hormones, transit issues, dehorning and castration of our calf-crops, or the lowly subject of manure, we want to hear your concerns. They simply reinforce our own concerns. To a large extent we have been focusing on these same issues for many years. Production efficiencies drive our industry; they have allowed us to reduce our carbon footprint. The United States cattle industry continues to be a model for the rest of the world in terms of greenhouse gas mitigation. According to the Environmental Protection Agency, beef production accounts for 2.8% of the country's greenhouse gas emissions, compared to 26% for the transportation industry.

Protecting that which gives us life (water, the environment, the economy, animal production and management—including welfare, and nutritious grasses and grains, etc.) is an ongoing and vital concern. When you truly know the extent to which we protect, nourish and support our lands, our cattle, and our forages; you just might find some humor in the remarks of the critics. If we were even one-tenth as bad as we are portrayed to be; we would not have survived. Our industry would be dead and gone. It is only through the extension services of the various universities, university research, professional nutritionists, animal health advisors, and advancing technologies that the cattle industry has survived the economic challenges that have been put in front of us. Had we not truly cared for the lands and water resources that sustain us, we would not still be here. Our lands and their resources, as well as the cow herd, are the "golden goose." In the future when you hear some of the remarks and statements made by our critics (who know absolutely nothing of our industry) telling you how poor a job we are doing, let it bring a smile to your face. Recognize that you really do know better; and if you have any future concerns, you know where to seek answers.

#5. "What about the impact of cattle producers' pervasive use of antibiotics on both bovine and human health—including worries about resistant-strains of bacteria?"

FIRST: Antibiotics (except for two, first generation antibiotics—penicillin and tetracycline, which are available at feed-stores) are only available as a prescription item, as prescribed by veterinarians. A valid client/patient relationship must be present in order to qualify the creation of a prescription. Regarding food animals, antibiotic residues are in the fore-front of our thoughts, anytime animal health matters are focused upon. Compliance is a key term that should be fully appreciated. If a veterinarian does not think he or she can get compliance in the proper administration a product by the producer; a prescription should never be written.

Do all veterinarians practice the same way, under the same philosophies? No. The world of private clinical practice and the world of veterinary consulting relative to feedyards are very dissimilar. At the feedyard (largely because we are creating a food product) very exacting treatment protocols are in place. Treatment personnel are strictly limited to pharmaceuticals that are a part of the designated treatment protocol for a particular condition. Everything is entered into the computer. This electronic system keeps up with everything, including the necessary withdrawal times that accompany every pharmaceutical product; and inventory volumes as well. A treated animal cannot simply leave the feedyard as long as there is any pending pharmaceutical withdrawal period that is not yet expired. The two exceptions include their being turned out into a pasture environment, or if bought by a "railer-buyer," who can assume the legal responsibility of an antibiotic residue. The system in that regard is near fool-proof. The system is in place (by USDA personnel) to monitor and identify any foreign substance in meat. Every great once in a while, a residue is found. Inspectors trace back the animal as to its origin (usually the feedyard). Serious discussions occur. Infractions bring stiff penalties. This is not a system that is intentionally abused by anyone.

SECOND: The days of administering multiple, different treatment protocols (one behind another), trying to find resolution regarding a chronic respiratory condition, ARE OVER. The worst part of that protocol is that the animal was allowed to suffer, while waiting for drug (usually antibiotics) residue periods to expire. That is no longer an acceptable philosophy.

Today, the vast preponderance of our treatment protocols (across the industry) are one treatment and you are out; or two treatments and you are out. I personally prescribe to something in the middle. Let me share a little of how I manage these issues.

When an animal is "pulled" (removed from the pen for medical reasons and is on its way to the hospital) there is accompanying paperwork indicating exactly why this animal was pulled. Every individual animal has a unique number assigned. Upon arrival at the hospital that unique number is entered into the computer. Any past medical history is now immediately available. If this is a fresh, not previously treated, respiratory diagnosis; the prescribed treatment (usually an antibiotic that lasts for seven days) is administered. An additional "med-tag" is applied, which clearly shows the date of this treatment, and the animal is returned as gently and efficiently as possible, back to his or her home pen.

If that animal is pulled again for the same reason (a respiratory condition) that animal is closely scrutinized and evaluated. We need to ascertain if this sickness is still a part of a residual condition still present (relating to the original infection), or is this an entirely new condition. The other aspect involves whether or not this animal is immune-compromised (a weakened immune system), or not.

If this animal is evaluated and determined to be a good candidate to continue at the feedyard, it will be treated with a different antibiotic (usually lasting 14 days), and returned to its home pen with an updated med-tag.

Otherwise this animal is considered to be immune-compromised, and will be removed from the feedyard as quickly as possible. Ideally, we would like to place these individuals in the low-exposure, pasture environment, where they can regain their health and perhaps will be successful at a later date.

It is critically important to physically remove these animals as quickly as possible. To do otherwise will cause pain and suffering on the part of the animal; and create an economic blood bath for the owner. We called this program of removal, "Selective Culling." With an aggressive attitude this program is supported by the associated economics if it is accomplished "sooner" rather than "later." Some additional individuals are culled simply because they are not good candidates to stay. Wild cattle in particular should be culled, as well as any individual expressing a chronic lameness.

Indiscriminate use of antibiotics is not a part of any acceptable policy involving feedyards. I am however at odds with most of my colleagues involving "mass treatments." Though a fully acceptable protocol, I believe that it compounds health issues, and creates more negatives than positives regarding getting the cattle straightened out (health wise), and back on the road to become a successful feeder. I know that pharmaceutical companies are overly involved in encouraging mass treatments. For clarification purposes: mass treatment simply means that every animal on a particular load (commonly 70 to 120 head depending upon their current weight) is to be treated with antibiotics. The proponents would have categorized them as "high-risk" cattle, and believe that a significant proportion of them will have to be ultimately treated anyway.

Our industry like most evolves as to how and sometimes why, we do things. In the past some feedyards have justified low-level antibiotics administered in the feed (in the early days of the feeding period). This was a combination product that also supported rumen function; and greatly reduced a clinical condition known as coccidosis (which could rather quickly spread through a group of cattle). Though it was an efficacious product, the idea of feeding antibiotics for more than just a very few days, simply met with too much resistance (from within the industry).

Now, returning to our original question regarding the perverse use of antibiotics, let us look at the word by definition. PERVASIVE (PERVERSE): willfully determined or disposed to go counter to what is expected or desired; wayward or cantankerous; persistent or obstinate in what is wrong; turned away from or rejecting what is right.

No, we have no pervasive use of antibiotics in the feedyard industry; none. It is all accomplished in a prescribed manner, fully documented, and fully accountable. Antibiotic usage (at the feedyard level) occurs only under protocols designed by that particular consulting veterinarian. Do we have differences of opinion? Sure. Are we all held accountable? Certainly. Do we over a period of years change our thinking regarding how antibiotics should be used? Of course. The day I left veterinary school I was told that the half-life of what I had learned was ten years. Meaning that in ten years, half of what I had learned had become outdated. Staying abreast of new developments and evaluating new trains of thought is vitally important to our effectiveness. The knowledge level within any field of study/interest is constantly evolving. Consulting veterinarians certainly have differences of opinion. There is nothing wrong with that; as long as we are all staying focused on what is best for the animal given the economic constrains that we must live under. As long as we are focused on the animal first, then the owner (costs), before ourselves, we will be in a perfectly legitimate position.

LASTLY: Regarding "Resistant Bacterial Strains" in human medicine.

This issue has not been resolved to where all facts of contributing elements are known, regarding why it exists, or how it was initiated. We know that some bacteria can mutate away from pressure. We know these resistant strains are principally sourced in hospitals, where strong disinfectants are used. We know that at least a few physicians have long continued to administer antibiotics for conditions that were still viral in nature. We know antibiotics are effective against bacteria, not viruses.

In veterinary medicine we know that to administer antibiotics before a secondary, bacterial infection (following an initial viral invasion) is present; causes the entire infective process to become more profound—worsened. Bacterial strains, by the way, are very host specific. The very same bacteria that might cause sickness in a dog, does not cause sickness in a cat. Strains that infect domestic animals are much the same; a few exceptions, yes; but not many. Sheep, goats and cattle do share some common strains of bacteria and some viral conditions as well.

Historically, resistant strains of bacteria in general, get that way because they were allowed to survive (given time to mutate); because someone failed to treat at the prescribed level, for the proper length of time. That we know. Every bottle of antibiotic pills that you get clearly tells you to use them all. If disinfectants were not of adequate strength; nor applied correctly; they could allow some of the bacteria present to survive and mutate; that we know.

We may also ultimately find that the immune systems of the patients involved, may play a part of this dilemma. This is a complex issue. With no more than is really known about the etiology of these resistant strains; I find it ludicrous that one of our industry's critics could blame antibiotic residues in beef as being the culprit. However if I were an "animal rights activist," who desired the demise of animal agriculture, I would shout to the roof-tops that antibiotics in our meat sources were the cause of resistant forms of human bacterial strains.

This is yet another great incentive on my part to write this book. I want you to have sources of information other than the media and our critics. I am sharing the story of beef as I know it to be; my lifetime of personal experiences with no punches pulled.

Let me conclude this question with a thought regarding what our future holds in regard to residues in general. Given how our technology (over the years) has advanced from finding residues in "parts per thousand," all the way to "parts per trillion" literally; we should prepare ourselves for some surprises regarding just how long residues of any kind remain present in animate bodies, and inanimate objects (crops for instance). Are these tiny, tiny residues meaningful? Are they significant? I am talking about resides of any sort: drugs, including antibiotics, narcotics, distillates, pesticides, petroleum bi-products, heavy metals, and other possibilities. Can they play a part in the transmission process of a disease, or other health issue? I do not know.

The very fact that they exist in these tiny, tiny amounts would likely cause an emotional, blow-torch issue to one person, and hardly an item of interest in the next. Perhaps we should keep these new findings (and they will come) in the "interesting category" until additional facts arrive. Do not allow a few critics of our industry (or critics of other industries for that matter), including the media, to emotionally affect you until certainties are eventually provided.

#6. "Is the bovine, ruminant animal more stressed consuming grain rations, than pasture-based forages?"

This is a difficult question to answer simply because of the scope of influencing factors that must be examined as well. Let me break it down into separate avenues of thought; each influencing the answer.

Professional ruminant nutritionists are very bright people; they have to be. Simply balancing a ration to meet the specific issues of the animals involved is complicated. Each ingredient is chosen based on availability, price (including transportation), protein content, energy potential, and nutritional make-up. PH (the acid-base balance within the rumen in particular) and its estimated rise and fall cycle through multiple feeding periods per day must be accurately anticipated. The length of time the PH might drop below 5.7 (for example) is especially critical, and potentially reverberating with repercussions.

REGARDING PASTURE CATTLE:

Just because animals are pasture-based does not mean that nutritional challenges are not present. They may not be instantly critical; but they are certainly important as to individual cow productivity. The ruminant digestive system cannot exclusively handle forages like alfalfa or clover, when these plants are in an active growth phase. Bloat (gaseous distention of the rumen) and death loss is a common sequela.

Poor quality grass forages (below 6% protein) also causes a build-up (accumulation) of this material in the rumen; because it is not being properly broken down into nutritional components. It is a common condition in some parts of the country that can be life-threatening, but usually just results in lost productivity.

Some grasses become "toxic" in the fall when frost occurs for the first time (producing high nitrate levels which tie up the oxygen carrying capacity of the blood). This toxicity often results in death. In most grasses the nutritional levels substantially deteriorates as fall and winter approaches. The nutritional quality of each and every grass that creates the grazing opportunities for a cowherd varies dramatically from one geographical area to the next, across the country. This is largely due to varying rainfall levels and mineral deficiencies of one sort or another in the local soil. This array of locally available grasses often varies depending upon the time of the year and specific moisture conditions. It can be an ever changing panorama as to type, quality, and availability.

The environmental aspects of winter, snow in particular, critically depresses grass/forage opportunities. Weed toxicities in the spring (in particular) when cattle are craving something green, can certainly have detrimental effects on life and/or productivity.

The grass environment (for pasture based cattle) is often not the pristine environment that our minds envision. Life is often not easy in these environs. It may be good at times; but challenging during other periods. Any and all of these mitigating changes can and do cause stress to the animals and to the digestive abilities of their rumen in particular.

Given the drought situation that is still occurring, particularly in the mid and south-western states over the last few years; we have experienced a new calamity associated with a lack of normal grazing opportunity. Cattle and horses for that matter have long enjoyed eating the mesquite beans (fruit of mesquite trees) that are a seasonal variation from their usual diet. When a drought persists long enough, the new presence of mesquite beans is just too enticing for the cattle to resist, and they over consume. Initially it appeared to be a compaction problem. That proved not to be the case. With massive over-load it appears that there is just enough of some toxic principal to cause loss of nerve function relative to the intestinal tract (the rumen in particular). The digestive system looses it normal abilities concerning "peristaltic movement." The ingesta (mesquite beans in this case) now does not move through the system as it should. Even surgical removal did not solve any issues. Most of these cows died; some few that lived are having an extended period of recovery. Life in the pasture is not without challenges.

REGARDING THE FEEDYARD ENVIRONMENT:

It is especially critical to understand that when we refer to feeding cattle (including when cattle are consuming grasses/forage in the pasture); we are actually feeding the "micro-flora" content of the rumen. These microscopic organisms are actually responsible for breaking down the feed-stuffs (sources of grain and forage) into metabolically active, nutritional substrates—the components of nutrition.

When their diet changes so too does the micro-flora array of organisms. Some adjustment period is required; but it all happens naturally—a wonder of nature. When feed changes are anticipated, ideally it should occur gradually (rather than abruptly); allowing for a transition into populations of new micro-flora with the necessary abilities to proceed with metabolic break-down. As we move forward with discussions concerning feedyard rations, remember that in many instances, the bulk of their growth (new animal arrivals weighing 800 pounds, for instance) has already occurred prior to arrival.

Historically, feedyard rations were actually five different rations, sometimes more. Ration # 1 (the starting ration) would be high in fiber (roughage/hay) content, and relatively low grain content. As they were moved up in ration numbers, the level of fiber would be decreased, and the level of grain would be increased. The #5 ration could be as much as 80% corn.

Today, is a new world relatively speaking. Today, distiller's grains, the by-product of ethanol production, has become a significant portion of the basic ration. Though it was originally a corn based product, the carbohydrates of that original corn have largely been removed by the distillation process. Just about everything else is still in place, including the protein levels.

Today's feedyard ration #5 may have as little as 30% additional corn added. This by-product is higher in fiber and lower in carbohydrates. The starch load thus has been greatly reduced from the rations of old. Yes, it is a by-product; but that does not mean it is not a very good product. In most ways, it is a superior product to what our rations used to be. Most of us also believe that the animals like it better as well. Obviously every aspect of the ration is balanced by the nutritionist; with careful additions as necessary to make sure all essential elements, vitamins and minerals are present at appropriate levels. Decisions regarding rations and ration changes are made by the nutritionist and the feedyard manager. They must necessarily work together to coordinate all the necessary activities required to make any changes.

Now, let us return to the original question concerning "stress" factors involved in dietary alternatives. Management is the key to minimizing nutritional stress at any level of production—on pasture or in the feedyard. Sometimes, at the pasture level, producers have few if any options; at the feedyard level, options are always being scrutinized. Performance parameters of the cattle are always being evaluated; production efficiencies reign supreme. The dietary needs of the cattle are met twice a day, every day. Health issues and gastro-intestinal problems cost the owner, performance. Thus their health and wellbeing is an essential ingredient to success. Happy cattle perform better. There is no incentive whatsoever to diminish their sense of wellbeing, regarding each and every calf at the feedyard; or out on pasture for that matter.

#7. "Bovine bodies are designed to live and eat in a certain way, i.e. pasture land. How can you confine them, and stuff them, and still make them happy in the feedyard?

In an effort to answer this question, let me break it down into parts.

Are bovine bodies designed to live in a certain way—any given way?

I consider the bovine especially adaptable: from the Scottish Highlander, to the bos indicus (Brahman); from the extremely meaty Charolais, to the queen of the dairy—Holstein; from the survivor (American Breed), to one that appreciates soft environments, the Jersey. I am not sure there is any specie more adaptable across the world than the bovine animal. They adapt and they provide us meat, milk, and hides that add great pleasure and functionality to our human lives.

American Tarentaise cattle.

Jersey cattle.

Florida cattle.

New Mexico mother with twins.

A young lady with her 4-H Show Steer.

A young man showing his calf at a Jr. Livestock Show.

How can we confine them? Confinement, whether it is the feedyard, the dairy, show cattle, or the backyard; just means that we (caretakers) have to do a better job of managing and meeting their needs. Having a lot of room to roam does not necessarily equate to quality of life issues. Some of the saddest sights I have seen are cattle held too long during an extended drought; all the room in the world and nothing to eat. Does management get the blame? Sure. Poor judgment is the ultimate causal agent every time. It simply does not have to rain on a regular basis, if at all. I have been on a fair amount of country that received less than 2.5 inches of rain per year for multiple years in a row, with cows still present and decently performing, but they did not look good.

Regarding their happiness? What makes cattle happy? A full stomach so they can lie around and chew their cud; properly hydrated so they do not thirst; and healthy, including being free of internal and external parasites. These are the easy ones. What else?

They need to be comfortable in their environment, which is a bit more complicated. What I know for sure is that if you can maintain their good health, and reduce the stress in their lives as much as is practically possible, their transition from one environment to another is reasonably short, and their performance parameters are good.

They have long lived in a predator/prey relationship. Reduce their predator anxieties, and treat them kindly, and they will follow your feedsack anywhere.

Yes, I can make them happy in the feedyard. I have to have management fully supporting the desired goal; but attaining their happiness is no longer a debatable issue. The implementation of "Genuine Care & Concern for the Individual" has proven that.

#8. "Is the fat associated with pasture-fed cattle, healthier to consume, than fat produced from a corn-fed diet?"

What we know is that each has a little different make-up of its fatty-acid content. That they are simply different is about all we know. Work (investigations) has been done, and to date neither one appears appreciably better or worse than the other regarding the fatty acid content as it relates to the health of the consumer.

When this becomes an issue in your life, please remember that marketing is everything, and everything is marketing. You may be allowed to believe that one is better because of pristine images and words depicting idealistic scenes. That does not change the facts as we know them today.

Heidi, the Grow Heifer that was obviously raised on a bottle (at the dairy).

In closing may I say that I am proud of our beef cattle industry? It has a long and colorful history. You will not find better people in any walk of life. We are now in transition, involving the very core of our activities, and the very philosophy under which we work. Why the change? You.

We are not the enemy. Our enemy is misinformation; and a general lack of knowledge concerning our industry by the public. That makes us vulnerable, because you do not know us. This book is an effort to enable your intellectual acquisition of facts, regarding our people, our product, and our way of life.

Thank you for being a beef consumer, if you are. If you are not, I hope you chose becoming a vegetarian for personal reasons that had nothing to do with the fact that beef is healthy, nutritious and very satisfying. Beef consumers, the next time you enjoy a great beef entrée, please remember all the effort that went into helping that beef source animal become all they could be.

You will not find another industry working as hard as we are, in bringing you the products that you desire. There are no real excuses not to. It benefits us all to do so. Our critics (Humane Society of the United States, and People for the Ethical Treatment of Animals) though few in numbers are powerful (enabled by war-chests of dollars), and have friends in the media. Hiding behind false banners of animal welfare, they desire the demise of animal agriculture. They do not believe that we should be eating protein sources from animals. They cannot win a battle over beef with a frontal assault; they must "peck" at your emotions to back-door, beef consumption. They are beneath contempt; showing television advertisements depicting poor, malnutrition and abandoned animals to elicit your donations, while actually spending a very small fraction of your donations on the animals involved in their advertisements. Under false pretenses, they (HSUS in particular) accept monies that you gave (to assist neglected pets), and utilize it as a tool to influence elected officials in Washington.

So, when you hear or read negative stories involving beef, recognize that very commonly these stories are designed to minimize the popularity of beef. If there are enough stories, enough times, they can achieve some degree of success. It all depends upon you. Yes, you. When you hear "fire" shouted enough times, you begin to smell smoke. It does not matter that "fire" was shouted by an individual simply desiring the theater be shut down because of the traffic congestion that was created on movie nights. Either way it is one person or actually a relatively small group of people desiring to influence the masses concerning an issue they are emotionally involved with—the demise of animal agriculture. Your defense and ours is to expose them for what they are—cheap racketeers and hustlers that exploit you and your sympathies concerning animals in dire need of assistance. If you do personally support these animals, and we all should, donate your monies to local animal shelters, not the national money gathering factories.

I'll let you pick your own descriptive terms regarding PETA; but it is obvious that they operate under the philosophy of "the means are justified by the end." They will stoop to any level to find a way to embarrass the cattle industry. They make any and every effort to demonize our industry; conjuring up assaults on an industry they know nothing about. If one looks at our future—a growing world populous reaching 9.5 billion, coupled with a shrinking agricultural base—do we not have more meaningful issues that our society needs to deal with?

William Jennings Bryant was a leading American politician and lawyer from the 1880s until his death in 1925. Because of his great faith in the wisdom of the common man, he was called "The Great Commoner."

Red Steagall, a cowboy poet and songwriter, in addition to his television production activities, often quotes William Jennings Bryant: "Burn down your cities and leave our farms, and your cities will spring up again as if by magic; but destroy our farms and the grass will grow in the streets of every city in the country."

Pause a moment, and reflect on that statement. The implications of its truth should startle us. In our efforts to "police" the activities of Americans regarding social and environmental issues, are we strangling agriculture? Is the price of a pristine ecological world the demise of agriculture? If agriculture dies do not our cities follow? Then, it is not hard to imagine "green gruel" becoming commonplace for most of the survivors; not the world leaders of course. The EPA is currently leading a new charge to put agriculture under even greater restraint. With their history it appears that they are the ones that need to be put under restraint.

You have come to know us through this book. We are not the enemy. Our lives and that of our industry are in your hands. We need your support. If William Jennings Bryant was correct, our end and ultimately your end are in sight. He was also right in his support of the common man. Our populous can make the right decisions; but we have to look beyond the polarizing single-issue personal priorities; and ask ourselves what is best for the country first. A lot of wars have been fought, and lives lost, to preserve our way of life. Surely, we can individually look past personal objectives long enough to insure that grass does not grow in the streets of our cities.

If you have a health issue, where would you go for information? If you had a mechanical problem with your automobile, where would you go for assistance? It would not be to people without medical training, or to people with no automotive knowledge. Please, utilize the sources of information and people from within agriculture to answer your questions. If they do not have the answer personally, they will refer you to someone who likely does have the answer. Not all questions have single or simple answers. Few things in life are simple and easy. But with open lines of communication between you and ourselves, we will find answers; we will find solutions; and we will prevent the grass from growing in the streets of America. It cannot be done without your support and understanding. Your knowledge base, and your faith in people—not governments—shall see us successfully through troubled waters.

Post Script

For consumers, I'd like to leave you with a final thought. Our efforts to date have been about the beef cattle industry; just one of the segments that make up agriculture. There is a very important, far larger, subject that involves food in general. Let me share a glimpse into the near future.

At an international (twenty-six countries represented) livestock congress sponsored by the Houston Livestock Show and Rodeo, many industry experts shared opinions and thoughts concerning where our food is going to come from as we begin to nearing that time (2050) when our planet's populations peaks. No government representatives were involved; just a variety of agricultural experts focused on how all these people are going to get fed given current state of affairs regarding malnutrition and going to bed hungry at night that exists across our planet. These are men that know what they are talking about. Their thought processes were very similar, only the percentages of need that each forecast, varied. What I shall share with you was taken from several speakers, but principally from Paul Genho, PhD, an internationally known individual with as much real world experience as any individual alive. If I can share his information so that you can understand and appreciate it, this material may well be the most important aspect this literary effort brings forth. Opinions might vary but many would say that this subject is the most important on the planet.

Dr. Genho began his presentation with a soils map of the world, depicting those areas of the world that had the proper soils for serious agricultural production, available moisture (rainfall or irrigation), and the necessary sunshine to make it all happen. Most soils of the world only allow equivalents to create subsistence diets. Today, there are 7.2 billion people in the world. Today, one billion across the globe go to bed hungry. One out of seven people worldwide go to bed hungry. Where? The primary areas would include Africa, India, parts of the mid-east, and China. Yes, China does have very large grain (rice and wheat) producing areas but not enough to even satisfy their own current population. Of course every other country in the world has some starving people. Right now, six million people a year die from starvation. And, as Dr. Genho continued, "during the one hour I will speak, somewhere around 1,000 kids will die of malnutrition. It is a real problem. To me, a moral problem as well as a production problem."

How much more food will we need to be able to produce, to meet the needs in 2050? I heard numbers that varied from twenty to seventy percent. We do know that today, six million people already die per year from malnutrition. Our planet's increasing population per year is roughly equivalent to that of Germany's current population. The further removed we are, individually, from starving peoples, the less we think of it. As we begin approaching the 9.0 to 9.5 billion people who will be present in 2050, everyone, everywhere, will be impacted.

Yes, you will. And your children will. You may not starve, but food will be much more critical even in the best of locations. Food and starving people will be at the top of conversations and the news. It will not be puppies exhibiting malnutrition, possible pollutants, or genetically engineered seeds. We will all want all the food we can produce.

Dr. Genho went on to share that there are only two places on the planet with the soils, moisture, and sunshine to truly feed the world: North America and South America. South America has its political issues on a country by country basis that will limit its ability to be an effective source of food for the world. That just leaves North America. Mexico limits farming activities to small operations. Canada's awesome potential is limited by the length of its growing season. They can certainly help but can't do it alone.

The source of production that could do it, fairly easily the experts say, is the United States. Under current governmental oversight and restrictions, it cannot be done. Dr. Genho pointed out that there are three things that will greatly and negatively impact production increases anywhere near where they should be if the planet's forecasted starvation is to be averted.

WATER CRISIS: We are in a water crisis that is not currently being addressed. There is no national commitment to water. Water is going to be an issue. The longer the subject is neglected, the more serious the issues pertaining to water. Too many people fail to see it coming; but it is coming. How can we not address something as critically important as water?

VIOLENCE ACROSS THE WORLD: Military activities cost money, often taken from areas that would have been focused on food production and distribution. Regardless of the size of the country involved, war takes the focus away from where it is needed.

OUR OWN GOVERNMENT: Agriculture in general and the farming segment in particular, coupled with advancing technologies that could drastically enhance production yields, could do the job that needs to be done in feeding the world, if the government were not in the way.

During World War II 48% of Americans were involved, one way or another, with agriculture. Today, that number is less than 2%. It is no wonder you have lost contact with agriculture in general. As you became more estranged from those who actually produce the food, your lack of knowledge has allowed you to be influenced by groups opposing agriculture on many levels. As you then began to develop "concerns," you wanted government to protect you. Government knows no more than you do, but they do have the power to make laws and develop oversight agencies to monitor issues. All of which slowly began to limit production aspects of all segments of agriculture. Consumer "fears and concerns" have created an environment such that these exciting new areas of interest cannot be fully researched and implemented. Fear is literally proving to be a barrier to much needed research.

Were it not for new production operational efficiencies, we would already be in trouble. Agriculture has many, many experts in the various segments that make up agriculture. These are smart people. There are many other prospective developments that could significantly increase production parameters. Yet, these new areas of interest cannot be fully researched because of your "concerns." American consumers are afraid of what "might" happen. I ask you to consider two things. One, the families of these experts also have families that will be eating the foods produced. Think they want them harmed? Two, we only have a few years to gear up for feeding the world. We can't wait until the problem is obvious to everyone—even politicians. If we are going to feed the world, we need to begin now. Otherwise, food issues even in America will become a primary concern, involving how your children and grandchildren are going to be fed. Support agriculture; it's the only hope we have to actually feed the world.

I thank you for the time you spent in reading of this effort. You and only you were the basis for this three year effort aimed at allowing consumers to get to know a small part of agriculture—the beef cattle industry. Let me close with a final thought: "If it's not good for the animal; it is not ultimately good for us either." Maximum rewards for us are directly proportional to maximum sense of wellbeing regarding the animals under our care.

Resources and an Appreciation

We want to put the face of our industry on that beef product you are consuming. We want to answer your questions, and give insight as to where your beef comes from. We are proud of our efforts, proud of our product, and welcome your feedback.

You have or will have questions. We include below a list of websites that might prove useful when following a story concerning beef.

But first I'd like for you to meet a friend of mine whom I hold in great esteem. He perhaps best represents the university level of competence and knowledge regarding beef cattle in general, and the stocker segment of our industry in particular. Dale Blasi, PhD is a positive and much appreciated influence on the lives of the young people graduating from Kansas State University. He is a great example of university staff that enables producers to stay abreast of new technology, new science based information, and new opportunity.

Dale Blasi, PhD.

Dr. Blasi was raised on a farm and ranch in southeast Colorado, near Trinidad. He received his BS in Animal Sciences, and his MS in Beef Systems Management from Colorado State University. His

PhD (Ruminant Nutrition) was earned at University of Nebraska-Lincoln. His first appointment was at Kansas State University as a livestock specialist; later transitioning into a State Beef Specialist.

At the time of the publication of this book, he is manager and director of the Kansas State University Beef Stocker Unit and Center for Animal Identification. This is a research center designed to evaluate health and nutrition practices in addition to the performance of existing and emerging animal identification technologies.

He has long interacted with and provided training/seminars for beef producers far beyond the borders of Kansas. He has an international reputation regarding his knowledge and concern for the individuals that make up our beef cattle industry. He is bright, articulate and a joy to work with. I have enjoyed his friendship for many years.

His ongoing research continues to open doors of opportunity for Kansas producers in particular. He continues to stay in touch with and support past students as they make their own mark in the beef cattle industry. The industry is lucky to have him. In his words: "From an educational perspective I am impressed with the beef stocker producer's willingness to learn and apply the latest of management techniques and technologies to their operations to insure that every calf that is received, obtains the best care and attention possible. In general, beef stocker producers understand the important relationship between animal wellness, performance and ultimately, delivering a quality product to the consuming public."

Here are the websites:

FOOD SAFETY NEWS:
www.foodsafetynews.com

FOOD SCIENCE & TECHNOLOGY:
www.foodinfo.ifis.org

FOOD:
www.itsaboutfood.com

FOOD WORLD NEWS:
www.foodworldnews.com

MEAT SCIENCE:
    www.meat.tamu.edu

THE BEEF INDUSTRY:
    www.beefmagazine.com
    www.beef.org
    www.beefusa.org
    www.agweb.com
    www.idbeef.org
    www.iacattlemen.org
    www.beefnutrition.org

BEEF CATTLE INSTITUTE:
    www.beefcattleinstitute.org

UNITED STATES DEPARTMENT OF AGRICULTURE:
    www.choosemyplate.gov

The "extension services" of state supported universities with schools of agriculture are a great source of information. Utilize these sources to answer your questions.

Acknowledgements

We are largely a product of our environment. Considering all the aspects of an environment, people must stand out as the most significant. As I grew up, I had my heroes. But, my dad, Walter Perry (Perk) Peirce, was always the center of my universe. He was a great father; who was loyal, honest, and a man of serious integrity. I believe that his generation was the last of the great cowboys, and he was among the best. My siblings: Jimmy, Jerry, Joe, Jan and Judy, each enabled me, past and present, to accomplish my own dreams and I thank them all.

Since those early years, I have been influenced by a lot of people as I developed my professional career, but none so much as Dr. John Lynch. All that I am really proud of knowing, and all that I am really passionate about, today, I owe to him. He is a great human being, a great friend, and a great feedyard consultant. I owe him a tremendous debt of gratitude.

The most rewarding years of my life, were those spent in the feedyard. For this opportunity I owe AzTx Cattle Company, founded by Bob Josserand; and, John Josserand who hired me, a serious debt of gratitude as well. I found my home in veterinary medicine when I found the feedyards. To be a part of a great cattle feeding company was extremely rewarding. In these tough economic times even a great company can stumble and fall. I fully expect it to reorganize, refocus and return to prominence; perhaps producing a product for someone other than the packers.

Next, I add the name of Kurt Landis. Kurt is a professional, animal (cattle) nutritionist, articulate and very bright. I have appreciated his advice on many occasions, and his personal friendship for a long time. I hold him in the highest of esteem and sincerely appreciate his thoughts and assistance, concerning the subject material of this manuscript.

I would like to thank Dr. Ashby Green, High Springs, Florida, for being the friend he has been to AzTx Cattle Company and to me personally. His personal credentials, contact base, and people skills are unsurpassed. If the beef industry were to have but one ambassador, it should be he. He was additionally the inspiration for this book.

I now add the name of Larry Bilberry (whom the book is dedicated to) who was the manager of Garden City Feedyard for many, many years. He was a great feedyard manager and a great friend. We actually grew up in the same general area, fifty miles apart. His dad was well known and much appreciated as an individual. I could not possibly have got done all the things that needed to be done at Garden City Feedyard, without his support and leadership. He often found solutions when answers were scarce. Few men could have enabled the program I envisioned; he did. He is a great man.

The name of Olivia Campbell Barton too must be added to this list, as well as the small populous of residents at Matador, Texas, in general, for their literary contributions, support, friendship, strong character, and sterling qualities that made life there a joy, and produced a very fond remembrance. Wayland Moore in particular should be mentioned.

From time to time special people, touched by the Grace of God, enter our lives; and enrich the quality of our lives. I sincerely appreciate and thank Francie and Ryan Ruppert for their support, encouragement, and efforts directed at getting this manuscript published.

Developmental Editors: Kim Weiss & Carol Rosenberg (Florida), Dianna Vela Peters (Texas), and Aleisa Schat (Nebraska)—thank you all.

And to friends and family who made significant contributions: Bruce Fleming, Marty Gilchrest, Joe and Lanita Peirce, Wayne Stewart, Darren Robertson, my sons Will & Joe Peirce, Kimbra OKeef Danley, Kara Peirce McClendon, Ann Bilberry, Albin Peters, Joey Freund, and Benjamin Falk who helped to assemble all the pieces of this manuscript—I sincerely appreciate and thank each of you for your invaluable assistance. I would also like to thank Sherry Cherryhomes, Bill Scott, and Sunstone Press and all the wonderful people who work there; especially Jim and Carl. Thank you!

Last, but certainly not least, I thank the Seminole Tribe of Florida, Inc. for their long-term support both of the company I worked for, and for me personally. They are a great people who are hard-working and dedicated to achieving economic prosperity for the tribe as a whole. Alex Johns in particular has enabled their cattle activities to achieve many milestones that few might have imagined twenty-five years ago. Their cow-herd is now one of the largest and best in the United States. Do not be surprised when they bring to the marketplace a beef product that sets new standards relative to the term "natural." Their cattle in fact have immune systems capable of withstanding the rigors of a high-exposure environment (feedyard), without the need for antibiotics. When we were feeding their calves at AzTx Feedyards there were at least two years that not a single calf of the thousands involved, received antibiotic treatment. Their support of my personal efforts in bringing you this book is greatly appreciated.

About the Author

I was ranch raised in the historically-rich cow country of north-west Texas, where values, personal integrity, and honesty were the foundations of life. As kids, all we wanted to accomplish was to walk in the footsteps of our fathers. I graduated from high school at Matador, Texas. Later, I received a B.S. and Doctor of Veterinary Medicine degree from Texas A&M University, College Station, Texas. After a few years in large animal practice, I moved to Clovis, New Mexico, where I became focused on beef cattle. Initially, I was in a clinical environment, but moved into a mobile ranch practice that covered much of north-west, and west Texas as well as the south-eastern quadrant of New Mexico.

Some twenty years later, I was employed by AzTx Cattle Company, Hereford, Texas, which was at that time, the fifth largest cattle feeding company. Heavy focus was placed on preventative health programs, initially at the feedyards, then focusing upon source producers. Approximately 40% of my time was spent in feedyards, 30% with source producers, and 30% involved with owner cowherds, and health issues involving outside (pasture) cattle owned by the company and/or their feeding customers. I was routinely in ten different states attending to company business.

Particular areas of interest included the issues of stress and their effects, critical support of the immune system, and proper calf preparation at the ranch level. Over the years I developed a passion for elevating animal care levels. The more we elevated their sense of wellbeing, the better was their performance. It evolved to become a program where we elevated care standards because it was "the right thing to do." But, it did allow us to enjoy performance parameters that had previously been unattainable. The feedyard is a data-rich environment; anything, everything can be measured.

Ultimately, I evolved into focusing on supply-chains that will provide branded-beef products to consumers. Necessarily, much emphasis was placed on carcass evaluations and performance criteria. Today, I am singularly focused on those issues that our consumers deem important; bringing their desired products to the marketplace, and developing interactive lines of communication with our consumers. The more they really know, and understand our industry, the better off, we will both become.

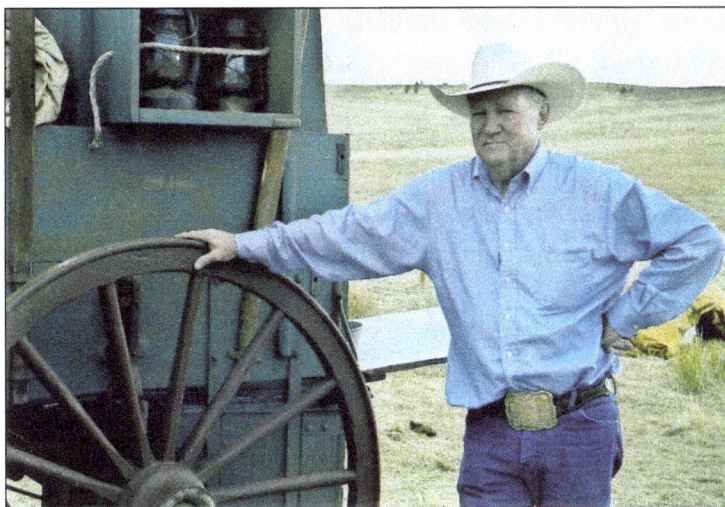

Your Author (standing at the rear wheel of chuckwagon).

As I ponder the future of the cattle industry it leaves me with mixed emotions. Direct and indirect assaults on our industry, continues. If there is a future, if there is a solution, it can only come from you—our consumer. Somehow we must enable you regarding our industry—informed decisions rather than emotionally derived decisions.

Perhaps the most concerning aspect of our world as we know it today involves the fact that giant corporations seem to be in control. They seem to have replaced our lost sovereignty. This new world seems to be whatever they want it to be. Our world has become complex, and vastly intermingled, in the creation of this one-world marketplace. Whether it is good or bad is not the issue, now. The haves (usually big business) will always want a larger playing field. The have-nots may suffer the consequences. Add in corruption, at all levels, lost integrity, lost transparency, as well as lost accountability and you have the marketplace as we know it today. Everything is a deal; everything is give and take; everything becomes looking out for themselves; doing whatever you have to do to get the objectives of the company met. The only exception that comes to mind lies in rural environments where cattle producers in particular, continue to make serious efforts to pass down from one generation to the next that inner-core of personal integrity where your word is your bond.

Given our world as it exists today it becomes more evident as to how and why various small groups, desiring specific goals, gain prominence. Using the art of mass-media noise they clutter our minds daily. They could gain little by sharing their specific goals upfront, so they mislead us through the back door.

If one desires the demise of animal agriculture, focus on the issues of inhumane treatment, environmental polluting, global-warming contributions, magnifying any prospective health issues, and make hidden camera footage front page news. If one does it long enough and often enough, they have created questions in your mind.

There are many other areas and historical topics from which today's groups have learned: the Viet Nam "police action," racial inequality, relationships outside the historical norm, energy issues, and environmental topics. Today these small groups are professionals at marketing. They know how to make the required money to obtain change. Size of the group does not determine their power. Money determines their power. If they cannot sell you on their beliefs, they will sell you on something you do support, making the money that brings them power. So when the Humane Society of the United States raises well over a hundred million dollars per year, and only spends a small fraction of that money on the dogs and cats of their television commercials, how do you suppose they spend that money?

The point is that things often are not as they appear to be. What one might propose as being the center of their objectives may not even be close. These activists are smart, creative, and realize that political consideration today is bought. They also, though few in numbers, write more letters to our elected representatives in Washington, than you would believe. Most of our "party politicians" vote according to who donates the most money to their coffers; and, these same politicians are very good at talking out of both sides of their mouth.

You and I cannot change the world today. But, we can begin by sharing and absorbing real facts about the cattle industry. The beef industry is not perfect; show me any group or industry that is. But, no one works harder than the beef cattle industry does in bringing you the safest, most wholesome product available anywhere in the world. The product we hand off to the packers is the best available product possible given the economic circumstances placed on us by mandatory cost efficiencies, and the constraints of the packers themselves.

No one works harder at doing the job right, shouldering personal responsibility, and supporting quality assurance programs than the men and women of your cattle industry.

Thank you for being a beef consumer and/or simply educating yourself regarding the story of Beef. May you and yours enjoy.

"Happy Trails."